Arthur Nussba

A History of the Dollar

Columbia University Press
New York and London

First printing 1957
Fourth printing 1967

Library of Congress Catalog Card Number: 57-11693

Printed in the United States of America

Preface

THE HISTORY of the dollar, marked as it is by the experimentation and struggle involved in the democratic process, reflects the history of the United States. From the time of the colonial era, when, after brief resort to barter, the early settlers adopted monetary devices alien to European thought, Americans were never reluctant to press for new solutions to the monetary problems peculiar to their expanding civilization. Many of our monetary institutions were largely shaped by leading figures of American history—Jefferson, Hamilton, Jackson, Franklin D. Roosevelt—and the contests preceding their adoption were hard-fought, sometimes bitter, and always dramatic. To my mind at least, few other aspects of the American scene are so dramatic as that unfolded in the history of the dollar.

This book tries to indicate the political, economic, and psychological factors underlying the monetary history of the United States. Glimpses of contrasting foreign experiences have been added. It also includes some numismatic lore, much of it perhaps not new to numismaticists, which I hope the general reader will find interesting.

The book does not offer a financial history, on which much literature is available. It is not concerned, for example, with taxation, tariffs, or government budgets, and considers only a few aspects of banking. Also, the discussion is limited to the more important points; the notes, with their bibliographical references, which include foreign literature, will give access to the details.

In 1950 I included as an appendix to the revised edition of my *Money in the Law, National and International* an inquiry into the legal history of American currency. The research involved gave rise to a desire on my part to reach a fuller understanding of the spirit of this great, free, and hospitable country. The present study is the outcome of that desire.

My deepest thanks go to the Columbia Council for Research in the Social Sciences for its kind encouragement and support of my undertaking.

April, 1957 ARTHUR NUSSBAUM

Contents

A History of the Dollar

The Colonial Era

WHILE MONEY represents an outstanding factor in American history, it is a curious fact that at the beginning of the colonial period there was perhaps less money in circulation than in any other civilized community of the Western world. The small amounts which the settlers had brought with them from England were soon expended for English imports. Hence the settlers resorted to barter.[1]

THE PREMONETARY PHASE

They were accustomed to reckoning in terms of £, sh., and d., and goods as well as services were evaluated on that basis. In such a barter system goods which are available in large quantities, are generally useful, and are somewhat durable will assume some monetary features. Thus corn and beaver skins and, in the South, tobacco [2] and rice became, so to speak, media of payment. Costs of local governments could be defrayed by no other means. Hence these goods were declared acceptable in payment of public dues at rates fixed by the colonial governments in terms of £, sh., and d. Called "country-pay," they became thereby a money substitute. The rule requiring acceptance in payment only on the part of government institutions was quite ingenious and became an ever-recurrent element of the American monetary system; in default of a better term we shall call it the rule of "public receivability." However, as early as 1631, Massachusetts went a step further and prescribed that corn had to be accepted by everyone in discharge of monetary debts (though stipulations for beaver skins as a medium of payment and other special arrangements were not affected). In modern terminology, corn was made legal tender. Other colonies followed the example of Massachusetts, declaring certain commodities receivable in public payments or by every creditor at fixed rates.

Inflationary and other disturbing features were inherent in the system of country-pay. Debtors were inclined to make payments in the lowest quality of the eligible commodity and overproduction of the latter would ensue. At the same time debtors and producers would exert pressure upon the authorities to increase the official rate. Market prices at variance with the official rates developed. Sometimes the colonists tried to provide remedies. For example, in Connecticut the official rate of wheat proclaimed as country-pay was declared binding only in public payments; in private dealings the price was to be determined by the parties and eventually by an arbitrator. In fact, differences between the official rate and the market price were the rule, with the latter being higher, but at the same time requiring better quality.[3]

The inflationary feature is impressively illustrated by the fate of the tobacco currency in Virginia.[4] There a steady decline of the value of tobacco was caused by the overproduction of poor tobacco. It led to such measures as restrictions on tobacco cultivation and to a decree ordering the destruction of half the crop. These measures proved ineffective, and in

1683 riots broke out which led to widespread devastation on tobacco plantations and also to a prohibition against contracts made in terms of money. A new way was opened when warehouses were built in which sworn commissioners had to supervise the quality of the stored tobacco and even to destroy the poor grade: payments on tobacco debts could be made through the warehouses warranting a proper quality. The first enactment of this device, which was clearly progressive, took place as early as 1632, but little is known about its actual effects. More information is available about the activities of the warehouses which were utilized in the eighteenth century for the issuance of tobacco notes—a new development which will be discussed in a later section.[5]

Bartering was practiced on a large scale throughout the colonial period. In Europe there was also much bartering as a substitute for money payment in the seventeenth and eighteenth centuries, but it was only in the American colonies that the monetary use of commodities resulted in an elaborate and long-lasting system. Rendering commodities legal tender demonstrates the ingenuity of the settlers in the premonetary phase. The establishment of tobacco warehouses in Virginia presents another example. On the other hand, the inflationary trend indicates a less favorable feature of the American spirit.

John Winthrop, first governor of Massachusetts, tells this story.[6] It concerns an argument between a certain Howley and his servant:

The master being forced to sell a pair of his oxen to pay his servant his wages, told his servant he could keep him no longer, not knowing how to pay him next year. The servant answered him, he could serve him for more cattle. "But what shall I do," said the master, "when my cattle are all gone?" The servant replied, "You shall then serve me, and so you may have your cattle again."

The argument gives us some illustration of the barter period, but at the same time is also a symptom of what has been called the "democratic equalitarianism" inherent in the Pilgrims' and Puritans' faith.[7]

Bartering was brought nearer to a monetary transaction by the use of wampum, beads made from certain shells.[8] Strings of them were used by the North American Indians of the Eastern seaboard as ornaments, tributes, and adornment as well as for bartering. They were similar to the well-known cowry shells which were employed by other American Indians, as well as by African and Asian primitives.[9] The settlers used wampum in trading with the Indians, selling them weapons, rum, cloth, etc., and purchasing beaver skins and other furs. Soon wampum was also employed among the colonists. They themselves started the manufacture of wampum, especially on the eastern end of Long Island where suitable shells were to be found. Since the settlers possessed better tools than the Indians they were able to produce wampum of greater uniformity and in far greater quantity. Typical wampum was one quarter of an inch in length and one eighth of an inch in diameter. Strings or belts of wampum developed into a kind of substitute for coins. Massachusetts elevated wampum to the status of legal tender in 1643. Other colonies followed suit, and in New York wampum remained legal tender until 1701. In frontier districts it is said to have been used until the early nineteenth century.

The inflationary factor is evident in wampum, too. In addition to being overproduced, beads were often made, by both Indians and colonists, of minor sorts of shell and even of bones, stones, etc., a practice amounting to counterfeiting. All this resulted in insecurity, vacillation, and depreciation. Massachusetts canceled the legal tender status of wampum as early as 1661. But there seems to be no other instance where beads or shells were made an object of statutory regulation.

CIRCULATION OF COINS DEVELOPS

The scarcity of English coins continued more or less until the American Revolution. The balance of trade with England remained heavily in favor of the mother country. Moreover, since 1695 exportation of specie from England was forbidden by English legislation.[10]

The English government did not even permit the colonies to produce coins. In 1652 Massachusetts proceeded on its own initiative to establish a mint for coining silver pieces of 12 d., 6 d., and 3d., among which the "pine tree" shillings, so called after their design, are best known.[11] But in 1684 King Charles II ordered the mint closed on the ground that it violated the royal prerogative of coinage. Attempts by other colonies to establish mints proved unsuccessful.

Some attempts to introduce certain coins of an English type into the colonies on the basis of special privilege had little success. In 1722 an English speculator, William Wood, obtained in some corrupt way a royal grant to make copper coins for Ireland and the American colonies.[12] The latter coins were called Rosa Americana after the rose engraved on them, the rose being the well-known emblem of the English monarchy. After a few years, however, Wood renounced the grant for a pension of £3,000 from the English government, and not many of these "roses" entered circulation. Some silver and copper coins, exclusively designated for Maryland, were created by her proprietor, Lord Baltimore.[13] The coins have an aspect of grandiosity, the proprietor's picture appearing with the circumscription "Dominus Terrae-Mariae," but the English government soon stopped their further production.

However, the colonies gradually succeeded in acquiring and circulating foreign specie. This was primarily the result of their maritime trade, which began very early; the first vessel serving that purpose was launched at Massachusetts Bay in 1631.

The main goal of the colonies' Atlantic trade—apart from England—was the Spanish West Indies. There, as in other American possessions of Spain, more coins were in circulation than probably anywhere else. This was the result of the vast output of the Mexican, Peruvian, and Bolivian silver mines, especially as the minting was done within the Spanish colonies themselves. The conquest of Jamaica by the English in 1655 gave to the colonists a trade station within the West Indies, facilitating not only their regular trade but also the smuggling which was done on a large scale, for the West Indian islands were thinly populated and lacked efficient coast guard. The Spaniards themselves took it as a point of honor not to betray their smuggling friends.[14] The balance of trade was favorable indeed for the North American colonies. The goods they sold included dried fish, whale oil, pickled beef, grain and, for a while, lumber and tobacco (Virginia); but from the beginning of the eighteenth century these and other dealings were far overshadowed by the slave trade. The slaves were brought from West Africa to the West Indies; from there many were exported, chiefly to Virginia and other southern colonies.

Foreign currency was also supplied by piracy. At least during the seventeenth century piracy flourished in the Atlantic along with privateering, that is, the licensed capturing and looting of enemy ships. Inasmuch as the Spaniards were, or were long considered, the main enemy, their ships became the chief target of piracy and privateering. The pirates liked to spend their loot in Massachusetts and other Northern colonies at the attractive rates provided there for foreign coins, and they sold the looted goods for whatever they could get. All this occurred with the connivance of the local authorities. The people themselves were prone to look at the pirates, not so much as common criminals, but rather as daring adventurers. The specie brought to the colonies by trade and piracy was, however, not entirely Spanish. Piracy spread to all the seas, and the regular maritime trade of the colonies extended early to the southwest coast of Europe and to the Mediterranean countries.

The Spanish silver coins were soon to become dominant within the growing circulation of specie.[15] Their basic unit was the "real" (royal), a silver coin weighing about 53 troy grains.

The most popular pieces, valued at eight reals and weighing 423.7 grains each, were termed "pesos." In English-speaking countries the pesos came to be called "pieces of eight" or "dollars." Dollar is an anglicization of the German "Thaler." Thaler, again, is an abbreviation of "Joachimsthaler," Joachimsthal being a Bohemian county whose counts in 1517 produced the silver coin which gained wide reputation as the Joachimsthaler. Its pattern was adopted by the Reich, whence the "Reichsthaler" or in English, "rix-dollar." The rix-dollar, which developed into a standard type of European mintage, was of approximately the same size and silver content as the peso. The London dealers in foreign exchange extended the name "dollar" to the peso, which became thereby the "Spanish dollar." Its best known type was the "pillar dollar," so called from two pillars engraved upon the obverse of the peso, on either side of the royal coat of arms, showing the "pillars of Hercules" at Gibraltar; a legend, "Plus ultra," indicated that beyond the pillars set as limits by Hercules there were other lands. The term pillar dollar was adopted in colonial monetary ordinances, and the same is true of some other peso types, the "Seville" and the "Mexican" dollars. Silver coins of four, two, one, and one-half reals were likewise in circulation.[16]

During the seventeenth and eighteenth centuries the use of Spanish silver coins spread to most countries. Owing to the profuse output of the Spanish colonial mines, these coins were not so heavily subjected to the debasement customary in this period—a fact further favoring their widespread use.[17] They even spread to East Asia. As late as 1797 the Bank of England, in order to supplement the English currency, circulated Spanish dollars stamped with a tiny head of George III upon the Spanish king's bust and valued at the rate of 4 sh., 4 d.[18]

The Spanish coins were not the only specie which made its appearance in the American colonies. Gold coins came in from Portuguese Brazil where gold mines had been discovered; French louis d'ors and Venetian sequins, too, found their way to the colonies. Great variety existed among the copper coins, which also included a number of spurious private tokens, such as English "tradesmen's tokens," which consisted in part of lead and had long plagued the British government.[19] But all this did not affect the extraordinary position of the Spanish dollar. Strangely enough, separation from England started in the monetary field.

However, this separation was not complete. The traditional practice of the colonists of reckoning in £, sh. and d. persisted. It proved necessary, therefore, to establish legal ratios between the dollar and the English units. The parity of the dollar on the basis of its silver content was at that time put in the American colonies at 4 sh., 6 d., but owing to the scarcity of coins, the actual rate was higher. In fact, each colony tried to attract coins by favorable valuation. Massachusetts took a relatively conservative attitude by placing the dollar at 5 sh. and sometimes at 6 sh., but other colonies went further by adopting a rate of 7 sh. or more. The same method was applied to other foreign coins.

The specie so rated was declared to be "lawful money," that is, it had to be looked upon as the full equivalent of English specie and had to be received at the proclaimed value by each creditor, especially so in the case of debts stated in £, sh., and d. Since that time "lawful money" has remained a technical term of the American monetary system—in a somewhat confusing way as its premises have long disappeared.[20]

The overvaluation of the dollar and of other foreign coin in terms of the official English units constitutes another evidence of the inflationary trend, and one which caused particular harm to the English creditors. Therefore, England intervened. By a proclamation of 1704, Queen Anne, while stating the "just proportion" of the dollar to be 4 sh. 6 d., limited the "current rate" permissible for the colonial governments to 6 sh. In 1708 the new ruling was confirmed and strengthened by Parliament through threats of punishment to transgressors; but the effect remained slight.[21] The colonies interpreted the proclamation as related to coin only and accorded a higher parity to silver bullion. People dealing with sizable amounts of money would now resort to scales and compute the coins on the basis of their silver content. In 1708 the New York Assembly permitted to a certain extent the clipping of standard coins so that application of the official rate would result in a higher ratio.[22] The home government was rather helpless in the face of these and other methods of resistance and evasion. The fact that it needed contributions from the colonial assemblies for Queen Anne's War against the French (1701–13) further aggravated the situation. Since the contributions ran in terms of £, sh. and d., the assemblies would insist on the application of rates exceeding the proclaimed rates.

It is remarkable that the colonies, despite such extreme handicaps, succeeded in maintaining a coin circulation worth mentioning. But the situation was complicated and confusing enough. An illustration is offered by the itinerary of a Boston schoolmistress, Madam Knight, who passed through New Haven, Connecticut, on a journey in 1704 and commented on the monetary conditions encountered there: [23]

The traders . . . Rate their Goods according to the time and spetia they pay in: viz Pay, mony, pay as mony, and trusting. *Pay* is Grain, Pork, Beef, etc. at the prices sett by the General Court that Year; *mony* is pieces of Eight, Ryalls, or Boston or Bay shillings (as they call them,) or Good hard money, as sometimes silver coin is termed by them; also Wampom, viz. Indian beads which serves for change. *Pay as mony* is provisions, as aforesd, one Third cheaper than as the Assembly or General Court sets it; and *Trust* as they and the mercht agree for time.

Now, when the buyer comes to ask for a comodity, sometimes before the merchant answers that he has it, he sais, is *Your pay redy?* Perhaps the Chap Reply's Yes: what do You pay in? say's the merchant. The buyer having answered, then the price is set; as suppose he wants a sixpenny knife, in pay it is 12d—in pay as money eight pence, and hard money its own price, viz. 6d. It seems a very Intricate way of trade and what Lex Mercatoria had not thought of.

"Pay" in this story meant country-pay, and the "General Court" was the Connecticut Assembly. "Pay as money" signifies the same goods rated at the market price (pork and beef were probably pickled meat which we know was used in trade); [24] the Boston or Bay shillings were the pine tree and other Massachusetts shillings which were not withdrawn after the closing of the mint. It also appears that in 1704 wampum was still used in Connecticut. Madam Knight certainly used reserved language in describing the situation as "very Intricate." The Lex Mercatoria to which she refers is England's venerable law merchant which was considered a kind of universal law.

BILLS OF CREDIT

Ingenious though colonial regulations on coins and their commodity substitutes might appear, the story of the colonial paper money is even more impressive.

In order to contribute to the financing of King William's War (1688–97) against the French colonies, Massachusetts issued in 1690 printed "bills of credit" reading as follows:

> No. 5 sh
>
> This Indented Bill of Five shillings due from the Massachusetts Colony to the Possessor shall be in value equal to money and shall be accordingly accepted by the Treasurer and Receivers subordinate to him in all public payments and for any Stock at any time in the Treasury.
>
> New England, February the Third, 1690. By order of the General Court. [There follow the colony's seal and handwritten signatures of the three members of the "Committee."]

Other bills were of sh. 10 or 20. As the text indicates, they had to be accepted by the Massachusetts authorities not only in the payment of public debts but also for "Stock," that is, in the creation of funds. ("Indenting" is a protective device against counterfeiting.) The notes are very precisely phrased and attractively designed.[25] It may be mentioned that in England bank notes, the first paper money, were printed, it seems, about 1729.[26] As early as 1692, the Massachusetts bills were made legal tender. Issued in limited amounts (in 1690 no more than £7,000), they proved for two decades a sound substitute for coin. They were never considered as infringing a prerogative of the Crown.

The issuance of these bills constitutes one of the most important events in monetary history. China had a kind of paper money since the 10th century A.D. It was based on imperial authority and its common acceptance was ordered under threat of capital punishment. The great Venetian adventurer Marco Polo had reported its existence,[27] but in the West it was never considered an example of currency-making. However, the conception of paper money had been discussed before 1690 in England as well as in Massachusetts.[28] In Massachusetts a Rev. John Woodbridge proposed the issuance of money notes secured by mortgage or merchandise, such as lumber. (Prior to the start of economic theory, monetary problems were frequently treated by theologians, usury being an important subject of canon law.) In addition to such proposals, the early and widespread use of bills of exchange and of promissory notes brought the idea of paper money nearer to the colonists. Endorsable as these bills and notes were, they circulated among the merchants far more extensively than they do in modern times. In fact, owing to the scarcity of coins, the bills of exchange and promissory notes constituted in the colonies something akin to a money substitute. However, it hardly need be added that bills of exchange and promissory notes can never be real money, if only because of the variety of persons, sums, and periods of time involved. Real money requires round sums and complete standardization.

A more direct antecedent of the Massachusetts bills of credit may be found in a peculiar Canadian event of the period. For the payment of soldiers, officials, etc., the Canadian government ordinarily used specie which was shipped to the colony annually by the French government. When a scarcity of currency arose in 1685, the intendant, highest civilian official of Canada after the governor, resorted to a strange expedient. He issued under his own name small notes in round sums (12, 50, 100 livres) [29] which were to be redeemed immediately after the arrival of the next money shipment from France. The notes had to be accepted, under threat of a fine, at their nominal amount. Writing paper was apparently not available in sufficient quantities, but playing cards were. Their pictures could also be helpful to the many illiterates for the identification of the various denominations. Hence, the intendant had playing cards cut and the text of the notes written by hand upon the cards. Such "playing-card" notes,[30] which were subsequently disavowed by the French government, may have been discovered by the English colonists invading the French territories and may have drawn their attention to the idea of paper money. Still, the differences from the bills of credit are significant. In absolutist France the high official would proceed solely on his own authority and even prescribe fines, while in Massachusetts the measure was taken by a parliament-like body of self-government. This difference is significant, of course, from a political point of view. Monetarily other differences are more important. The playing-card notes merely indicated, in addition to being numbered, the amount of money represented without mentioning how they would be redeemed or otherwise discharged; by contrast, the bills of credit defined in a juridically correct manner the right of the "possessor" (bearer). Moreover, the playing-card notes, as was mentioned, were stripped of their legal force through the rejection by the home government. Altogether, the playing-card notes were no more than an approximation of paper money.

The same may be said of the notes issued in 1661 by the Bank of Stockholm on the initiative of a Dutch financial schemer, Johan Palmstruch.[31] They, too, were issued in round sums payable to the bearer, and they were, like the Massachusetts bills, in printed form with the exception of the signatures. Still, there was no legal provision to the effect that they had to be accepted in payment of debts, public or private. Actually, they circulated first at *a varying premium* above the utterly cumbersome Swedish standard coin which was made of copper; for example, a piece worth two "dalers" (dollars), the most usual denomination, weighed more than seven pounds.[32] But inflation followed and the notes suffered a discount of 8 to 10 per cent; after two years their issuance had to be discontinued. The Swedish experiment, long unknown, is symptomatic of the trend toward paper money. However, the Massachusetts bills of credit may well be said to have definitely created that formidable instrument, paper money, which was later to affect so seriously the economic and even the political fate of men.

The bills of credit soon spread throughout the colonies.[33] They were ordinarily made legal tender, and this feature was strengthened by various ways of legal pressure; not only fines, but forfeiture and even imprisonment, were threatened to repudiators. On the other hand, and at variance with the original Massachusetts type, the later acts providing for bills of credit promised redemption in specie at definite dates, or retirement within definite periods; also, special taxes were prescribed in order to guarantee such redemption.[34] In part, suggestions of earlier writers were revived by basing the bills on securities, issuing them as personal loans with the prerequisite of mortgages on land and sometimes of pledges of commodities. In the case of such loans, the sources resort to the expression "bank," which, however, used in a wide sense, applied to issues of bills of credit and extended to the loans granted by the colonial governments through bills of credit and to the pertinent government institution. This is true particularly of the Pennsylvania and Rhode Island "banks."[35]

The freedom of creating bills of credit led to grave inflationary abuses by way of overissues and of violation of promises made to the holders. The period of redemption was sometimes extended unilaterally, the stated maximum of issuance exceeded, the collection of taxes securing the redemption omitted. The resulting depreciation was welcomed by the debtor class, which was numerous and powerful everywhere. "Half of the nation if not more are debtors," said John Adams in 1775.[36] Hence, the inflationary trend received strong support and led to severe conflicts. The degree of depreciation differed widely according to colonies and the various issues ("old tenor," "new tenor," "new tenor second," etc.) of the bills of credit. The deepest depression was reached in 1740 by Rhode Island where one "tenor" finally circulated at 4 per cent of its sterling parity. That colony often took a radical attitude, rooted in its tradition of religious freedom, in monetary matters also, as will appear more clearly from later developments.

Massachusetts, too, ran into serious trouble. By great effort and various artifices, the colony escaped depreciation of the bills until 1713; but then a gradual decrease set in, which reached its nadir in 1749 when the bills were worth no more than 11 per cent of their sterling parity. In the royal colonies the governors appointed by the Crown succeeded somewhat in stemming the tide; in New York, for example, the depreciation amounted to no more than 25 per cent. For Massachusetts it is characteristic that the assembly at one time refused to vote the governor's salary unless he would assent to an inflationary measure.

A step of theoretical interest was taken in 1742 when Massachusetts issued its "new tenor."[37] At the same time it authorized its judges to increase equitably the amounts payable in case the bills should depreciate in relation to English silver coins. In 1747 the reference to silver coins was broadened to include the "prices of provisions and other necessaries of life." Unconsciously the notion, then not yet clearly seen, of purchasing power—and even of purchasing power parity —was used, but the experiment met with difficulties and was ended in 1749. Massachusetts was then able to redeem the notes in coin, since she had received a considerable reimbursement from England for war expenses.

A more satisfactory picture is presented by Pennsylvania.[38] There the first bills of credit were issued in 1723 by a government "bank" [39] which gave "public loans" in such bills secured by land up to 50 per cent of its value. Through wise management this undertaking proved a complete success and contributed greatly to the prosperity of Pennsylvania. Benjamin Franklin's name is connected with it. In 1729 when a slump occurred in Pennsylvania, Franklin, then twenty-three years old and a newcomer in Philadelphia, published an anonymous pamphlet in favor of Pennsylvania paper money, "A Modest Inquiry into the Nature and Necessity of Paper Money," [40] which contributed to the adoption of the measure. It was here that Franklin used the striking term "coined land" for the notes. He tells us in his autobiography that he was then charged by the Pennsylvania assembly with the printing of the notes, "a very profitable job and a great help to me." Technically his notes proved an outstanding performance.

While the original Massachusetts scheme was designed to establish a credit in favor of the colonial government for the payment of soldiers, purveyors of war material, etc., the Pennsylvania device enabled the government to grant credit to the public at large at "easy conditions." [41] Such use of the bills of credit was by no means confined to Pennsylvania, although the outstanding pattern was set there. Here again we are confronted with a novel and progressive development, the public organization of credit. This conception appeared in Europe much later, first in Prussia under Frederick the Great, but characteristically as a favor to the nobility. Similar credit opportunities were extended there to peasants only in the middle of the nineteenth century; until then a paternalistic government felt that peasants should be prevented from "accumulating debts." [42]

A peculiar type of paper currency was employed in Virginia. There a legislative act of 1730 authorized the tobacco warehouses to issue transferable tobacco notes which would be "current and payable in all tobacco payments within the district," that is, these successors to the original tobacco currency ought to be a kind of legal tender, namely, with regard to tobacco debts (as distinguished from debts expressed in monetary terms), but within a definite area. The notes, whose actual circulation started in 1742, proved successful and were adopted by Maryland where they were quite stubbornly kept in circulation long after the United States had been founded and had established the U.S. dollar as a monetary unit.[43] Apparently it was felt that carefully controlled tobacco offered the best protection to the public.

In a number of colonies efforts were made to create private "land banks" for making loans in their own notes, in accordance with the theory which favored private institutions for such purposes.[44] The movement had little success. In 1740 a land bank was established in Boston which actually issued monetary notes redeemable in various goods; but this venture lasted only a very short time. As early as 1741, when about £17,000 of the notes were outstanding, the English government closed the bank on questionable legal grounds,[45] thereby creating a ruinous situation for the subscribers and their payees and arousing bitter resentment.

Far more important was another step taken by the homeland. Reinforcing the policies of the governors, Parliament prohibited in 1751 the further issue of legal tender notes by the New England colonies. Withdrawal of circulating bills of credit was likewise ordered. These measures were extended to the other colonies in 1763.

We are not much concerned with bills or notes bearing interest, as the bearing of interest destroys the monetary character of these bills or notes. Circulation as currency is impossible where the payer and the payee first have to compute the interest due. However, the confused state of colonial currency tended to obliterate the difference. Even the nature of the early Massachusetts bills of credit was obscured by the grant of an "advance" (premium) of 5 per cent if the bills of credit were used in *public* payments. New York tried the same practice in 1709, but gave it up in 1710. The misconception is even more evident in the field of "treasury notes." Treasury notes were and are issued for a short period, perhaps one year or half a year; they bear interest and are not intended to be legal tender. Their issuance by the colonies was expressly permitted by Parliament in 1773. Still, colonial treasury notes had sometimes been circulated in small amounts and were equipped for this purpose at least with public receivability.[46] The resulting confusion in the nature of treasury notes persisted in this country far into the nineteenth century and has even affected writers of our time.

Although the province of New York took a secondary position among the American colonies at least until the middle of the eighteenth century, a few words may be added regarding its monetary history,[47] in view of its later prominence. The protracted circulation of wampum has been mentioned previously. Regarding coin, preference was long given, not to the pillar dollar but to the "Lyon (lion) dollar," perhaps due to a lingering Dutch tradition, for that dollar was probably made as a trade coin in the Dutch province of Gelderland and brought to New York in obscure ways.[48] These coins were also called "dog dollars," because the lion looked like a dog, due to poor craftsmanship. Moreover, the common practice of clipping led to the establishment of a new unit of account, the (silver) "plate." Thus, a New York bill of credit emitted in 1709 begins: "This indented bill of eleven Ounces of plate, or Sixteen Lyon dollars." Later the pound unit was readopted and new emissions followed, based on involved legislation. The poor design of the notes indicated a low level of artistry and was an encouragement to counterfeiters.

Nowhere did the English government's monetary policy meet with stronger resistance than in New York. We have mentioned the strange attitude of the New York assembly in the matter of clipping. In 1771, because of the scarcity of currency, Parliament was compelled to permit New York to issue "paper bills of credit." These "bills of credit" were actually treasury notes bearing public receivability. The act was therefore a forerunner of the general enactment of 1773. Various copper coins were likewise used in New York, some of which, as well as some treasury notes, bore such inscriptions as "Nova Eboraca," "Neo Eboracus," and "Neo Eboracensis."

CLIPPING AND COUNTERFEITING

The "clipping" of coins by cutting or boring into their edges, as well as outright falsifications through use of base metal, has probably existed as long as coins have circulated.[49] The crime spread widely, especially since the last centuries of the Middle Ages. Favored by war conditions, they became in the seventeenth century a menace to the evolving economic systems to such an extent that noted historians, like Macaulay [50] in England and Gustav Freytag [51] in Germany, described in well-known publications these criminal activities and their effects and repercussions. Princes with independent minting power, especially in Italy, participated in the falsifying of coinage.[52]

In the American colonies a very large part of the coinage was criminally clipped or falsified. The colonies were too large and too sparsely settled to allow an effective supervision and prosecution. Counterfeiting of paper money proved particularly attractive to the criminals and dangerous to the communities. Again, this experience was by no means limited to the American colonies, though there it gradually assumed the character of a lasting plague. In the latter part of the colonial era organized counterfeiting bands were working throughout the colonies. A careful monograph devoted to this subject refers to a report of 1768 according to which a clan of 500 counterfeiters was working from New Hampshire to North Carolina, but the author of the monograph considers this number too small in the light of subsequent revelations.[53]

In Europe counterfeiters had been threatened with gruesome torture and death since the Middle Ages.[54] In some colonies, too, capital punishment was enacted as a penalty. New York bills of the colonial period carried the inscription, "'Tis death to counterfeit this bill." Other penalties consisted in branding cheeks or cutting off an ear. Rewards were promised to informers, and North Carolina, which suffered particularly from the counterfeiting of her notes, authorized persons confronting a counterfeiter to kill him if he would not surrender within a certain time. Still, the effect of all these measures was greatly limited because of the variety and numerous flaws of genuine money. Forgery was too easy and too profitable. While in England clippers "were hanged by the half dozen,"[55] nothing similar is reported from the colonies. Only half a dozen executions of counterfeiters, in addition to some suicides, are known for the entire colonial era. In addition to the inefficiency of the colonial system, a certain connivance of the people, who found the death sentence too harsh, might have been a contributing factor to the continuance of counterfeiting. And clipping especially was not looked upon as a grave crime. In 1699 a person convicted of clipping was made clerk of the New York assembly and the governor had to abide by the appointment.[56] This was a kind of prelude to the legalization of clipping.[57]

In the later part of the colonial period the clipping of coins was rather effectively curtailed by corrugating their edges through a milling procedure, a measure first applied in France during the seventeenth century and later adopted by Spain. The "dollars" so improved were called "milled dollars" in the colonies and naturally were given preference over the earlier (handmade or stamped) type. Also, counterfeiting of notes was made more difficult by improvement in the engraving methods. Nevertheless, counterfeiting remained a major crime far beyond colonial times.

A practice different from falsification was the cutting—mostly halving—of the familiar Spanish coins as well as of paper money in order to obtain money of smaller amount. Such "cut-money," apparently rather a local than a general phenomenon, was more used in the early nineteenth century, mainly with respect to bank notes.

GENERAL APPRAISAL OF THE COLONIAL CURRENCY SYSTEM

According to Pelatiah Webster, a noted contemporary writer,[58] currency worth about 12 million dollars was circulating in the colonies at the beginning of the Revolutionary War, or in silver value perhaps not more than 10 million dollars, of which at least two fifths were coins. Later estimates are higher: 22 million dollars, of which 6 to 12 million was in specie.[59] But even so, the amount of circulating media does not appear excessive, since the population at that time was about 2½ million.

In 1764 Benjamin Franklin, in answer to a report of the English Board of Trade, made this remarkable statement:[60]

Pennsylvania, before it made any paper money, was totally stript of its gold and silver. . . . The difficulties for want of cash were accordingly very great, the chief part of the trade being carried on by the extremely inconvenient method of barter; when, in 1723, paper money was first made there, which gave new life to business, promoted greatly the settlement of new lands (by lending small sums to beginners on easy interest, to be repaid by instalments), whereby the province has so greatly increased in inhabitants, that the exports from hence thither is now more than tenfold what it then was; and, by their trade with foreign colonies, they have been able to obtain great quantities of gold and silver, to remit hither in return for the manufactures of this country. New York and New Jersey have also increased greatly during the same period, with the use of paper money; so that it does not appear to be of the ruinous nature ascribed to it.

In later times and especially during the flourishing period of the gold standard, prevailing opinion condemned the colonial system of paper money rather unreservedly. More recently, however, Benjamin Franklin's appraisal has been generally reestablished. Of course, the many imperfections and abuses of the colonial monetary management are evident, but without paper money the colonies would never have attained their astounding progress. In fact, the bills of credit offer another evidence of colonial resourcefulness and vigor. The opportunities offered to the common man were greatly enhanced by the easy access to currency and exerted a lasting influence upon popular thought as crystallized by Benjamin Franklin in his *Poor Richard's Almanack.*[61] "Time is money" is a slogan coined by him, based on a moral approach influenced by the Quaker religion.[62]

The prevalence of paper money, which persisted for many decades after the creation of the United States, probably explains why gold in this country did not have the symbolic significance it had in European countries. Rather, it was taken by the common people as the symbol of dangerous financial power.[63] The practice found widely in France and other European countries of hiding gold in stables, under trees, etc., seems not to have existed in this country (except during the Revolutionary War). Whenever we shall speak of "hoarding" gold, nothing else is meant but keeping it under lock and key. Goethe's "Am Golde hängt, nach Golde drängt doch alles," does not fit into the American picture.

A more serious psychological effect of the prevalence of paper money was a strengthening of the gambling spirit, which had been stimulated by the instability of most of the bills of credit. The inflationist tendencies, so long a threat to the monetary structure of the United States, definitely had their roots in the colonial period.

Politically, monetary (as distinguished from financial) problems became the subject of controversy and strife much more than in any other country. The colonial struggles over the bills of credit were only the beginning.

The monetary picture was influenced also by the fact that the reciprocal relations of the American colonies were practically those of independent states. Although the colonists reckoned in terms of £, sh., and d., the official rates of the silver dollar and other circulating coins varied with the rules and customs of the different colonies. Professor Nettels gives the following figures, with 100 indicating the sterling value of the dollar, for the period after 1708:[64] New England and New York, 155:100; Pennsylvania, 178:100; Maryland, 133:100; Virginia, 120:100; South Carolina, 161:100. Actually, the variations were greater because of the prevalence of paper money which, we know, was always the product of a single colony. It is also characteristic of the semi-sovereign relations among the colonies that the courts handed down judgments in terms of their *local* £, sh. and d., and that in 1744 Massachusetts forbade by legislative action the importation of Rhode Island paper money.

THE COLONIES AND THE MOTHERLAND

While English tradition secured to the colonies the inestimable values of personal freedom and self-government, a different spirit prevailed in the economic field.[65] There the English policies required the colonies to serve exclusively the motherland. For this purpose they had to be kept as far as possible in a state of agriculture, with the raw materials to be exported to England for manufacturing. The English attitude stiffened in the eighteenth century. Thus the erection of slitting or rolling mills and of steel furnaces in the colonies was prohibited, measures preceded by an irritating restriction upon colonial hatmaking. Colonial commerce, too, had first of all to serve England. Elaborating on earlier policies, the Navigation Act of 1660 prescribed that a number of "enumerated" articles might not be directly exported to foreign countries but had first to be sent to England; sugar, tobacco, and raw cotton belonged to this group, to which were later added other more important products, such as naval stores, rice, beaver skins, pig iron, and lumber. Legally, then, commerce with the West Indies and other foreign countries was confined to nonenumerated items, such as slaves. Moreover, under the Navigation Act colonial exports had to be carried on English ships and, with certain exceptions, only English ships were allowed to bring European exports to the colonies, the main purpose being the exclusion of Dutch ships from the colonial trade. The colonists, considered to be English, participated in the various privileges of the English shipowners, but they were greatly curtailed in the development of their non-English trade.

The English regulations form part of what is generally termed a "mercantilist" system—a nationalist policy aimed at strengthening the economic position of the home government. In the case of the North American colonies the officials, British and colonial, exhibited great laxity ("salutary neglect") in the enforcement of the English restrictions. Nevertheless, the restrictions would have been sufficient to keep the colonists in a debtor status toward the English; and other circumstances operated even more in the same direction. The colonists depended on English sales and loans for preserving and improving their living standard; not only did they buy from the motherland better tools and plows than they produced themselves but, remarkably enough, also many little things such as candle sticks, handkerchiefs, calendars, etc. Moreover, since the time of Queen Elizabeth English investment in this country had been considerable. "Taking all the centuries together, this country was the greatest foreign field of financial adventure for the British capitalist." [66]

The effect of the colonies' unfavorable balance of trade, of which we have sketched only the most important aspects, was even aggravated by the prohibition against exporting specie from England. Under Charles II exportation of foreign bullion and coins was made possible under certain conditions requiring a special license, but the new regulations did not include English coin, nor did the colonies otherwise profit from them. The "sinews of war," namely hard money, were too badly needed for English expansionist policies, especially since the motherland herself during the seventeenth century suffered from inadequate currency. Financial relations between England and the American colonies were for the most part carried on by bills of exchange. Thus, colonial exporters drew bills of exchange upon their London correspondents and sold them to colonial importers. Even the English government paid for goods and services received in the colonies by bills of exchange or promissory notes redeemable at the Treasury or at other government agencies, an arrangement leading to many complaints because of bureaucratic and careless handling on the part of the English authorities.

The colonial habit of reckoning in £ gave rise to a strange monetary usage which long persisted in the United States.[67] Under Queen Anne's Proclamation of 1704 the (Spanish) dollar was rated at 4 sh., 6 d., or 54 pence, hence the pound sterling at 4.44 4/9 dollars. Strangely enough, this rate was preserved in the United States as a reckoning method far into the nineteenth century. The rate was then used as a "technical par" to express the value of the dollar in terms of the pound sterling. A quotation of 1 £ would mean $4.44, a quotation of 1.50 £ would mean $6.66. This parity was even adopted by Congress in 1799 for customs purposes, to be abandoned in 1842 because of the change of the gold dollar caused by the American legislation of 1834 and 1837. Nevertheless, businessmen made further use of the "technical par," but this method proved so confusing after the issuance and depreciation of the greenbacks that Congress in 1873 replaced the 1:4.44 and 4.44 4/9 by a 1:4.8665 ratio and declared contracts invalid which still used the old ratio, a curious measure which Congress apparently deemed necessary to break the old and actually awkward custom. At the same time that custom was remarkable for the stability it revealed of the financial ties to England, and, generally, of the strength of tradition, another English inheritance.

Incidentally, an opposite phenomenon, the £ being adjusted to the dollar, occurred in 1804, when under the pressure of the Napoleonic War the Bank of England issued with the consent of the government silver dollar coins of 5 sh.[68] Because of their unofficial character, they were called "tokens," though the use of the foreign unit in coining remains somewhat strange. In 1811 the tokens were called up to 5 sh. 6 d. because of the inflationary depreciation of the English currency, but they were soon withdrawn, it seems.[69]

While policies of the home government in the monetary affairs of the colonies were negative and prohibitive, it was perhaps only the closing of the Massachusetts mint which in historical perspective might be called highhanded and overbearing. Plausible reasons were not lacking with respect to Queen Anne's proclamation or for the suppression of the Massachusetts land bank or the prohibition of the bills of credit. But it was particularly the last measure which proved definitely impolitic. Testifying in 1766 before the House of Commons, Benjamin Franklin called this measure one of the causes why the respect for Parliament was greatly lessened in the colonies.[70] One may perhaps allege as another monetary reason for the growing estrangement from the motherland the fact that England insisted upon receiving American customs duties and other taxes in the hard money so difficult to obtain.[71] Still, the monetary conflicts were to a great extent merely the expression of a deeper discontent. A famous monetary case is illustrative.[72] In 1758 the Virginia assembly resolved that public dues payable in tobacco should thenceforth be paid in money at a rate of 2 d. for the pound of tobacco, the actual value of which was 6 d. Virginia being a royal colony, the measure affected many English officials as well as clergymen. The King vetoed the bill, but apparently an attitude conforming to the veto was not established in Virginia. In 1762 several clergymen brought a suit (the "parsons' cause") for the tobacco amounts originally accorded to them. The defendants were represented by Patrick Henry, the later Revolutionary leader who became famous for his aggressive rhetoric. The lawsuit against the Virginia clergymen gave him his first opportunity for such oratory. He called the bill passed by the assembly a salutary law; by disallowing it, the King had, he asserted, "degenerated into a tyrant" and "forfeited all rights of obedience." The jury could not very well disregard the royal action entirely, so the clergymen had to be awarded damages, but the amount was determined by the verdict at one penny. In this case there can be little doubt that the royal veto was fully justified. The real motive behind Patrick Henry's attack and the jury's scornful verdict was a dislike of royal interference, a dislike especially violent in the financial field, where any burden imposed "without representation" was deeply resented. It was an attitude very much in the English spirit.

Revolution and Reorganization

ON THE American side the outbreak of the Revolutionary War in 1775 immediately raised a fundamental problem in the monetary field, namely, how to finance the war.[1] The Continental [2] Congress at Philadelphia, central authority of the belligerent colonies, was no more than an assemblage of diplomatic delegations, and of delegations not authorized to obligate their principals, the colonies. Congress was therefore unable to raise taxes or to impose any other levies: the colonies even declined to contribute to the treasury of the Congress. Hence, a desperate attempt was made to defray the costs of warfare by a new type of bill of credit.

THE CONTINENTALS

The "continental bills" or, briefly, the "continentals," as these bills of credit came to be known, were based upon a Congressional resolution which pledged the faith of all the confederated colonies for the redemption of the bills. Moreover, it was provided that the colonies should carry out the redemption between 1779 and 1782 in amounts corresponding to their population—assurances of little legal or practical value. The typical continental read as follows:

The United Colonies Three Dollars
This bill entitles the Bearer to receive three Spanish milled

> dollars according to the Resolution of the Congress, held at Philadelphia the 10th of May, 1775.
> [Signatures follow]

At the left and right of the text the words "Continental Currency" were printed. Instead of the customary coat of arms, a design was engraved on the bill showing an eagle (England) fighting a subdued crane (the colonies), whose long bill seems to be piercing the eagle's breast. The picture was not very encouraging, nor was the motto of the bills: *Exitus in dubio est* (The issue is in doubt).[3] The design was changed in later issues. Subsequent to the Declaration of Independence on July 4, 1776, the heading "United Colonies" was replaced by "United States." The bills were originally issued in denominations of from one to eight dollars; later, fractional parts (one half, one third, two thirds of a dollar) were added.

The choice of the "Spanish milled dollar," the common circulating medium, signifies the turning away from English units. It has been asserted that the choice was caused by the different valuation of the £ in the various colonies,[4] but such a difference also existed with regard to the dollar. The English units, however, continued to be used in business and accounting.

The bills were made legal tender by the individual colonies, Congress having no power to do so, and in the colonial tradition, punishment such as penalties and forfeiture of the debt were threatened to those who refused to accept the bills. Congress itself declared that a person convicted of such an offense should be treated as an enemy of his country and be "precluded from all trade and intercourse with the inhabitants of these colonies." Strangely enough, the main sufferers were Quakers who, for religious reasons, would not accept this war money.

In the beginning Congress approached the issuance of the bills hesitantly. The first emission, authorized on June 22, 1775, on the basis of the earlier resolution, amounted to $2 million; $4 million followed in the same year. From 1776 on, under the pressure of unfavorable events, the issues grew rapidly until in 1779 they reached a sum of more than $241 million.[5] Depreciation started in 1776 and proceeded rapidly, driving gold and silver coins out of circulation. In March, 1780, Congress decided to admit the breakdown. It declared its willingness to redeem in specie, at the ratio of 1 to 40, the dollar loans made to the United States, but not much was achieved along this line. The value of the continentals faded entirely, particularly when the states began to cancel the legal tender status of the bills, a measure recommended by Congress itself in May, 1781. It was no more than an honorable burial when the United States, by the Funding Act of 1790, allowed the continentals to be accepted in the subscription of stock (bonds) at the rate of 1 to 100; but only $6 million were used for that purpose. Estimates of bills destroyed or otherwise withdrawn from circulation vary from $70 to $200 million. Stories have been told about barbers who papered the walls of their shops with continentals. The phrase "not worth a continental" became a synonym for utter worthlessness.

We are presented here with an example of a typical "pernicious" inflation, one which in a relatively short time destroys the currency altogether. The same fate overtook the French assignat a few years later and, perhaps most drastically, the German mark after World War I. In the American situation the catastrophe was hastened by counterfeiting to such an extent that Congress had to call in entire issues. Counterfeiting was especially carried on in New York when it was under English occupation.[6] In fact, the English encouraged and practiced counterfeiting in order to crush the rebels. As stated by Congress, "large sums of Continental bills of credit have been counterfeited and issued by the agents, emissaries and abettors of Sir William Howe," the English commander in chief.

Inevitably heavy inflation undermines respect for law. In addition to counterfeiting, it fosters fraud of all kinds, reckless speculation, and provocative luxury by the profiteers. It is one of the most instructive lessons in the history of inflation that even Washington became confused. As early as 1777 he advised the manager of his real estate to adapt the rents to the "intrinsic worth" of the money, and in August, 1779, he decided "to receive no more old debts" at "the present nominal value of the money." The law, he stated, could never "have been intended to make a man take a shilling or sixpence in the pound for a just debt, which the debtor is well able to pay, and thereby involve himself in ruin." [7] Washington's objection became the point of departure of the "scaling laws" which, originally devised by Congress, were enacted by the states after the war. These laws prescribed "scales of depreciation" for the settlement of debts according to months of contracting during the depreciation; the amounts so calculated had to be paid in specie. Practically the device did not work out too well, though it reduced somewhat the damage done by the inflation. In fact, the underlying principle was adopted by France in the regulation of the aftereffects of the assignat's inflation. The claims of the English prewar creditors against American debtors were settled by the peace treaty of 1783, which granted them the full specie value of their claims; but this arrangement met with difficulties and had to be replaced by later less favorable conventions.

OTHER MONETARY TYPES OF THE PERIOD

Paper money was not only emitted by Congress but also by the states.[8] According to colonial tradition, it ran for the most part in terms of £, sh., and d., the relation to the dollar being established by way of decree. The issuance of the state bills was temporarily halted when in 1777 Congress required the states to desist in favor of the continentals; but the issuance was resumed in 1780 following the collapse of the continentals. Hence, the greater part of the states' paper currency was circulated in the eighties, until 1789, when this practice was prohibited by the Constitution. The colonial restrictions of "bills of credit" no longer existed during the Revolutionary period, and the Southern states, especially Virginia and North Carolina, indulged in gross inflationary excesses. The total of state issues was not much below the total of the continentals; depreciation was heavy but, on the whole, not entirely destructive; in Connecticut and in Delaware it was even insignificant. The tenors issued by North Carolina in 1781 and 1782 were an exception; they became entirely worthless. Their poor quality had greatly facilitated counterfeiting.

In 1780 Massachusetts resumed her remarkable experiment of granting protection against inflationary depreciation. The purchasing power of the Massachusetts bills of credit was reduced by the war to a fraction of their face value. The soldiers who were paid with these notes and their families were thrown into utmost poverty and distress by this development. Thereupon the Massachusetts legislature decided to compensate the soldiers (and later some other groups) by the grant of "depreciation notes." These notes, however, were not bills of credit or any other type of paper money but bonds bearing 6 per cent interest and due at various times in the following years. In contradistinction to the 1742 bills of credit, which were subject to equitable adjustment, these depreciation notes or, rather, anti-depreciation bonds, are comparable to modern bonds secured by index clauses. There was no official index at that time in Massachusetts, but a "table of depreciation" was based on the price of beef, corn, wool, and leather. Principal and interest of the bonds had to be computed and paid according to average changes of prices in these commodities. Following an act of 1786 the depreciation notes were exchanged in 1787 and 1788 for ordinary bills payable in coin. There is no information concerning the practical use of the table of depreciation. Apparently the scheme did not function as expected. It is noteworthy, however, for its underlying theory.[9]

While the depreciation notes, in one way or another, actually took care of the soldiers and their families, the frightful inflationary upheaval in prices led to strong reactions on the part of those who were not so protected and were not wealthy. In 1786 the misery which the rural population in particular suffered and which was attributed to the scarcity of paper money led in Massachusetts to an insurrection, Shays's Rebellion.[10] The rebellion was put down by the militia without much bloodshed, and in an accommodating spirit concessions were made to the very needy. The interesting point historically is that here was a rebellion directly connected with the problem of paper money.

The same problem led to another remarkable conflict in Rhode Island.[11] There the government was more under the influence of the inflationists (the "paper money party"), and in 1786 it issued, by means of a "bank," bills of credit which soon depreciated heavily. Under the law the bills had to be accepted by everyone. However, a butcher named Weeden refused to do so. He was indicted, but a special tribunal established by the Rhode Island assembly for such cases absolved him on the ground that the act providing the penalty was unconstitutional. Thereupon, the assembly formed itself into a tribunal and summoned the judges for trial on the ground of disobedience. As in the case of Shays's Rebellion (and often, it seems in this country), the outcome was not as formidable as the preceding events would seem to indicate. Nothing happened to the judges except that some of them were not reelected. The questionable enactments were repealed and the bills were redeemed at a rate of 15 to 1. The

Weeden case is the first to demonstrate in the monetary field the power and independence of the judiciary, unknown to such an extent in countries outside the English tradition.

Sometimes local, nongovernmental paper money made its appearance. A curious example, the only one of its type known, is the "church money" of Schenectady, New York. There, in 1792, because of the scarcity of small coins, the church issued 4-pence (not cents) notes.[12]

Regarding specie we know that gold and silver coins had disappeared during the inflation caused by the continentals, but the situation improved when, in February, 1778, the alliance with France was concluded. French assistance, which created a lasting pro-French sentiment in this country, was also effective in the monetary field. France paid subsidies in gold and silver, while Spain, connected with France by "family compact," allowed specie to be sent from Havana. Moreover, $3 million came from Holland. Curiously enough, England herself involuntarily improved the American currency situation. The English soldiers stationed in New York and other places, as well as the pro-English loyalists, were paid in specie and often used it for purchases from the local population; a feeling of kinship between the enemies, observable also in other respects, made contacts easier. And when the coins from foreign sources appeared, the American hoarders too released their treasures, especially after the military situation had improved. Hence, the early eighties witnessed the circulation of specie in larger amounts, which would have been satisfactory had not the coins been so diverse and so differently rated in the several states. For instance, in addition to the coins mentioned earlier, other gold coins now appeared in circulation, such as the Portuguese Johannes ("joe" and "half joe"), the Spanish doubloon, and English and French guineas.[13]

Confusion existed especially with regard to copper coins valued at 1 d. or ½ d. Some states, especially Connecticut and New Jersey, issued such coins, but to a large extent the copper coins were of unknown private origin. English copper coins, also mostly of private origin, circulated widely, and in 1786 their circulation was prohibited by the Continental Congress.[14] People generally considered copper pieces as tokens rather than as real coins, an attitude which persisted in this country into the nineteenth century.

In 1783, as the result of an unfavorable balance of trade, gold and silver coins left the country, but a new inflow took place in 1785.

Though conditions remained unfavorable for years, the effect of the Revolutionary inflation should not be overrated, especially when it is compared with the pernicious inflations of recent times.[15] There were no savings or other depository banks in the fighting colonies and no bonds or shares exposed to inflation; also, the state issues of paper money were partly saved. Losses were heavy and unfairly distributed; but all things considered, they were worth the sacrifices, and after victory was won they did not greatly delay the economic reconstruction of the country.

PRIVATE BANKS OF ISSUE

In 1780, a year of American defeat, the Bank of Pennsylvania was founded in Philadelphia, seat of the Continental Congress, under the leadership of Robert Morris, "financier of the Revolution," with a capital of £300,000. Its purpose was to give the Continental government financial assistance in the conduct of the war and more especially to establish the necessary contacts with France.[16] The bank also issued a small amount of notes in terms of £, sh., and d., then still the monetary unit in Pennsylvania. Conceived as a temporary institution, it was replaced in 1781 by the Bank of North America. This bank, again located in Philadelphia, was chartered by the Continental Congress after the Articles of Confederation had gone into effect. Again Robert Morris, then Superintendent of Finance, was prominent in its creation; he also caused Congress to issue the charter, whereas the Bank of Pennsylvania had been established under the law of Pennsylvania. The capital of the new bank was determined in dollars; originally $10 million were authorized and $400,000 fixed, but the government was unable to subscribe more than $254,000, and this only after a considerable subsidy had arrived from France. Other subscribers added $85,000. The bank issued monetary notes in very small denominations in order to offer a substitute for the unsatisfactory small coins. Inasmuch as under Pennsylvania law the dollar was worth 7 sh. and 6 d., that is, 90 d., the notes were issued by the bank to the amount of a ninetieth or thirtieth of a dollar, called "one penny specie" or "three pence specie" respectively. The "cent" was not yet known, but these notes were the first to be issued on a dollar basis. The bank operated successfully, establishing for Philadelphia a high standard of commercial punctuality, but was handicapped by doubts about the legality of its Congressional charter. In 1787 it received a Pennsylvania charter and became a local institution.

Following the example of Philadelphia, private banks were set up in 1784 in Boston (Massachusetts Bank) [17] and New York (Bank of New York).[18] The Massachusetts Bank, which was chartered by the state, issued notes in terms of dollars. Since the dollar was worth 6 sh. in Massachusetts, the fractional notes were denominated in pence on the basis of $1 being equal to 72 d. They proved to be a failure because of overissue. The Bank of New York was planned by Alexander Hamilton, who prepared its constitution and became one of its directors. It started business, including it seems the issuance of notes, in 1784 without a charter. This was done on the basis of a common law tradition under which private banking was considered a business, like any other, and the issuance of notes a part of such business; in fact, these notes were not looked upon as money but as credit instruments like bills of exchange. This practice was narrowed down in England during the last decades of the eighteenth century and abandoned altogether in 1823, though in Scotland it lasted until 1844. State legislation in the United States after the enactment of the Constitution made the banking business ordinarily a "franchise" which required a charter, but in early times banking, including the issuance of notes, was considered lawful in the absence of a charter,[19] inasmuch as a charter might merely offer certain advantages such as the limitation on the personal liability of stockholders for the debts of the bank. As a matter of fact, the Bank of New York received a charter as late as 1791. Its notes ran in terms of dollars as well as pounds.[20] The bank was very strict in its regulations and practices and became rather unpopular, but it proved to be prosperous and was able to weather all financial storms. The Bank of New York is the oldest bank still existing in the United States.

THE RISE OF A NATIONAL CURRENCY

The dollars referred to in the bank notes mentioned above were still related to the English unit, though in different ways. The Articles of Confederation (1781) had given Congress the exclusive power to regulate the alloy and value of coins including those struck under state authority, but no such regulation was actually attained.[21] In 1782 Robert Morris, as Superintendent of Finance, in a report [22] to the President of Congress, suggested the adoption of the decimal system, although proposing an infinitesimal unit (1/1440 part of the dollar) to provide the basis for determining the value of the various circulating coins according to the ratios prevailing in the various colonies. In a comment Jefferson declared himself in favor of the decimal system while rejecting Morris's reckoning unit. He proposed the Spanish dollar as the unit and also recommended that the dollar be defined in terms of silver as well as gold; in this respect he referred to the proportion of 1:15 as "eligible." Thereupon Congress in 1785 passed a resolution to the effect that the "money unit of the United States of America be one dollar" and that the dollar should be divided on a decimal system. A resolution of August, 1786, dubbed the hundredth part of a dollar a "cent"—a Jeffersonian term—and the tenth part, a "dime" (*dixième*). More important, the dollar was defined in terms of silver (375.64 grains) as well as gold (24.6268 grains), at the awkward ratio of 1:15.253. All this was mere pronouncement. In September, 1786, Congress took a more businesslike step by ordering the establishment of a mint, but little work was accomplished. Only some copper coins of one cent, one-half cent, and two cents were produced. However, they were remarkably well designed. One side showed thirteen circles (the thirteen states) linked together and surrounding a small circle containing the words "United States" and "We are one"; the other side revealed a dial with a meridian sun above and "1787" at the right, with "Fugio" at the left; below were the words "Mind your business" (since I [the Sun] fly). This inscription, in the spirit of his "Poor Richard," is said to have been suggested by Benjamin Franklin.[23] The coins, also known as "Fugios," are therefore called "Franklin cents"; but due to their scarcity, their significance is only numismatic.[24]

A few states did some coining, as the Congressional ordinance establishing a mint had not entirely abolished the minting power of the states.[25] Massachusetts's copper cents and half cents were outstanding. They were issued on a large scale and, together with the Fugio cents, are the first coins ever produced in terms of the decimal system; they therefore take an important place in the world's monetary history, though it might be mentioned that John Law's notorious French notes (1716–20) included denominations of 10, 100, and 1,000 livres. New Jersey and Connecticut likewise issued copper coins. The New Jersey as well as the Massachusetts coins indicate the link with the revolutionary Confederation by displaying features of the Great Seal which had been adopted by the Continental Congress in 1782.[26] Thus, the Massachusetts coins show, like the Great Seal, an eagle with arrows and an olive branch, and the New Jersey coins, the motto of the Seal, "E Pluribus Unum," which also appears on various tokens and patterns. Vermont, which likewise issued copper coins in the same period, does not belong to this group.

The Constitution of the United States, in force since March 4, 1789, again brought little progress. In Section 8 (5) of the fundamental Article I, the power of Congress to coin money and regulate the value thereof, as well as the value of foreign coin, is reasserted. Furthermore, in Section 10 (1) the states were now forbidden to coin money or, more important, to emit bills of credit.[27] Another provision of the same section prevents the states from making "any Thing but gold and silver Coin a Tender in Payment of Debts," a provision not easy to understand. Apparently the intention was to preclude the states from making copper coins or notes of state-chartered private banks legal tender, but there remains the implication that the power over legal tender was otherwise still left to the states. Actually, that loophole proved innocuous, but the general incompleteness and weakness of the Constitution in the monetary field was destined to become a source of serious trouble.

At least the movement for national unity was by now immensely strengthened, and the newly established government of the United States soon took the first steps toward the creation of a Federal monetary system. When Washington took office, he appointed Alexander Hamilton, his former aide-de-camp, as Secretary of the Treasury. Hamilton, half French and half Scotch by descent, possessed an unusually vigorous and brilliant mind, especially in the financial field. Politically he favored the monied class, partly because he felt its assistance to be necessary for the frail Federal government but also because he considered wealth a partial substitute for aristocracy, an attitude which was to prove disastrous for him. One of his achievements was the funding of the war debts, not only those incurred toward foreign nations—on this there was no controversy—but also internal war debts incurred by the Confederation as well as by the individual states. This measure greatly favored the many speculative holders of old debt certificates but certainly strengthened the credit of the new government. Two other great Hamiltonian accomplishments are more closely related to our inquiry: the establishment of the Bank of the United States and the Coinage Act of 1792.

The Bank of the United States [28] was planned by Hamilton to be much more than the Bank of North America had been. It is true that the new institution, too, was to serve the Federal government. But this task in itself was now far more comprehensive because the Bank had to assist the government in the collection and disbursement of larger and expanding revenues. More important, according to Hamilton's plan, a truly "national" institution was to be created accessible to the public at large and serving the entire community. National commerce and national finances were to be fostered, and last, but not least, the position of the Federal government was to be strengthened. The enterprise was not to be what was later called a "central bank," equipped with monopolistic and other privileges and charged with the preservation of the country's monetary structure—according to Keynes,[29] a "sun" circled by bank-planets. Actually, the concept of a central bank developed many decades later. However this may be, the bank projected by Hamilton was to have a prominent position and a nation-wide influence.

Following the example of the Bank of North America, the Bank of the United States was to be chartered by a Congressional enactment. However, Hamilton's Federalist position led to a bitter struggle in Congress. The Anti-Federalists, at that time called Republicans, and led by Jefferson, were opposed to the curtailing of state power in the financial field. Moreover, they were less interested in trade and industry, which the Bank was designed to serve, than in agriculture, and they were afraid that the wealthy merchants of the Northern seaboard would primarily profit from the new institution. Still, the Republicans, predominantly Southerners, were in the minority. Hence the bill was passed. There was still the constitutional problem of whether Congress had the power to charter a bank at all. Washington felt that in the absence of such power he would have to veto the bill, but Hamilton, whose highest qualities of knowledge, skill, and energy developed in the struggle over the Bank, was able to convince Washington of the constitutionality of the bill, a view which was later judicially confirmed. The act was signed on February 25, 1791. The charter was to expire after twenty years.

The capital was fixed at $10 million, $2 million of which the Federal government subscribed, a step that was taken more for speculative than for political reasons. The Bank was authorized to issue notes receivable in payments to the Federal government. This sole legal prerogative over other bank notes was even made dependent upon the continued redemption of the notes in silver or gold coin, an obligation which was invariably carried out by the Bank. Lack of experience explains the fact that important regulations were left to the judgment of the administration, such as the amount of reserves to be held for the notes. Also, there was no statutory provision concerning the denominations of the notes.

Actually, notes of $5, $10, and above were issued. In design and appearance they resembled very closely commercial instruments.[30] The name of the individual endorsee appears on each note, though with the decisive addendum, "or [payable] to bearer on demand." The signature of the president and the cashier, as well as the name of the endorsee and the date, are handwritten; while the rest of the text, including the denomination of the notes, is printed. The reverse is blank. In the upper left corner, one sees an emblem reminiscent of the Great Seal (two eagles, one with arrows, the other with an olive branch; and the striped shield).

The central office of the Bank was in Philadelphia; gradually eight branches were opened, for example, in New York, Baltimore, and New Orleans. From the beginning the outlook for the Bank was very favorable. The stock was oversubscribed and to a great extent taken by foreign, especially English, investors. In fact, the Bank was a complete success commercially and paid high dividends to the stockholders.

In the technical terminology of American legislation, bank notes as well as other paper money, such as the later U.S. notes, national bank notes, and Federal Reserve notes, are called "currency" (a term meaning simply circulation in early legislation), whereas the term "money" is generally reserved for coins. This is a residue of the common-law tradition which considered bank notes simply as commercial instruments. The old terminology, however, has not been sustained in more recent legislation and, in conformity with the economic and legal literature of our day, we shall speak of "paper money" and, on the other hand, include coins in the term "currency."

THE COINAGE ACT OF 1792

An even more lasting achievement of Hamilton was the Coinage Act of April 2, 1792, officially entitled "Act Establishing a Mint and Regulating the Coins of the United States." The act was based on Hamilton's *Report on the Establishment of a Mint*, a document of outstanding value.[31] Hamilton and Congress followed in many respects the resolutions passed in 1785 and 1786. The "dollar" was to be the monetary unit, defined in terms of gold as well as silver, thereby making the American system bimetallistic. Likewise the decimal principle was accepted with the denominations of quarter, dime, and cent. The name "eagle" for the ten-dollar gold piece referred to the emblem on the coin, which had been proposed in 1786 by a committee of the Continental Congress.

In addition to the eagle, the issuance of gold half-eagles and quarter-eagles was provided for by the act. The silver coins were to be one "dollar or unit," a half dollar, a quarter of a dollar, a dime, and a half dime. Cents and half cents were to be made from copper. Up to the present day, the cent is colloquially called "penny."

Regarding the metallic equivalent of the dollar coin, Hamilton proceeded in a more realistic way than Congress had in 1785. He caused the Treasury to weigh a random assortment of Spanish dollars and found their average pure silver content to be 371¼ grains, at variance with the official Spanish rate of 377 grains, the difference being the result of abrasion. The 371¼ grains were taken as the basis of the prospective American dollar. The gold value of the dollar was determined on the gold-silver ratio of 1:15, as set forth in Newton's famous report of 1717 on the coinage. The pure gold equivalent of the dollar was therefore fixed at 24¾ grains. It is not necessary to elaborate on the circumstantial provisions concerning the alloy, which was and is not taken into account in computing the value of the coins. The main point is the definite separation of the American dollar from its Spanish forerunner, in other words, *the establishment of a new monetary unit of the United States.*

Following the English example, free coinage was introduced. Any holder of gold or silver was entitled to have it coined free of charge by the Mint. The intention was to increase the amount of circulating media and to buttress the accepted gold-silver ratio. There was therefore no "seigniorage," meaning a charge by the government for the coining of the metal offered. However, the gratuitous character of the procedure was impaired by the provision that if the holder of the metal wanted to receive the equivalent in coin immediately, ½ per cent would be deducted. Even so, the burden on the new and inexperienced Mint was heavy enough, and the plan did not work out satisfactorily.[32]

Copper coins of one cent and a half cent, as provided by the act, turned out to be too large, the idea being that they ought to represent the full metal value. Hence, the one-cent coins were about two thirds the size of the silver dollar, which itself was a very big coin. On January 14, 1793, the size of the copper coin was reduced by an amendment to the original act.[33] In later times a number of new coins were added: (*a*) gold—double eagle, $3, quarter eagle, and $1; (*b*) silver—20 cents, half dimes, and 3 cents; (*c*) copper, bronze, and nickel—3 cents and 2 cents.[34] Most of the new specimens proved shortlived.[35] By contrast, the types provided by the Coinage Act of 1792 remained permanent components of the monetary system.

Bimetallism,[36] as adopted by Congress, exposes the monetary system to convulsions whenever the legally adopted gold-silver ratio deviates from the actual market price. The legally undervalued metal, say gold, will be exported rather than offered to the Mint, while the legally overvalued metal will flow into the Mint and depress the value of the monetary unit. However, these effects depend not only upon the scope of market fluctuations but on the development of the technical facilities for issuing, trading, and transporting the metals. It was only in the nineteenth century that the problem became an acute object of controversy. As a matter of fact, the term "bimetallism" was apparently invented as late as 1869,[37] and even the earlier term "double standard" was not yet employed in Hamilton's time. In sponsoring bimetallism he was influenced by the idea that simultaneous admission of gold and silver coins would be helpful in overcoming the scarcity of circulating media. The contrary happened, as will be shown in the next chapter.

Some misunderstanding has been raised by the fact that the Coinage Act of 1792, at the suggestion of Jefferson, called the one-dollar coin the "dollar or unit." Apparently Jefferson and following him, Hamilton, wished to offer an alternative denomination to the Spanish coin. It has sometimes been assumed that the term "unit" should indicate a prevalence of the silver dollar over the gold coins, but this assumption is unfounded. If Hamilton had a preference, it was for gold, as his report clearly indicates. The people never used the term "unit."

The Coinage Act of 1792 provided that "all accounts in the public offices and all proceedings in the courts of the United States" had to be kept in conformity with the new regulations; the decimal system was stressed to such an extent as to provide for accounting purposes a minimal unit of a "mille," [38] or a thousandth of a dollar. Nothing was said about the accounting by state authorities. In fact, the states were slow in adopting the new system. Massachusetts did so in 1794 and New York in 1797; Maryland deigned, as late as 1812, to pass an "Act recognizing the coin of the United States and the value of foreign coins as established by the Acts of the Congress of the United States." And New Hampshire, whose 1784 constitution provided for the establishment of the shilling as the monetary unit, did not do away with this constitutional provision until 1948, by a popular referendum vote of: yes, 62,949; no, 28,038! [39] Actually the people had widely reckoned in dollars before 1792, and the change from the Spanish to the U.S. dollar was generally ignored. But the calculation in £, sh., and d. continued here and there, particularly before the states had adopted the new system. The foreign coins remained in circulation, and the more important among them, especially the Spanish (including the Mexican) dollars, were declared by Congress on February 9, 1793, to be legal tender. The dollar sign, $, is connected with the peso, contrary to popular belief, which considers it to be an abbreviation of "U.S." The two parallel lines represented one of the many abbreviations of "P," and the "S" indicated the plural.[40] The abbreviation "$." was also used for the peso, and is still used in Argentina.

Congress was not bothered much by monetary problems. Its chief concern was the establishment of a new Federal authority, the Mint. (The mint of 1786 had closed down.) Hamilton himself, as the title of his bill indicates, was aware of the political preeminence of this question. The Mint was finally provided for, and its erection as the first public building of the United States was started in 1792. Yet the Mint was treated by Congress with a niggardliness which impeded its operation.

The greatest interest among the people was aroused by the question as to whether the dollar should carry the image of Washington,[41] the first President, or of the Goddess of Liberty. The Goddess won. The Senate favored the portrait of Washington but yielded to the House of Representatives and to popular opinion. The English coins bore the King's image, and the people did not wish to be reminded of the sovereign of the past or even to allow the first citizen to take his place. They preferred to look again and again at the symbol of the liberty which they had won so dearly. This attitude persisted for more than a century.[42] When in 1863 two-cent pieces with the head of Washington and in 1866 five-cent pieces with the head of Lincoln were introduced, they did not find favor with the people. A change occurred, however, in 1909, the centennial of Lincoln's birth, when a one-cent piece adorned with Lincoln's head, the Lincoln penny, was eagerly accepted. Only since then have regular coins as distinguished from commemorative pieces been engraved with figures of the great men of American history—Franklin, Washington, Hamilton, Jefferson, Franklin D. Roosevelt, and, again, Lincoln. Living persons have never received that honor.

Under the Coinage Act of 1792, which is still the law, the

obverse of the coin has to show "an impression emblematic of liberty, with an inscription of the word Liberty." Obviously, the heads of Franklin, Washington, etc. were accepted as emblematic in this sense, a legally questionable theory because of the controversy in Washington's time; but it may be said that he and the other portrayed leaders have *become* symbols of Liberty. The word Liberty has been added to the portraits. Some of the coins still show the goddess either as a figure or a bust or a head; from 1840 to 1878 the figure appeared seated. For the reverse of the gold and silver coins the Coinage Act recognizes the figure or representation of an eagle with the inscription "United States of America." Originally the eagle, as in the Great Seal, holds arrows in one claw and an olive branch in the other. This conditional reference to war has been omitted in recent coins. Moreover, Congress has dispensed with the eagle emblem for a number of coins, especially for dimes, nickels, and cents. Stars are sometimes added, representing either the original thirteen states or the states existing at the time of coinage. One-cent and five-cent pieces show an Indian head on the obverse and a buffalo on the reverse. Artistically the progress achieved since the last decades of the nineteenth century is evident. Up to and through the time of the Civil War the engravings were rather unsatisfactory; the busts and heads of Liberty were particularly unattractive.

Unlike the creation of the Bank of the United States, the Coinage Act of 1792 was not a complete success, due chiefly to the limited extent of general monetary experience. Moreover, events which could hardly be foreseen delayed the development of the new monetary system.

In 1795, Hamilton, then thirty-eight years old, resigned as Secretary of the Treasury largely for personal financial reasons, but still maintained great influence with President George Washington. However, John Adams, who succeeded Washington in 1797, although a Federalist like Hamilton, resented and ultimately curbed his attempts at policy making, and, of course, when Jefferson became President in 1801, Hamilton lost his influence on the government altogether.

Without overlooking the merits of Morris and Jefferson, it may well be said that the creation of a national monetary unit was preeminently an achievement of Hamilton, and one which has stood the test of time until the present day; the silver dollar still contains 371¼ grains of silver. Likewise, the decimal system, as worked out by him, finally prevailed and proved to be an advance of more than national significance. As early as October 7, 1793, France adopted a law prescribing the *calcul décimal* for monetary denominations. This was, it is true, no more than a verbal pronouncement, but the year 1803 (17 Germinal of the Year IX),[43] which also adopted bimetallism, saw the decimal system become a reality. Since then that system has spread all over the world, with the exception of England and countries strictly adhering to the English tradition.

Until far into the nineteenth century "dollars," but not U.S. dollars, remained the principal coins in many English colonies and especially in the Far East.[44] While the English colonies preferred the Spanish dollar, the Mexican dollar prevailed in the Far East. In fact, its value was higher because Mexico, following its establishment as a republic in 1824, and after some vacillation, reverted to the higher standard of the old Spanish peso ("old die"), at least for foreign circulation. On the other hand, the contents of the Spanish peso suffered a slight reduction in the first quarter of the nineteenth century. In the Far East dollar signified the Mexican rather than the U.S. dollar. This is the meaning of dollar, for example, in the important Anglo-Chinese Treaty of 1842 which opened certain Chinese ports to European commerce and, at the same time, obligated China to certain payments in "dollars."

Confusion and Crude Action

THE PERIOD 1795–1837 is the least satisfactory in the history of the dollar. The effects of the breakdown of the colonial regime had still not been overcome at the beginning of this period; authorities and sound policies were widely lacking. These defects are evident in regard to specie as well as to paper money.

SPECIE

The 1:15 gold-silver ratio of the Coinage Act of 1792 was originally in accord with market conditions.[1] But after 1794 the market price of silver started to decline, making the statutory ratio an undervaluation of gold. In 1794 the market ratio was 1:15.37 and in 1808 it reached a climax of 1:16; by 1811, the last prewar year, it was 1:15.53.[2] Nevertheless, gold entered this country until 1807 because of favorable foreign trade conditions during the Napoleonic Wars and because of foreign investments. The Mint coined $128,000 in 1797 in gold coins and $206,000 in 1798; in the following years the annual average was $200,000 to $400,000 and in 1810 and 1811 it was $500,000.[3] But to an unknown extent the gold coins were exported or hoarded as they were worth more than their nominal value. Beginning in 1805 gold coining was restricted to half eagles and quarter eagles, which were less attractive for export and hoarding. Circulation of gold coins, nevertheless, remained unsatisfactory.

Unfortunately, silver currency likewise encountered difficulties. The silver dollars were well designed and looked much better than the Spanish dollars, which had also suffered from abrasion. Hence, the silver dollars were taken on a large scale to the Spanish West Indies and exchanged for Spanish pieces which, in turn, were brought to this country. Thus the excellent quality of the silver dollars [4] proved to be a disadvantage, certainly a remarkable experience. In 1806 the coining of dollars was also discontinued. In this case it is known that the discontinuance—an action hardly in accord with the Coinage Act—was ordered by President Jefferson. Thereafter, the Mint concentrated upon the production of half dollars and lower fractional silver coins which were not exported to the same extent.

Copper coins, chiefly cents, were produced on a small scale. In most of the period prior to the War of 1812 the average annual output was about $10,000. And there was little call for half cents, as the people found them to be too small in size.

On the other hand, there were considerable amounts of foreign coins in circulation. In addition to the familiar Spanish specimens, other foreign coins, especially French ones, became available as a result of the flourishing foreign trade. In 1806 Congress renewed, with ineffective limitations, the legal tender status of the Spanish milled dollar and extended it to the French crown and the five-francs piece, both silver.

All this did not keep pace with the rise in the population,

which, 4.2 million in 1792, rose to 5.2 million in 1800 and to 7.2 million in 1810. The bank notes, to which we shall recur, were to a great extent defective. Nevertheless, monetary conditions prior to the War of 1812 were, on the whole, better than those of European countries during the Napoleonic Wars, or of this country during the War of 1812 and the decade following.

In 1814 gold coinage was reduced to $77,000 and in 1815 to $3,000; and in 1816 and 1817 no gold coins were produced at all. After that a slight but steady recovery took place until the early 1830's when domestic gold production began in Georgia, North Carolina, and a few other states. Until then—the population had grown to 9.6 million in 1820 and 12.9 million in 1830—a monstrous paper money machine dominated the country. The production of silver coins, which in 1815 amounted to no more than $17,000 in quarters, was restored in the following years and rose in the late 1820's to between $1 million and $2 million annually. They were practically all half dollars, but according to a Senate report of 1830,[5] even the half dollars were to a great extent treated as "bullion" (that is, sold or hoarded); only those of the most recent emissions were left in circulation. Hence foreign coins were still in use, and several enactments regulated, although not consistently, their legal tender quality. The Spanish coins, of course, were in the forefront. Retail prices were fixed in amounts like 6¼, 12½, and 18¾ cents, a practice applied even to postal rates and local paper money.[6] The quarter dollar came to be called "two bits" and the dime "a short bit."[7] To complicate matters, the nominal amounts of the coins, including the statutory valuations of the foreign pieces, were little observed. Premiums were paid for "good" pieces,[8] especially pieces on which the inscription was legible.

REGIONAL PAPER CURRENCY

Although the states, under the Constitution, no longer had the power to issue bills of credit, they could charter private banks; and banks, we know, were supposed to issue notes.[9] The states indulged widely in such chartering. Twenty-eight of these banks existed in 1800 and 89 in 1811. Unfortunately, banking was thought of as a highly speculative enterprise with little responsibility. Nor was there, except perhaps for New England, an effective government control. Loans were commonly paid out by the banks in their own notes without giving much thought to specie or other reserves. It was a favorite device of bank directors, who were also big stockholders, to pay the first installment on the stock in specie, as required, but then in a few days borrow from the bank the same amount without security and pay the rest in their own promissory notes.[10] Fortunately, the Bank of the United States was of a different type. Its notes enjoyed a high reputation at home and abroad, and for good reason. It exercised a wholesome influence on other banks by favoring the solid institutions, and this, in turn, explains why monetary conditions before the war were not too unsatisfactory.

But the situation changed disastrously when the charter of the Bank of the United States expired. Despite the heavy burden which the War of 1812 placed upon the country, the state governments continued to grant new charters, heightened by a desire to fill the vacuum left by the Bank of the United States. Before long the specie situation and financial confidence deteriorated to such an extent that in 1814, again with the exception of New England, the banks throughout the country suspended redemption of their notes. Yet remarkably enough, the notes were not thereby eliminated from circulation. People accepted them at varying discounts, especially as the denominations were not too high—mostly $5, but sometimes as low as 25 or 12½ cents, especially in the South. This lenient attitude of the people, which persisted for decades, can perhaps be traced back psychologically to the colonial experiences with the bills of credit; in any case, it resulted in a calamitous situation. Bad experiences did not work as an impediment to the chartering of new banks; the rapidly expanding population and the heavy demands of the westward movement for money and credit offer some explanation. In 1815 the number of banks had arisen to 208 and by 1820 the number had climbed to 307.

No wonder that under such chaotic circumstances banking practices became more and more irresponsible and even fraudulent. Under the law bank notes still had to be redeemed on demand. Hence, the strangest tricks were invented to escape redemption. Banks were located in inaccessible places and came to be known as "wildcat banks," meaning banks in forests inhabited by wildcats; this name became a catchword for the type of inferior "bank" of the period.[11] A contemporary observer declared that "the imagination of an honest man can hardly conceive the stupendous villainies that have been contrived [by the banks]."[12] Nevertheless, since specie was so scarce and banks, whatever their standards, were needed by the communities, state and local authorities sometimes supported the resistance to redemption, especially when large amounts of notes were presented. Thus people seeking redemption were compelled by a state enactment to swear before a justice of the peace, and in the presence of five directors and a cashier, as to the ownership of each bill. Other state governments passed laws delaying payment in specie or suspending execution of judgments.

As if to increase the confusion, paper money of small denominations was issued by municipalities, by bridge and turnpike companies, and by other enterprises.[13] Commonly called "scrips" or "shinplasters," they were given and accepted in payment by the issuer and as circulating media by the people. In the spirit of the common law tradition, the issuance of such scrips was considered a perfectly permissible business affair.

Prices surged upwards due to the flood of paper money. The inevitable collapse of the inflation occurred in 1819, partly through the successful intervention of the Second Bank of the United States which insisted upon redemption of the bank notes. Circulation of the notes of state-chartered banks, which in 1815 amounted to about $100 million, shrank in 1819 to $49 million and in 1820 to $41 million. Many banks and other important business enterprises collapsed. Although the Crisis of 1819 removed some sore spots in the economic structure, the situation remained unsatisfactory throughout the 1820's and only improved slowly during the following two decades. William M. Gouge, an outstanding authority, says in his *A Short History of Paper Money and Banking in the United States*, published in 1833,[14] that "the banking system was the principal cause of social evil in the United States."

In some ways the outrages described are symptomatic of the period. Unprecedented opportunities, lack of authority, instability of living, and the roughness of pioneering contributed to a decay in public morals. Freedom widely degenerated into lawlessness.

But there were also honest reactions. An interesting though unsuccessful experiment was the circulation of "labor notes" in Ohio from 1830 to 1835 by followers of the English social reformer Robert Owen.[15] Representing the amount of time needed for the production of certain commodities, rather than definite sums, they were designed for the buying and selling of goods. They were at least another monetary instance of American experimentation.

More important, in some parts of the country the Crisis of 1819 led in the field of banking proper to progressive measures. In 1819 the Suffolk Bank of Boston, chartered in 1818, established the practice of redeeming at its office notes of New England country banks at par, providing these banks maintained a sufficient redemption fund with the Suffolk Bank.[16] This system proved successful, particularly after a consortium of Boston banks serving the same purpose had been established in 1825 under the leadership of the Suffolk Bank. Country banks unwilling to provide a redemption fund were presented with their notes in large quantities for immediate payment, a form of pressure which explains to some degree the resistance mentioned above. However, the fundamental purpose of the Suffolk system was to keep the New England notes at par, which was certainly an undertaking that served the public interest; and it was helped by a Massachusetts statute of 1810 which placed a penalty of two per cent a month on a bank failing to redeem its notes. Once again Massachusetts had taken the lead.

Meanwhile New York had more and more come to the fore due to the rise of the merchant marine and increasing immigration. Its population, 33,000 in 1790 and 79,000 in 1800, had grown by 1820 to 124,000 and in 1830 to 203,000. The New York banks at first adopted the Suffolk rule. In 1829, however, a new program was accepted by the legislature on the recommendation of Governor (later President) Van Buren. It was based on the "safety-fund" system, allegedly taken from a Chinese model.[17] The law required a charter for each bank of issue; in addition, the bank had to make an annual contribution to a "safety fund" administered by the government, a fund securing the redemption of the notes as well as the payment of other debts of the bank. The amount of the required contribution was made dependent upon the size of the bank's capital stock, imposing an unfair burden upon the larger and definitely solvent institutions. There were other defects and abuses, including fraudulent overissue of notes. Hence, after a few years the system decayed, though its basic principle became popular in other states, and was adopted in an improved form by Canada, where it is still in force.[18]

Another important principle embraced by many states, namely, the preferential right of the note holders over other bank creditors of an insolvent bank, was first introduced by Connecticut in 1831. In New York it was made a part of the state constitution in 1846.

All these measures contributed to the strengthening of public confidence in bank notes, but the fact remained that the value of the numerous types of the notes differed greatly. Discounts remained in use throughout the period, with rates varying locally. From the second decade of the century publications such as "Bank Note Reporters" and "Counterfeit Detectors" appeared and were to be found in all parts of the country. For example, a "Counterfeit Detector and Bank Note List" of 1839 enumerated 54 banks which had failed; 20 fictitious banks, the "notes" of which were in circulation; 43 banks whose notes were unsalable; 254 banks whose notes had been counterfeited or altered; and 1,395 types of altered or counterfeited bank notes supposed to be in circulation in denominations from $1 to $500.[19] The daily newspapers made it a practice to publish tables showing the discounts of the locally more important notes.[20] Here, again, we are confronted with a situation unique in monetary history.

THE BANK OF THE UNITED STATES —AND TREASURY NOTES

When the twenty-year charter of the Bank of the United States drew near its end, great efforts were made to obtain a new charter from Congress, but without success, and the Bank was compelled to liquidate in 1811. The opposition to the Bank was similar to that which Hamilton had been able to overcome in 1791. Now, however, the Republicans led by Jefferson were dominant. The Bank was also attacked because allegedly 16,000 of its 25,000 shares were owned by foreigners, who were mainly English. Under the charter, however, the directors had to be American citizens; foreign residents had practically no voting power since they were not permitted to vote by proxy, and no specific charges were raised against them. But the fact that many of the shareholders were foreigners presented an excellent opportunity for political attacks, and sponsors of the rechartering were charged with "selling the sovereignty of the United States to foreign capitalists," a phrase used by Senator Crawford, who later became Secretary of the Treasury. Jefferson himself proved to be a vigorous opponent.[21]

Seldom have party politics been refuted so fast by subsequent events. Shortly before the War of 1812 began, more than $7 million in cash had to be sent to the foreign stockholders in refund of their shares and $15 million had to be paid in specie to the holders of the withdrawn notes of the Bank. Thus at a critical time the available means of financing the war were severely curtailed. The local banks proved unable to fill the gap. The result was the 1814 suspension of specie payments and the protracted crisis that followed. The government resorted in 1815 to the issuance of "small treasury notes," beginning with $5; all such notes were below $100.[22] They were bearer documents (though like modern paper money, without explicit bearer clause) receivable in payments to the government with no time limit. They did not bear interest but were convertible in amounts of at least $100 into bonds bearing 7 per cent interest. Except for the two handwritten signatures (for "Treasury" and "United States"), they were entirely printed and showed in the corner a well-designed emblem representing the eagle with arrows and olive branch. The reverse was blank. The notes, also "small" in size (6 x 2⅝ inches), are historically remarkable as the first paper money of the United States. Their circulatory function, it is true, was hampered by the fact that the opportunity to obtain a 7 per cent government bond proved too attractive, but the government, after making the conversion into bonds, reissued the notes again and again as they were readily accepted by the public. Some circulation must thus have been attained. In addition to the "small" notes, the government issued "large" ones, namely, real treasury notes of at least $100, bearing interest, drawn on order, and redeemable after one year or earlier. They, too, possessed a monetary feature through the attribute of public receivability, but they did not actually serve as currency.

After the war experience, Congress passed on April 10, 1816, a law once more creating for twenty years a Bank of the United States of America, generally known as the Second Bank of the United States.[23] It was organized along the lines laid down in Hamilton's report of 1791. The capital was set this time, however, at $35 million, the fifth part of which was again taken by the Federal government; five of its twenty-five directors had to be appointed by the President. The Bank started business in January, 1817. Its principal office was again in Philadelphia, but more branches were established, especially in the West; their number finally reached twenty-five. As the result of unscrupulous management, the circulation of its notes increased in 1818 to more than $8 million, an expansion followed by a contraction which reduced the average circulation to about $5 million for the next few years.

After the blunders of the first years, a successful reorganization was begun in 1819 and led to a period of distinct prosperity after 1823, when Nicholas Biddle became president of the Bank. Like the act of 1791, the Bank Act of 1816 provided that each bank note had to be signed by the Bank's president and treasurer. During the 1820's the business of the Bank expanded greatly. The desirable amount of notes could not be supplied in the prescribed way, but Congress steadfastly refused to amend the law. The technique of facsimile signatures was not yet known. In this situation Biddle devised the "branch drafts": checks of $5, $10, or $20 drawn by a branch on the parent bank in Philadelphia, endorsed on bearer, and printed, colored, and designed like the notes. This obvious circumvention of the law was tolerated because it was felt that there was no other solution to the problem. Thus, it was possible to increase the Bank's paper currency to more than $21 million in 1832; but this expansion should not be called "inflationary," [24] in view of the growth of population and trade and the superiority of the notes over those of other banks. Nor was there any failure or hesitation on the part of the Bank to redeem the notes or branch drafts. The notes were issued in denominations of $5 or more and, though more amply decorated, displayed the same features as the notes of the First Bank of the United States, especially the named endorsee.[25]

Perhaps the most memorable event in the life of the Bank occurred prior to Biddle's administration. Since the Bank had to promote the soundness of the country's paper currency, it started to require payment in specie from state-chartered banks. The pressure sometimes exerted upon these banks, reminiscent of the Suffolk practice, rekindled the smoldering enmity of the states, and several of them decided to take stringent countermeasures. When Maryland and Ohio laid heavy taxes upon its branches, the Bank called the tax enactments unconstitutional and the resulting legal case was brought before the Supreme Court of the United States. In *McCulloch v. Maryland* (1819),[26] one of its most important decisions, the Court unanimously decided in favor of the Bank. The opinion, written by Chief Justice Marshall, held that contrary to Maryland's assertion, the Bank was lawful under the Federal Constitution and that the state's tax law, on the same ground, was unconstitutional. In this connection the Chief Justice used a phrase which became famous: "The power to tax is the power to destroy." Relying on Alexander Hamilton's report to President Washington, the opinion took the view that the Constitution granted to the Federal government the powers "necessary and proper" for carrying on its operations unless the power was clearly withheld by the Constitution. This doctrine of "implied powers" became a cornerstone of American constitutional law and the legal safeguard, not only of the Bank of the United States and its notes, but of the various paper monies later decreed by Congress.

Another decision based on the same kind of reasoning was rendered against Ohio; [27] in this case the bitterness of the conflict was emphasized by the fact that Ohio officials, who forcibly took the tax money from the Bank's branch, had been arrested on the order of a Federal court. The legal situation was clarified by the decision, but the political conflict persisted.

The conflict entered a new stage when in 1829 Andrew Jackson became President of the United States.[28] Born in the South, he had grown up primarily in what was then the West, whose prevailing political beliefs he passionately accepted. He disliked the wealthy capitalist class of the Eastern seaboard and the private banks altogether. Worst of all, in his estimation, was the Bank of the United States, which he termed "a monster" and "a hydra of corruption." This view exaggerated and vulgarized the Jeffersonian tradition, but it was increasingly accepted by the new Democratic party gathering around Jackson. It became a central point of attraction in what was felt to be a fundamental contest between the impecunious, as represented by the Democrats, and the monied classes. During Jackson's first administration (1829–33) his attitude remained reserved, but Biddle, who feared him, committed a political mistake by granting questionable loans or earnings to Congressmen on a large scale. Even worse, he prematurely asked Congress for a recharter of the Bank at the time of the approaching presidential election of 1832. Congress voted the new charter but Jackson vetoed the bill. Now the Bank controversy became an important issue in the election, which resulted in Jackson's overwhelming victory. Thereupon, Jackson decided to open the war against the Bank.

In 1833 the Federal government ceased depositing its money in the Bank. Instead, its new deposits were entrusted to various state-chartered banks (the "pet banks"). Inevitably, the Bank of the United States had to curtail the credits which it had given to customers, including state-chartered banks, and Biddle purposely reduced the credits more than was necessary. The result was widespread financial stringency, which aroused popular sentiment more than ever against the Bank. Pressed from all sides, it had to liquidate its affairs. Like the Bank of North America, it was turned into a local institution under a Pennsylvania charter and became known as the Bank of the United States of Pennsylvania. After a few years it failed and went out of existence in the depression which followed the Panic of 1837, contributing thereby to the shift of financial leadership from Philadelphia to New York.[29]

As mentioned before, its notes had always been fully redeemed. Their disappearance was a heavy blow to the economy of the United States. State-chartered banks sprang up everywhere; in 1835 they numbered 704 as compared with 330 in 1830.

The ideological background of the fight against the Bank of the United States is in an oblique way illustrated by certain happenings in Kentucky. Under the Federal Constitution, we know, states are prohibited from issuing paper money and from making anything but gold and silver legal tender. However, Kentucky worked out a sly plan to overcome these impediments and thereby get rid of its debts. It established a corporation, the Bank of the Commonwealth of Kentucky, with the entire stock belonging to the state, which also did the managing. The bank had no real capital stock. This institution was authorized to issue bank notes down to 12½ cents. Under the Federal Constitution the creditors could not be compelled to accept them. The Kentucky legislature decided therefore that if a creditor, unwilling to accept the notes, should bring suit against the debtor, the proceedings would be suspended for two years.[30] The underlying legislation represented an amazing expression of the spirit of wildcat banking; in fact, the Kentucky institution was "a caricature of a bank in every respect."[31] The Supreme Court of the United States was called upon to decide the constitutionality of the issuance of the Kentucky notes,[32] and Justice Story, internationally the most famous jurist in the history of the United States, delivered a truly monumental opinion denying their legality, but the majority of the Court, consisting of Jacksonian appointees, held the notes valid. The majority was probably influenced by the idea that the hands of the state governments ought to be strengthened regarding bank notes especially since the Bank of the United States had been eliminated at the time of the decision. Other states also established banks of their own, but in a somewhat fairer way and without forcing their notes upon the creditors. On the whole, however, these state banks did not prove to be superior to the average private institution.[33]

THE RETURN TO HARD MONEY

The defeat of the Bank of the United States had one favorable result. Since 1819 Congress had wrestled with the problem of how to change the gold-silver ratio of the Coinage Act in order to establish a satisfactory circulation of domestic gold and silver coins.[34] Now Congress could wait no longer. A statute of June 28, 1834, changed the gold-silver ratio to 1:16. To put it differently, the fine gold weight of the dollar was reduced from 24¾ to 23.2 grains. The silver dollar was left unaltered at 371¼ grains fine. The gold-silver ratio in the market of 1834 was 1:15.625. Hence, although bimetallism was legally maintained, the new regulation meant an overvaluation of gold, mainly in order to have the notes of the Bank of the United States replaced by gold coins.

An act of January 18, 1837,[35] further amended and supplemented the 1792 act. Gold and silver coins, following the French pattern, were to have a standard of 9/10 fine. The silver contents of the dollar being unchanged, its full weight was to be 412½ grains, a provision which is still the law, and the weight of the eagle was to be 258 grains, which meant an increase in the gold content from 23.2 to 23.22 grains. The act also ordered free coinage by abrogating the ½ per cent minting charge for immediate delivery.[36] Furthermore, a bullion fund of $1 million was established enabling the Mint to buy bullion for coining independently of minting demands by private owners.

The coinage of gold, we know, had already increased in the early 1830's; a production of $980,000 was reached in

1833. Now the overvaluation of gold under the law of 1834 exerted a great attraction. Gold flowed freely in from abroad and, in addition to the growing bullion produced in domestic mines, old coins were sent to the Mint for recoinage. Coinage of gold rose in 1834 to $3,950,000 and in 1836 to $4,140,000, foreshadowing, so to speak, the great events of the next period. Thus gold coins finally became part of the actual circulation, a great improvement. Silver dollars, we know, had been out of circulation since 1806. The coining and circulation of fractional silver coins, however, continued without great change. More serious troubles concerning the silver situation appeared in the next period; but for the years 1834–37, coining of silver remained at a level of $2 to $3 million, an amount which had been reached temporarily some years before. All in all, specie circulation was now much more satisfactory.

Jackson, it seems, did not interfere in the Congressional handling of monetary regulation, the details of which were probably too technical for him. Still, he was a definite adherent of "hard money" and therefore in favor of the new pro-gold legislation.

His "hard money" policy became manifest in the Specie Circular which, on his initiative, was issued by the Treasury in 1836. It provided that public lands must be purchased in gold or silver or notes recognized by the Treasurer of the United States as convertible into specie. This ruling affected primarily the lands in the West. They had been purchased by settlers and speculators on credit granted by Western banks through their notes, a situation which resulted in a wide overexpansion of credit. The Specie Circular was therefore based on sound considerations, but it contributed to an approaching crisis, which was caused, among other factors, by the elimination of the Second Bank of the United States, which had provided the only control over the credit structure.

Hard money, as sponsored by Jackson, became an important plank in the program of the Democratic party in the following decades. Certainly, under the conditions prevailing in this country there was much to recommend such emphasis. This great President, then, does not lack merit, even in the monetary field. However, there is a growing consensus of opinion among historians that he did not contribute to his glory by his furious fight against the Second Bank of the United States. There was little force to the argument that the existence of the Bank ran counter to the principles of democracy, even considering the political climate of the period. Jackson was influenced by prejudices rooted in his Southern and Western background. His mistake led to grave consequences.

4

The Strengthening of the Dollar 1837-61

THE YEAR 1837 witnessed the outbreak of one of the longest and severest economic crises which this country had ever experienced. Among the causes were crop failures in 1835 and 1837, the Specie Circular, and an English financial panic followed by withdrawal of investments and credits granted to this country. But the main cause was the boundless expansion of business, which led to a collapse when the yields proved inadequate and loans could not be repaid. Overspeculation was stimulated by the tremendous increase in immigration and land cultivation. The gambling spirit of the people had been aroused, in a disastrous way.

Ths Crisis of 1837 was inaugurated, so to speak, by a monetary event: in May, 1837, all banks suspended payment of specie; no less than $149 million of notes were outstanding. More than 600 banks broke down, among them the Bank of the United States in Pennsylvania, as was mentioned above. Had the Bank of the United States been upheld it might have been able to provide fast help. Instead, regular banking business was not restored until 1843. But meanwhile the circulation of notes shrunk to $59 million; the $100 million level was not reached again until 1846.

SPECIE

We have seen how in the preceding period production and coining of gold improved. A new era started in 1848 when, as a result of the California gold rush, production of gold rose from $889,000 in 1847 to $10 million in 1848, $40,900,000 in 1849, and $50,400,000 in 1850, and was to remain for decades at a level of $40 million to $60 million annually.[1] In fact, the 1850 production was above the average annual production for the entire world during the preceding decade.

The new situation found a monetary expression in Congressional legislation. An act of March, 1849, introduced a double eagle and, because of the scarcity of silver dollars, a tiny one-dollar gold piece as well; the eagle had been revived by the Treasury in 1838.[2] The double eagle (diameter 1 5/16 inches) was one of the largest, if not the largest, modern national gold coins ever circulated.[3] It was looked upon as a mark of American wealth and was apparently exported on a wide scale. More important than this legislative action was the general increase in gold coining which, with some divergencies, was in line with the rise of gold production. From $4 million in 1846 (there had been a jump to $8 million in 1843), gold coinage rose in 1847 to $20 million and, after two low years in 1848 and 1849, to $31 million in 1850 and to $37 million in 1856; an average of about $23 million was maintained in the following years to 1860. The rise in gold production and coinage far surpassed even the large increase in population, which expanded from 17 million in 1840 to 31 million in 1860.

Currency circulation was now saturated with gold, but this did not mean that the "gold standard" had been achieved. The bimetallistic silver-gold ratio preserved by the enactments of 1834 and 1837 proved to be more than a matter of legal theory. The statutory undervaluation of silver, it is true, did little harm during the first decade of this period. Mexico continued to export silver to the United States. Silver also flowed in from other Latin American countries. The coinage of silver as well as of gold therefore increased, though chiefly by means of the badly needed quarters and dimes; half dimes remained approximately at the same level.[4] In 1840 the coinage of silver dollars was resumed after an interval of more than thirty years, though in negligible amounts. Instead, the legal tender status of certain foreign coins, especially Latin American silver coins, was established. But it was all in vain. When the market value of gold took a definite downward trend, as a result of the California discoveries, silver began to leave the country. The scarcity of silver coin was keenly felt. Railway companies, for example, paid sizable premiums in order to obtain change for their ticket offices.

This new disturbance to the currency compelled Congress to look for a remedy. The first groping step was an act of March 3, 1851, which provided for a silver three-cent coin designated primarily for the purchase of postage stamps. Weighing about a quarter of the present cent, it was the smallest coin ever produced by the United States.[5] Its silver content was slightly *below the 1837 standard* and its legal tender quality was limited to payments of no more than thirty cents.

A far more important step along the same path was taken

by Congress on February 21, 1853. The fine-silver contents of the half dollar, quarter, and half dime were reduced about 7 per cent and the coins subjected to a legal tender limit of $5. Free coinage was excluded for these pieces.[6] The usefulness of such an arrangement was obvious. Cost of coinage was diminished, and the substandard silver content would work as a barrier against exportation. On the other hand, people at home would care as little about it as they had about abrasion, certainly where small sums were involved. And in the case of higher claims, the creditor was fully protected by the new legal tender limitation. The acts of 1851 and 1853 therefore marked the introduction of a momentous new element into the American monetary system, namely, "subsidiary" coins characterized by substandard contents of metal, by a limitation upon their legal tender status, and by the elimination of free coinage. It may be mentioned that instead of "subsidiary," the terms "fiduciary" or "token" are used (and in the past the French term "billon") for the same concept, and there cannot be much objection to that terminology. But it must be remembered that paper money, too, is "fiduciary" and that "token" often applies to private products.

Subsidiary coins were by no means an American invention. In 1816 England had made all silver coins subsidiary, establishing thereby the gold standard. Henceforth the value of the £ was exclusively defined in terms of gold. Congress expressly declined to follow the English example. Moreover, anything like a general theory of subsidiary coins was far from the minds of the legislators. The new measure was considered rather as a temporary expedient. The silver dollar remained legal tender. Actually, it was as little in circulation as before, but the Spanish dollars and some other foreign coins were still available and had to be accepted as legal tender.

However, in 1857 Congress finally canceled the legal tender status of all foreign coins. The same act made provision for a new copper-nickel cent which was far more attractive than the large copper cent.[7] For a period of two years the holders of the Spanish and Mexican reals (two, one, and one half) were allowed to exchange them for the new cents at a preferential rate. Since the nature of subsidiary coinage was not yet understood, the new cents were not made legal tender, not even for small amounts, but this did not prevent their circulation. The interchange of the foreign coins for cents was carried through until finally the currency was cleared of all foreign elements. The silver dollar was left on the statute books,[8] and bimetallism remained the official theory. It was only after the Civil War that the serious consequences of this contradictory situation made themselves felt.

So far we have been concerned with government coins. Strangely enough, there was still a vast amount of private coining, first of all in gold.[9] This "assaying" business developed especially after the discovery of the California gold fields, but it had started earlier, when gold had been found in Georgia (1830) and North Carolina (1831). On the whole, the coins were by no means fabricated in order to deceive the public; they were simply attempts, and successful ones, to commercialize the newly produced metal. They did not claim government authorization but indicated the name of the assayer (producer) and generally passed as money. Some, particularly those made by Moffat and Co., acquired a reputation throughout the country. There were also several types of private 50-dollar pieces, called "slugs." Among these was an octagonal piece produced in 1851 by the San Francisco Assay Office, predecessor of the San Francisco Mint. The Office, however, acted in this case apparently in a nonofficial capacity since such coins had not been authorized by Congress. After the Mint was established in 1852 at San Francisco, United States gold coins gradually replaced the private pieces, the production of which finally ceased in 1855. However, it is remarkable how fast the private producers of gold had been able to show their skill. It exemplifies again the technical versatility characteristic of the American way of life. And, of course, the large private gold coins are a notable expression of the gold rush. The octagonal 50 dollar piece especially has met with much numismatic interest.

The production of private copper coins was of an entirely different character. We know the indifference of the people toward the inferiority of copper tokens. Many pieces again made their appearance during the Crisis of 1837. Called "hard times tokens" and representing cents, the new copper pieces tried to exploit the scarcity of real cents by a lower copper content and often concealed the name of the producer.[10] Many of these tokens satirized President Jackson, a symptom of the resentment which the last years of his presidency had aroused in some quarters. Others, naming the issuer, were intended simply as advertisements; the numerous "cents" of a button factory in Waterbury, Connecticut, it would appear, belong to this category.

These private ventures with the currency were not illegal. Elsewhere in Western civilization coinage was the prerogative of the sovereign or other ruler. Emerich de Vattel, in his widely known work *Le droit des gens* (1758), considered the sovereign's prerogative over coinage to be self-evident, though he was a citizen of a free Switzerland.[11] The American freedom of coinage is so remote from European thought that one does not find it mentioned in the most comprehensive studies of European writers on the subject of money.[12] To some extent the American attitude can be explained on the ground that the Crown's prerogative of coinage was lost through the Revolution and that the authors of the Constitution neglected to establish a substitute. But there is also the cultural factor of extreme American individualism. As late as 1900 and 1901 an Oregon silver producer issued octagonal silver pieces for "commercial use," claiming this to be his right. He had already issued about 5,000 pieces when the United States government intervened.[13]

PAPER CURRENCY

There were no national banks in this period which could issue bank notes. Indeed, grave doubts existed as to whether the Federal government had the power to create paper money. As in colonial times, there were some experiments with treasury notes. In 1843 treasury notes of $50 and up were issued receivable for public dues and bearing .0001 per cent [*sic*] interest.[14] A committee of the House of Representatives declared them "unconstitutional bills of credit," but no further action was taken. In 1847, during the Mexican War, treasury notes bearing 6 per cent interest were issued which stated on the reverse the amount of interest due for one, three, ten, twenty *days*, for one month and one year, and with the additional words "pay to bearer"; at the same time, as in other issues, the notes contained the phrase "on order." [15] The purpose of the quasi-circulatory "bearer" clause is somewhat baffling, and all the more so since the Mexican War only slightly ruffled the country's financial surface.

The banks established under state law were the main sources of paper money during this period.[16] It is true that a few states, among them California, followed Jackson's hard-money philosophy to such an extent as to outlaw the banks of issue; but the great majority of the states took the opposite point of view and most of the other states abandoned their narrow policy after a few years. In fact the number of banks trebled from 1834 to 1861, when there were a total of 1,601 throughout the country with $207 million in circulating notes.[17] The banking reform movement had continued during the entire period, with New York State taking the lead.[18] The safety-fund system, as was seen, did not work out satisfactorily; but another defect of the state's banking law proved to be more harmful. Since common law tradition was no longer effective in New York, banks of issue had to ask for charters. Hence, the power over banks and bank notes fell into the hands of the state authorities. Chartering became an object of party politics and gross corruption. This situation led to a political revolt by the Locofocos, a radical faction of the Democratic party, and was followed by the adoption of more or less radical ideas by the Van Buren Democrats, who were victorious in the elections. The result was a state enactment of 1838 under which any person or association was allowed to start the business of banking, including the issuance of bank notes, without a government license.

Fortunately, this ultraliberal principle of "free banking," supported somewhat by the common law tradition, was only one of the features of the new legislation. The right to issue circulatory notes was made dependent upon deposits with the state comptroller. The deposits had to cover the entire issue intended by the bank and had to consist of eligible bonds, for example, bonds of the United States or New York State, or—a reminder of the colonial "land-bank" system—mortgage bonds on real estate.[19] In addition to the deposits with the comptroller, the bank had to keep a specie reserve of not less than 12 per cent for redemption, a prerequisite which had to be repealed after a few years. Failure to redeem a note under $1,000 was placed under heavy penalty. The notes were to be printed by the comptroller, who would then turn them over to the applicant, a procedure securing the uniformity of the notes.

At first the "free banking" feature of the new enactment led to numerous abuses and failures, and regulation by the state legislature was therefore made more stringent. For example, mortgage bonds were removed from the list of eligible deposits, and the state constitution of 1846 laid upon the shareholders, in the amount of their shares, an additional personal liability for the debts of the bank. Also, the noteholders were made preferred creditors. Thus, the safety of the notes was greatly increased. New York City, which had a population of roughly 390,000 in 1840 and 1,200,000 in 1860, became definitely the financial capital of the nation. The notes of its leading banks won prominence everywhere, and banks in other places, in order to maintain their credit, had to see to it that their notes would be accepted at par by the New York banks and be listed accordingly in New York bank note reporters. This was one of the reasons why out-of-town banks redeposited with New York institutions part of the deposits received from their customers. Thus, natural developments led to an interplay and organization which had been first introduced by the Suffolk Bank. The chief defect of the new system was its lack of elasticity. The amount of notes being tied to the deposits, the circulation could not be adjusted fast enough to the varying demands of business.

The free banking system was adopted by a great many of the states. In some states it led to a tremendous increase in banks and circulating notes, resulting in confusion and breakdown. This was especially true in Michigan, where the spirit of "wildcat banking" was still prevalent. On the other hand, Louisiana,[20] after some bad experiences, worked out a general banking law in 1842 which placed the banks under the supervision of a Board of Currency, to which each bank had to submit a detailed report weekly; a monthly report also had to be published. A bank director leaving the state for more than thirty days or absenting himself from more than five meetings of the board of directors was deemed to have resigned. More important, all liabilities to the public had to be covered by 33⅓ per cent specie and 66⅔ per cent qualified commercial paper. The minimum amount of a bank note was to be $5. While a number of the Louisiana banks which were unable to meet the new requirements had to be liquidated, others now won a high reputation throughout the country and were well prepared to meet the later crises of 1857 and 1860. It is surprising that Louisiana should have distinguished herself so in the banking field, considering that at the time of the enactment the state had a population of less than 400,000. It may be that the French-Spanish tradition, which was very strong in Louisiana, was more in accord with stringent governmental interference than the Anglo-American tradition. André Bienvenu Roman, Governor of Louisiana in 1842, was an intelligent and strongminded person of French descent and he seems to have had a thorough understanding of banking.

Generally speaking, the free banking system was of great historical importance. It influenced later Federal legislation on national banks and even on Federal Reserve banks.

In the state of New York banks and notes based on the safety-fund system were not abolished after the introduction of free banking, but despite their greater elasticity, they suffered from other weaknesses, particularly from the fact that the guaranty provided by the fund was not confined to the noteholders. In New York the safety-fund system gradually disappeared in this period.

Counterfeiting still caused much trouble, chiefly because of the great number of banks [21] and the variety of their notes.

Special organizations tried to fight the crime by paying rewards for arrests and convictions of counterfeiters. However, the authorities generally showed little interest and the punishment was not severe enough. Most of the criminals escaped punishment altogether.

The wildcat banks were finally weeded out. Enforcing the redemption of their notes became a specialized enterprise in the 1850's. There is an amusing story about a "Bank of Morocco" discovered by an agent, after a long search, in two Indiana log cabins which belonged to a smith, the proprietor of the bank. He had gold enough to redeem notes amounting to $1,000 presented to him by the agent, and he did so, but he implored the agent not to disclose the location of his "bank" to other people.[22]

CHECKS AND CLEARINGHOUSES

Checks are not paper money but negotiable instruments drawn for individual purposes; nevertheless, they do not have a credit function to the same extent as bills or promissory notes, which otherwise have the same character. The fundamental purpose of checks is to replace real money in payment; to this extent they have an immediate monetary effect. In this country it is a matter of common knowledge that 90 per cent or more of all payments are made by check, though this is a comparatively late development.[23]

In London check-like notes made their first appearance about 1675 as bills drawn on goldsmiths with whom the drawer had deposited gold bullion or coins. Though worded in monetary terms (£, sh., and d.),[24] *they were based on ac-*

tual gold deposits. Checks of the modern type, requiring merely sums of money paid into a bank but not kept separate by it, likewise first appeared in London, probably late in the eighteenth century, but it was about the middle of the nineteenth century that they developed into a national system.[25] Paying by check was long considered an exclusive characteristic of the wealthy. According to an English saying, paying by money or check marked the difference between a man and a gentleman.[26]

In this country checks were first used for payment probably during the 1830's in the large cities, but for several decades this practice remained limited and technically imperfect. Bank A having received from a client a check drawn on Bank B and endorsed to A, would send a messenger to Bank B, which had to hand the messenger the amount in gold. Since it was impossible to carry through this procedure in each case separately, settlements were made weekly, usually on Fridays when the messengers (runners) had to run from bank to bank. It was a splendid subject for cartoonists who showed them tumbling over each other.[27] In fact, the delays and risks involved were serious drawbacks to the use of checks.

This condition was greatly improved when in 1853 a central institution for the settlement of bank balances, the Clearing House, was established in New York, an example which was soon followed by other large cities, such as Boston (1856).[28] While clearing arrangements, in a wider sense, can be traced to the medieval fairs, the first vestiges of a regular meeting of bankers for clearing purposes, that is, for payment and adjustment of their reciprocal balances, appeared first in London soon after 1770.[29] These meetings seemed to have been quite informal. Organized clearinghouses developed in London, as well as in Edinburgh, during the first half of the nineteenth century. An outstanding American expert, Albert Gallatin, who had been Secretary of the Treasury under Jefferson, recommended in convincing terms the adoption of the English system in 1841,[30] but it took more than a decade before his advice was followed. Rivalry among banks, a factor observable also in England, may have produced stronger inhibitions in this country, due to the far greater number and diversity of banks. The New York Clearing House, however, proved to be a great success; it was later joined by the Treasury, though only to save the transfer of huge amounts of specie. While the English institutions in their early stages had more to do with promissory notes and bills of exchange, checks were from the beginning in the foreground of the activities of American clearinghouses. We are not concerned here with their other functions, except one which is peculiar to the American situation: their intervention by means of "clearinghouse certificates"[31] in monetary crises, a practice traceable to the absence of a central bank.

Clearinghouse certificates were originally issued by a clearinghouse association to the member banks on the basis of gold deposits in amounts of $1,000, $5,000, $10,000 and more, and they were used among the member banks in the regular settlement of balances. In times of financial crisis certificates were granted also on the basis of eligible assets, ordinarily of marketable securities; officially called clearinghouse *loan-*

certificates, they were not always on the same footing as the certificates of the first group.[32] However, they, too, were correctly considered as being supported by the "solidarity of responsibility" of the member banks which shared proportionately the "liability" arising from the certificates.[33] Hence, they also enjoyed the highest confidence; in common usage the term "clearinghouse certificates" was applied to them, too. But the certificates were not "money." Apart from their high denominations, they circulated only among the member banks. However, as will be seen, this solid foundation of the certificates was sometimes shattered under the pressure of emergency.

The United States and England have remained by far the leading countries in the use of checks and have thereby reduced the currency circulation in a most desirable way. Most continental countries, and especially France, have not developed in this direction, despite some recourse to clearing institutions; Germany, however, has made great advances in this field during the twentieth century.

THE INDEPENDENT TREASURY SYSTEM

Inasmuch as the system of "pet banks" could not be continued indefinitely and a national bank did not exist, the Federal government devised a new expedient. It became its own banker by taking care of its funds and managing its revenues and expenditures through its own instrumentalities. These instrumentalities were local "subtreasuries," including mints and customhouses. The resulting Independent Treasury System [34] was an innovation of President Martin Van Buren, successor to Andrew Jackson, and was based on the latter's "hard money" philosophy. First established in 1840, it was abolished in 1841 by the Whigs, who had been victorious in the national election of 1840. After the Democrats won the election of 1844, the Independent Treasury System was re-established, in 1846. It continued to function until 1920, although the Federal Reserve Act of 1913 may be taken as the point marking its true end.

The significance of the system is illustrated by the fact that in 1855 the Treasury possessed half as much gold as the 1,300 banks in the country put together, since payments to the government had now to be made in specie. The financial position of the government was thereby truly made more "independent." At the same time, specie reserves of the banks were curtailed. Moreover, the usability of their notes was reduced, as they could no longer be employed in payments to the government.

The dispersion of the subtreasury offices over the country was not easily accomplished. For instance, in 1855 William M. Gouge, then official supervisor, was strongly reminded by a subtreasury in Indiana of "what Robinson Crusoe's fortification was supposed to have been." He found the subtreasury

> in a tavern adjoining the bar-room, with which it was connected by a door with glass lights, so that the sub-treasurer might, when in the bar-room, see into his office. The entrance for the public was through a back passage under a stairway. The office was divided into two rooms by a temporary partition, lighted by a single window defended by iron grates. The silver was kept in wooden boxes, the gold in an iron safe. The sub-treasurer slept in one of the rooms with his weapons.[35]

Remarkably enough, the Independent Treasury System apparently suffered no loss through dishonest administration and little from burglary.

CANADA ADOPTS THE DOLLAR

In the first half of the nineteenth century Canada, then consisting only of Upper Canada (Ontario) and Lower Canada (Quebec), had no currency of its own. Monetary conditions were still the same as in the colonial days of this country, if not worse. There was more English and French currency, but this merely added to the variety since the greater part of the currency was foreign and subject to varying regional ratings. Private notes similar to the American "shinplasters" were also in use. Among the foreign currencies that of the United States came more and more to the fore, owing to the rapidly growing trade and financial relations with this country. While accounting was generally done in £, sh., and d., businessmen started to reckon in terms of the dollar with its decimal division. In the 1850's a popular movement for the official adoption of the dollar developed, supported by Prime Minister Francis Hincks.[36] The British government strongly resisted such an independent action but finally had to yield. Early in 1857 the Canadian Parliament passed an act requiring "accounts to be rendered to the Provincial Governments to be so rendered in dollars and cents,"[37] a formula reminiscent of the accounting provisions of the United States act of 1792. It omitted any reference to coinage, which was the prerogative of Queen and Parliament in Great Britain. The Canadian act also provided that the accounting in dollars might be accompanied by an accounting in £, an impractical provision which was obviously added to take care of sensibilities.[38] In 1858 the first Canadian silver coins made by the English Royal Mint were circulated in Canada; their denominations were 5, 10, and 20 cents, and were followed much later by 25- and 50-cent pieces. No silver dollars were coined, so that even in this respect the currency situation was practically the same as in the United States. In 1867, after Canada had become a dominion on a larger territorial basis, the law of 1857 was reenacted. In 1871 the American eagle was made legal tender, together with the English sovereign, the latter at the rate of $4.86⅔, which was, of course, unwieldy in a decimal system.

All these measures were taken without any pressure or even public interest on the part of the United States. Canada was led by a desire to facilitate intercourse with this country and to benefit from the decimal system. In fact, Canada's action amounted to a foreign approval of the merits of the American monetary system.

THE PANIC OF 1857

By strange coincidence the Canadian adoption of the dollar was very soon followed by a disturbance in the American monetary system. A panic developed in 1857 following the breakdown of a large Ohio insurance company,[39] an event which could hardly have caused nationwide consequences had not American overspeculation, this time particularly in railroad securities, again reached dangerous proportions under the impact of the enormous gold supplies from California. In the tense atmosphere the Ohio failure resulted in wide withdrawals of bank deposits and presentation of bank notes for redemption in specie; the accumulation of specie in the Treasury was a contributory factor. Many banks had to close their doors, and in October, 1857, even the New York banks, with one exception, suspended redemption. It was at this point that the New York Clearing House intervened by issuing clearinghouse loan-certificates. The New York banks were thereby given a breathing spell and enabled to resume specie payment by the middle of December.

Another disturbance occurred in 1860 when the election of Lincoln and the subsequent secession of the Southern states increased the danger of war. Cancellation of credits, especially those given to Southern businessmen, again resulted in a suspension of bank note redemption, affecting also New York banks. However, in this case the disturbance was more easily overcome, again mainly through the intervention of the New York Clearing House. As for the Federal government, with the Independent Treasury System it had been able to make its payments in specie without interruption.

By and large, the prewar period brought about considerable progress, especially with respect to specie. Silver dollars, American and foreign, were missing but there were sufficient gold coins and, at the end of the period, enough fractional silver pieces, as well as nickel-copper cents. With respect to actual gold circulation, this country was unique. In England the notes of the Bank of England were generally accepted as a gold substitute reducing thereby the use of gold coins.

The relatively satisfactory condition of metal currency was certainly no compensation for the absence of a central banking institution. The Panic of 1857 and the disturbance of 1860, though by no means as severe as the Crisis of 1837, pointed to a dangerous imperfection in the monetary system.

The Civil War

ON APRIL 12, 1861, the Civil War commenced when Fort Sumter was bombarded by the Confederates. In the North the opinion first prevailed that the South would not be able to fight for very long, and that the war could be financed mainly through loans. However, by the end of 1861 the military situation had not improved, and, moreover, the people feared conflict with Great Britain because of her stern reaction to the forced removal of two Confederate diplomats from the British mail packet *Trent* by Captain John Wilkes of the American warship *San Jacinto*. A feeling of uneasiness arose and gold was hoarded or withdrawn from circulation for other purposes. In December, 1861, banks all over the country suspended payment; no clearinghouse was able to restore order. Hence bank notes began to depreciate fast, and the Federal government was confronted with the necessity of providing another and better currency.

GREENBACKS AND OTHER TYPES OF GOVERNMENT PAPER MONEY

With this purpose in mind, Congress in the Legal Tender Act of February 25, 1862, resolved to issue $150 million of a new type of public money, "United States notes," colloquially called "greenbacks."[1] They ran in round numbers, $5, $10, $20, $50, $100 and above,[2] and did not bear interest. As in the case of the continentals, they promised to the bearer payment in the amount of dollars indicated on the notes without stating the time of such payment. However, like the "small treasury notes" of 1815, they granted the bearer the right to have the notes funded into bonds. These bonds of no less than $100 were to mature within twenty years, but would be redeemable by the government after five years; interest on these bonds (6 per cent) was to be paid in gold. The notes were declared "lawful money" and legal tender (hence the term Legal Tender Act) except for customs, which therefore remained a source of gold for the government. By later enactments the total of greenbacks authorized was raised to $450 million, including denominations of $1 and $2. According to a Congressional act of 1864 the figure of $450 million was to be the definite limit. A questionable measure was passed on March 3, 1863, when Congress without much ado canceled as of July 1, 1863, the convertibility of the greenbacks into gold bonds, leaving the holders with an ill-defined promise of redemption, almost as in the case of the continentals. However, since little use had been made of the conversion and some months remained for converting, the repeal was not censured much and has been little commented upon by writers.

The most conspicuous figure in the financing of the Civil War was Salmon P. Chase,[3] who had been appointed Secretary of the Treasury by President Lincoln. His known personal integrity had been an important factor in the choice, though, unfortunately, he lacked experience in matters of public finance. More disturbing were defects of his personality.

Dominated by strong ambition, he repeatedly tried to obtain the Republican, and later the Democratic, nomination for the presidency. Although his opinions were sometimes contradictory, he was distinctly dogmatic about them, an attitude which frequently led to conflict with the cabinet and Lincoln. Repeatedly he tried to force his ideas upon Lincoln by offering his resignation, but the magnanimous President would not accept it. However, in June, 1864, a new offer to resign was accepted, much to Chase's disappointment. In December, 1864, Chase was named to succeed the late Roger B. Taney as Chief Justice of the Supreme Court, a position in which we shall meet him again.

Chase originally believed that the war could be carried on financially through loans and a slight increase in taxes. The turn for the worse in military fortunes at the end of 1861 found him unprepared and rather helpless. The issuance of the greenbacks was originally provided for by Congressional action; Chase at first opposed the measure but afterward gave his qualified and finally his unqualified consent.[4] The withdrawal in 1863 of the convertibility of the greenbacks was carried through upon Chase's initiative.

The greenbacks became the common currency of the country; immediately after their issuance, they started to depreciate. Mitchell's figures are illustrative:

Average Annual Prices of Gold, Cost of Living, and Wages in Terms of 100 Dollars (Greenbacks)

Years	*Gold*	*Cost of Living*	*Wages*
1860	100	100	100
1861	100	103	100

Average Annual Prices of Gold, Cost of Living, and Wages in Terms of 100 Dollars (Greenbacks) (Continued)

Years	*Gold*	*Cost of Living*	*Wages*
1862	113	112	101
1863	145	129	112
1864	203	156	130
1865	157	168	150

It appears that during the war the cost of living did not rise proportionately to the price of gold; the lagging of wages, partly due to the absence of labor organization, is a striking feature. Holders of government bonds, of which $90 million had been issued prior to the war, suffered least of all, as under the act interest on such bonds was to be paid in gold. One of the causes for the increase in prices was, of course, the tremendous orders of the government for manufactured and other goods. However, the main reason for the price movements was the varying estimate of the greenbacks by the public in terms of gold. There was no difficulty in ascertaining and publicizing gold prices. Trading in gold was perfectly legal. The official center of the gold trade was the New York Stock Exchange, but soon some less respectable gold markets made their appearance in the city. Persons from all walks of life participated in the trading. In the first place, the development of the prices was, of necessity, influenced by military fortunes, and it does not testify to the soundness of speculative judgment that the dollar reached its nadir, 36 cents, in July of 1864 when the superior strength, military and otherwise, of the North had definitely become apparent. One month earlier, Congress, on the advice of Chase, had attempted to check the downward trend of the dollar by an enactment which might be taken as an early instance of "exchange control": transactions in gold dischargeable after the day of contracting and transactions in foreign exchange dischargeable within ten days were forbidden under penalty. However, the public looked upon the measure as a symptom of the government's lack of confidence in the dollar. The effect was therefore the reverse of what was expected, and the act was repealed three weeks after its passage.

The decline of the greenbacks seems to have given rise to the use of the term "inflation" in the sense in which it has come to be used all over the world and in various languages. Apparently, it was first employed with this meaning by Alexander Del Mar, an American monetary writer of questionable merit, in a propagandistic pamphlet, *A Warning to the People: The Paper Bubble* (New York, 1864), which shows quite impressively a puffed-up balloon with inscribed segments illustrating the "relative inflation" of labor, real estate, merchandise, etc.[5]

The greenbacks were not the first Federal paper money of the Civil War. They were preceded by the "demand notes" authorized by Congress on July 17, 1861, soon after the start of hostilities, as a part of Chase's war financing program.[6] Issued in amounts of $5, $10, and $20, like the "small treasury notes" of 1815, they resembled the earlier type of note in that they were not legal tender. The bearer was given the right to have the notes paid at any time, "on demand"; and such payment inevitably had to be made in gold since silver coin was not available.

However, the finances of the Treasury had been in an unsatisfactory condition even before the outbreak of the war, and it is strange indeed that Chase did not give thought to the fact that there would be a further decrease of the gold stock. Actually, gold soon became so scarce that the banks, as was mentioned, suspended redemption of their notes as early as December, 1861, and the Treasury could not help following their example immediately. No such disaster had befallen the small treasury notes of 1815. Nevertheless, Chase insisted upon the further issuance of his demand notes, which in March, 1862, were made legal tender and were kept for a while by traders for the payment of customs—a practice which lowered even further an important source of gold receipts. But this policy could not be sustained, and after May, 1862, the demand notes, amounting to $26 million, were withdrawn and replaced by greenbacks.

In addition to the issuance of the demand notes, the colonial tradition of employing treasury notes for currency purposes was resumed in a highly complicated manner by enactments of March 3, 1863 and June 30, 1864. The notes provided by these laws bore interest, could be redeemed after specified periods, and were declared to be legal tender for their face value only. To their first issues (in denominations of $50, $100, $150, $500, $1,000, and $5,000), interest-coupons were appended, which made their currency function practically impossible. These "interest-bearing notes" were therefore replaced by "compound-interest notes," in amounts of $1, $10, $20, $50, $100, $500, and $1,000. As with the treasury notes of the Mexican War, the reverse side of the notes showed the interest and redemption value, this time for a period of six months. The intention was to make the notes attractive to investors and thereby keep them out of circulation. Actually, it was a self-contradictory device. The notes served mainly as reserves for banks, which thereby obtained legal tender instrumentalities combined with interest. It has been officially asserted that considerable amounts of these notes actually circulated as money.[7] But this general statement is questionable, in view of the inflationary confusion. Circulation merely among banks and fiscal agencies would not fulfill a real currency function.[8] In any case, these additional types of notes were transitory and entirely secondary in importance when compared with the greenbacks.

The new paper money also raised technical and artistic problems.[9] In the past, bank notes, including those of the Bank of the United States and the small treasury notes of 1815, were essentially devised as commercial instruments. Now a new approach was taken, following the example of foreign paper money. Obverse and reverse were fully covered by vignettes, not only showing the amounts of the notes and certifying the issuing authority but also appealing to the sentiment of the people. The prevailing colors were black, white, and green, whereas in the earlier period only black was employed. The United States notes are outstanding in that they have continued as an essential part of the American monetary system from the time of the Civil War to our own day. In size they were originally about 7⅜ by 3⅛ inches and displayed in one form or another the seal of the

U.S. Treasury. In appearance the issues of the Civil War period were somewhat amateurish. The $1 note shows the head of Chase. Others have the portraits of Hamilton and Webster; on the obverse the legal tender character of the notes and its limitations are explained. After the war the artistry of the notes improved. They show the heads of Washington, Hamilton, Franklin, Jefferson, Jackson, Lincoln (in 1869), Webster, Clay, and a few less prominent personalities; frequently female allegories representing Victory, Architecture, Columbia, and the Capitol are added. Chase is the only person portrayed on the greenbacks during his lifetime. The aversion against portraying did not exist in the case of paper money, paper being short-lived still. On April 7, 1866, however, Congress prohibited the portraying of living persons on either notes or securities of the United States in a lengthy statute concerned with dozens of appropriations among which the prohibition was hidden, perhaps in order to soften the blow upon Chase.

The demand notes are generally considered to be the first paper money of the United States (the "small treasury notes" of 1815 being little known). The $5 demand note shows the head of Hamilton, and the $10 note, the head of Lincoln. He was then alive, but it had to be demonstrated that he was the representative of the nation, in contrast to Jefferson Davis. A rather large-sized bust of Chase is again reproduced on the "compound-interest notes" and the "interest-bearing notes." On other specimens the heads of Lincoln (after his assassination), Hamilton, and Washington are seen; the interest-bearing notes of higher denominations have a considerable variety of engravings, showing, among others, various allegorical female figures as well as warships of the War of 1812.

BANK NOTES

The greenbacks were not supported by any collateral, specie or otherwise, but were simply based on the credit of the Federal government. The maximum amount prescribed by Congress for the greenbacks was never exceeded; by the end of the war almost $433 million were in circulation. But more currency was needed. Specie had more or less disappeared from circulation and could not be expected for a long time to meet the exigencies of the economy. The structure of the state bank system clearly proved to be inadequate, and the war had aroused national sentiment, if not sufficiently to permit the creation of a central bank, at least to permit the establishment of a decentralized system of institutions regulated by the Federal government for the issuance of a safe paper money. It was Chase's idea, and in the monetary field his chief merit, that for this purpose the New York "free banking" system was put on a national basis. Inasmuch as New York had long been the country's undisputed financial center, the plan was based on sound experience.

On Chase's initiative Congress adopted on February 25, 1863, an act providing for a national currency designated, from 1874 on, after various amendments, the National Bank Act.[10] The act provided that any five persons might form a "national bank association" with the privilege of issuing notes ("free banking"); as if to exclude any vestige of centralization, a capital stock of $50,000 was declared sufficient for places of 6,000 inhabitants or less. Half of the capital of any bank had to be paid in before the start of business. In conformity with the New York law, bonds covering the full amount of notes had to be deposited with the Comptroller of the Currency, now an official of the U.S. Treasury, who also had to take care of the uniform design and the printing of the notes and to supervise, to the extent provided by the law, the management of the banks. The bonds had to be exclusively Federal, a rule strongly supporting the finances of the Federal government, and on this basis notes could be issued at 90 per cent of the market value of the bonds, but not in excess of 90 per cent of the face value. As a further guarantee, the banks had to maintain cash reserves of 15 to 25 per cent of the total of their notes and deposits. But a considerable amount of these reserves could be kept as credits with authorized banks in "reserve cities," among which a central role was assigned to New York. Finally, as a further guarantee to the noteholders and following the New York example, stockholders were made responsible for another amount equal to their stock ("dual liability").

The notes, in denominations of $1 to $1,000, had to be redeemed at the counter of the bank in "lawful money," including greenbacks, and were receivable at par for all dues to the United States, except customs. A new feature was introduced which declared these notes receivable for all payments *by* the United States (for example, salaries), except interest on Federal bonds.

The national bank notes are by far the most colorful type

of American paper money ever issued. In addition to various allegories on the bi-colored reverse, elaborate pictures are to be found—the landing of the Pilgrims, the discovery of the Mississippi, the baptism of Pocahontas, the signing of the Declaration of Independence.[11] The notes also contained the coat of arms of the state in which the issuing bank was located, a fact which did not prevent some state courts from treating them as notes of "foreign banks" lacking the full legal status of domestic banks.[12]

The first national bank was established in June, 1863, but progress was very slow. On April 9, 1865, when General Lee surrendered, not quite $100,000,000 of national bank notes were in circulation. But the fact remains that these banks had helped the government by their absorption of bonds and of greenbacks. The main development of the national banks belongs to the postwar period.

Regarding state bank notes it is obvious that the suspension in 1862 of bank note redemption placed many banks in a difficult position. The suspension was not supported by legislation. Quite the contrary. The law of New York and of other states provided penalties for refusal to redeem bank notes. In many cases when noteholders insisted on their rights, the banks were compelled to pay out of their reserves of gold and other specie, which the recipients would then hoard or sell at premium prices. Under this pressure the banks naturally tried to restrict the circulation of their notes by issuance of certified checks and in other ways. The situation was somewhat relieved when the greenbacks appeared, since they were legal tender and could be employed therefore in the redemption of state bank notes. Thus, most state banks now resumed redemption and even expanded circulation of their notes. In 1862 the state bank notes amounted to $184 million, which constituted the greater part of the circulating currency. By 1863 they were exceeded by the greenbacks ($239 million as against $312 million of greenbacks). They took part in the depreciation of the dollar, in many cases with additional discounts. This situation provided further evidence of the need for a national currency.

From the beginning the National Bank Acts had offered the state banks special opportunities for conversion into national banks, but with little success. The Federal rules and regulations were so much stricter than those of the various states that the incentives offered by the National Bank Acts were of no avail. It was necessary to resort to coercion. On March 3, 1865, Congress imposed a "death tax" of 10 per cent upon state bank notes paid out by any bank and even by private persons. The state banks were now compelled to make their choice. The majority of them simply gave up the issuance of notes. Quite a few, however, became national banks. There had been only 638 national banks at the end of 1864; one year later there were 1,582 and by the end of 1866, 1,648. State bank notes gradually disappeared from circulation.[13]

The constitutionality of the "death tax" was affirmed by the Supreme Court, with two justices dissenting, in *Veazie Bank v. Fenno*.[14] Chase was now Chief Justice and wrote the opinion. He could not and did not cite Chief Justice Marshall's words: "The power to tax is the power to destroy." But one must admit that the Federal government had to possess greater power in the monetary field than did the state governments. The Chief Justice correctly emphasized the "power of Congress to secure a sound and uniform currency for the country" and "to restrain by suitable enactments the circulation as money of any notes not issued under its own authority." The decision offers another striking instance of the task of the Supreme Court to adapt the insufficiently phrased rules of the Constitution to the needs of an advancing nation. It also marks an important change in the structure of American banking: the long obsolete common-law tradition was broken and the typically commercial banks [15] were no longer identical with banks of issue, a distinction long known in other countries.

FRACTIONAL CURRENCY

By the middle of 1862 the dollar had depreciated to such an extent that the exportation of subsidiary silver coins was profitable. Many went to Canada. Because of the previous adoption of the dollar there, they were readily accepted at full value with undiminished purchasing power; in part, it seems, they were exchanged for gold coins, which were then sold on the New York market. It was a lucrative business and did not require the expense of melting the coins. Even larger amounts of fractional coins went to Latin American countries, where they served as a welcome addition to the inadequate local currency. As a result, the small silver coins so badly needed by every one for food, transportation, etc., disappeared entirely from circulation. A serious situation developed, and help was necessary. A minor expedient was the "cutting" of $1 and $2 notes, a procedure all the less desirable since these notes had been issued only by some of the smaller banks. Many city councils, for instance, those of Newark and Jersey City, started the issuance of fractional money notes in spite of legal objections.

Private copper coins again made their appearance, and on a much larger scale than in the past.[16] A catalogue was later published listing more than 5,000 specimens of this period. They were one-cent pieces, often imitating the official cent, or containing patriotic inscriptions. Other specimens were again of the advertising type. In New York, with its large German-speaking population, 25 million cent-tokens allegedly circulated. One side of one token carried the picture of a patriarchal German with a long, pointed beard, and on the reverse side appeared a beer mug over the name of "G. Lindemüller," probably a brewer who would accept them in payment.

In addition, "shinplasters" once more appeared on the scene.[17] They were issued mostly by hotels and transportation companies, but also by barber shops, drug stores, etc. The issuance of private notes of less than $1 had been prohibited by Congress by an act of July 17, 1862,[18] and many states, including New York, had declared them illegal. But the public did not care and the authorities proved unable to enforce these laws during the critical years.

However, the Federal government tried to relieve the situation by constructive measures which, for various reasons, are of particular historical interest. At the suggestion of Chase, Congress in the act of July 17, 1862, made postage stamps in amounts less than $5 receivable in dues to the Federal government except for customs; in addition, the stamps were made redeemable in greenbacks. This "postage currency" [19] was a most unusual and awkward expedient. Postage stamps do possess an intrinsic value but they are not suitable for circulation. The first effect of the enactment was a rush to the post offices which placed a new burden upon them and soon exhausted their stamp supplies. A conflict arose between Chase and Montgomery Blair, the Postmaster General, especially after people started to ask for redemption of the stamps. Moreover, the stamps were to a great extent cracked or so dirty as to make them unusable and unreceivable. The government therefore decided to issue stamps without glue and printed on tough paper in sheets, with the result that many were mutilated. A private invention was more successful: the stamps were put in a round brass frame with transparent mica as cover and a metal back for advertisements, such as "Ayers Sarsaparilla," or "Take Ayers Pills." These "encased postal stamps" [20] were accepted by the public as currency and they seem to be highly valued by collectors today. They were certainly another instance of American ingenuity. The entire postage currency experiment may be placed in the same category, though rather in the sense of a failure. Apparently the greater part of the postage currency was destroyed through wear and tear, loss, or other accidents, with a corresponding damage to the public. But at least this currency served to drive out the shinplasters.

By an act of March 3, 1863, the postage currency was gradually displaced by "fractional currency" notes of the Treasury of 3, 5, 10, 25, and 50 cents, all receivable for dues to the government. These notes were somewhat larger than postal stamps. The 3-cent note was $1\frac{13}{16}$ by $1\frac{1}{16}$ inches and the 50-cent note was 3 by $1\frac{1}{2}$ inches. They were made of stronger paper than the postage currency and contained the inscription "fractional currency." Obverse and reverse were well designed. The portrait of Washington and of various Secretaries of the Treasury appeared on many of these notes. This fractional paper money remained in circulation until its redemption in silver was ordered by a Congressional enactment of April 17, 1876.

Fractional coinage was likewise improved by the Federal government. U.S. copper cents were in wide circulation at the beginning of the war. When the silver coins vanished, the cent pieces were employed in bundles of 25, 50, or 100 pieces and were readily accepted by restaurants, theaters, etc. A store in New York, we are told, had to take so many of them that the floor of the storage room collapsed.[21] These coins were soon at a premium, though their metal content was below a cent; people had become disgusted by the many flimsy types of fractional paper currency passing around. Hence, on April 22, 1864, Congress enacted a law providing for the coinage of one and two cents, to be made of bronze (95 per cent copper, 5 per cent tin and zinc); also, private production of one- and two-cent pieces was now prohibited. The new bronze pieces were made legal tender only up to 10 or 20 cents, as the legislators were still groping in this field; but actually the first "subsidiary" copper coins had been created.

On March 3, 1865, a three-cent copper-nickel coin was introduced. Under the distress of the war the act also provided that the motto "In God We Trust" be placed on these and other coins. This motto was widely, though not invariably, placed on the coins. Emphasizing the religious trend in American public life, it was made obligatory by an enactment of July 11, 1955.

Fractional-money legislation was completed by an act of May 16, 1866, which created the five-cent copper-nickel piece, a specimen that has preserved its content and weight up to the present day.

All things considered, the war had brought about at least one fundamental achievement in the monetary field: the currency had become nationalized. Moreover, after shinplasters, private tokens, and postage currency had been eliminated, the condition of the currency was fairly good from a technical point of view. The chief problem consisted in the stabilization of the monetary system through redemption of the greenbacks. The difficulties which it raised and its final solution will be discussed in the next chapter.

CONDITIONS IN THE WEST

Railroads to the Pacific Coast did not exist at the time of the Civil War. In fact, the people of California and Oregon were little affected by the changes produced in the East through the Legal Tender Acts.[22] The Mint in San Francisco manufactured gold coins and the dollar did not depreciate. When debtors started to offer large amounts of greenbacks in payment of their debts, acceptance of which would have meant heavy losses to the creditors, the latter developed strong resistance against greenbacks. The resistance became organized when the pressure of inflowing greenbacks increased. The Portland Merchants Association threatened to blacklist debtors who would insist upon their acceptance. It also became common usage to insert into sales, loans, and other contracts gold clauses obligating the debtor to make payment in gold. Such clauses were declared lawful by the California and Oregon legislatures. The states even required payment of taxes in gold. Thus, the price level on the Pacific Coast did not rise much during the war. This fact had to be recognized even by Eastern courts. For instance, the highest New York court admitted, at a time when gold was still at a premium, that the value of a plain California dollar bond had to be determined on a gold basis.[23]

More important, Congress by an act of 1870 authorized the Comptroller of the Currency to permit individual national banks to issue bank notes redeemable in gold rather than simply in "lawful money." In accordance with the purpose of the act, the Comptroller granted that permission to certain Californian banks so as to extend the local gold standard to the Californian bank notes.[24] Characteristically, these notes were "yellowish" like the later "gold certificates."

Actually, the resistance movement amounted to open disobedience of the Federal government. This point of view was admitted by many people in the Pacific states, among others, by the treasurer of the state of California. But the Federal government was too much concerned with the enemies in the South to pursue new quarrels in the West. From an economic point of view it is, of course, easy to understand the attitude of the people on the Pacific Coast; but a noted economist, we think, misses the point when he states that only those people "could decide whether they should have pulled in their belts in order to support the cause of the North." [25]

THE LEGAL TENDER CASES

The Constitution dealt with legal tender only insofar as it barred the states from making "any Thing but gold and silver Coin a Tender in Payment of Debts," and from emitting "Bills of Credit." The majority of the Constitutional Convention had been averse also to Federal bills of credit, but no express interdiction of this type was enacted. Hence, the question remained open. In addition, many creditors, and not only on the Pacific Coast, refused to accept the depreciated greenbacks on constitutional grounds. This situation resulted in numerous law suits. No less than seventeen of the highest state courts were confronted with the problem. Sixteen decided in favor of the greenbacks. The only exception was the highest court of Kentucky which, in a divided opinion, took the view that the Legal Tender Acts could not be applied to contracts made before their enactment. Thereupon the Kentucky case, *Hepburn v. Griswold,* was taken in 1867 to the Supreme Court.[26]

A general sentiment prevailed among the people that on this question, which was so fundamental to the federal form of government, the highest court of the United States would uphold the main measure used in the financing of the war.

Almost all of the highest state courts had done so. Further, the memory of the case concerning the Bank of the Commonwealth of Kentucky could hardly evoke a high evaluation of the Kentucky dissent. And the Secretary of the Treasury, with whose consent the greenbacks had been issued, was now the Chief Justice (abstaining from participation in the case, which one would consider normal procedure today in such a situation, was little practiced at that time).

Instead, something unexpected, in fact something startling, occurred. The man who bore prominently the political and legal responsibility for the greenbacks and had his portrait engraved on them now became their severest enemy—after they had inundated the country and affected the life of each and every inhabitant!

It has been conjectured that Chase had been irritated because Congress did not take the necessary steps for the promised redemption of the greenbacks. Perhaps Chase also resented the fact that he had been compelled by events and by Congress to declare his consent to the issuance of the greenbacks (though in that case he should not have taken the unusual step of having himself portrayed on the notes); [27] now after victory was won, he wanted to exhibit a remote and lofty attitude. And, as often happens when a person feels, perhaps subconsciously, the weakness of his point of view, particularly if he is of a stubborn and pompous character, Chase fought for it with an excessive passion and ferocity. The result was an unparalleled personal hostility between him and other members of the Supreme Court, and mutual accusations were placed upon the record.

Because of this friction, it took more than two years, until February 7, 1870, to decide the case of *Hepburn v. Griswold.*[28] It was a victory for Chase. By a four to three vote, the Legal Tender Acts were declared inapplicable to contracts made before their enactment. Chase himself wrote the opinion which, in addition, implied the unconstitutionality of the acts so as to render them inapplicable even to contracts made after their enactment! An intolerable burden would have been placed by this ruling upon the numerous debtors who had paid their debts since 1862 and to a lesser exent—the dollar stood then at about 87 per cent of its gold value—upon debtors who still had to discharge their inflated obligations. The value of gold would have been raised again and the value of the greenbacks destroyed, or heavily reduced, not to speak of the amount of litigation which the courts of the entire country would scarcely have been able to handle. Fortunately such an outcome was averted. At the time of the decision the Supreme Court consisted of seven members. Two more had to be appointed, and President Grant chose two well-qualified jurists who were known to be in favor of the Legal Tender Acts. Following their appointment, the Attorney General asked the Court in March, 1870, for a reconsideration of the Legal Tender Acts in some other pending cases. At this point the country at large knew that it need not be afraid of *Hepburn v. Griswold.* On May 1, 1871, by a five to four decision on the Legal Tender Cases,[29] the Supreme Court declared the Legal Tender Acts constitutional. The cardinal reasons set forth in the majority opinion, written by Justice Strong, read as follows:

. . . It would be difficult to overestimate the consequences which must follow our decision. They will affect the entire business of the country, and take hold of the possible continued existence of the government. If it be held by this court that Congress has no constitutional power, under any circumstances, or in any emergency, to make treasury notes [30] a legal tender for the payment of all debts (a power confessedly possessed by every independent sovereignty other than the United States), the government is without those means of self-preservation which, all must admit, may, in certain contingencies, become indispensable. . . . It is also clear that if we hold the acts invalid as applicable to debts incurred, or transactions which have taken place since their enactment, our decision must cause, throughout the country, great business derangement, widespread distress, and the rankest injustice. The debts which have been contracted since February 25, 1862, constitute, doubtless, by far the greatest portion of the existing indebtedness of the country. They have been contracted in view of the acts of Congress declaring treasury notes a legal tender, and in reliance upon that declaration. . . . If now, by our decision, it be established that these debts and obligations can be discharged only by gold coin; if, contrary to the expectation of all parties to these contracts, legal tender notes are rendered unavailable, the government has become an instrument of the grossest injustice; all debtors are loaded with an obligation it was never contemplated they should assume; a large percentage is added to every debt, and such must become the demand for gold to satisfy contracts, that ruinous sacrifices, general distress, and bankruptcy may be expected. . . .

. . . A civil war was . . . raging which seriously threatened the overthrow of the government and the destruction of the Constitution itself. It demanded the equipment and support of large armies and navies, and the employment of money to an extent beyond the capacity of all ordinary sources of supply. Meanwhile the public treasury was nearly empty, and the credit of the government, if not stretched to its utmost tension, had become nearly exhausted. Moneyed institutions had advanced largely of their means, and more could not be expected of them. They had been compelled to suspend specie payments. Taxation was inadequate to pay even the interest on the debt already incurred, and it was impossible to await the income of additional taxes. . . . There was then due to the soldiers in the field nearly a score of millions of dollars. The requisitions from the War and Navy Departments for supplies exceeded fifty millions, and the current expenditure was over one million per day. The entire amount of coin in the country, including that in private hands, as well as that in banking institutions, was insufficient to supply the need of the government for three months, had it all been poured into the treasury. Foreign credit we had none. . . .

It was at such a time and in such circumstances that Congress was called upon to devise means for maintaining the army and navy. . . . It was at such a time and in such an emergency that the Legal Tender Acts were passed. Now, if it were certain that nothing else would have supplied the absolute necessities of the treasury, that nothing else would have enabled the government to maintain its armies and navy, that nothing else would have saved the government and the Constitution from destruction, while the Legal Tender Acts would, could any one be bold enough to assert that Congress transgressed its powers? Or if these enactments did work these results, can it be maintained now that they were not for a legitimate end, or "appropriate and adapted to that end," in the language of Chief Justice Marshall? That they did work such results is not to be doubted. . . .

This opinion of the Court was based on the necessities of warfare; but in 1884 the constitutional power of Congress to issue legal tender notes, regardless of war exigencies, was affirmed by the Supreme Court, with only one dissent.[31] Chief

Justice Chase had died in 1873, but even in his last days he had continued to inveigh against the Legal Tender Cases.

Although the Supreme Court upheld the Legal Tender Acts, it did limit their effectiveness in some respects. For example, the Court recognized the validity of contractual "gold clauses," [32] and even the validity of the California and Oregon enactments which excluded greenbacks from the payment of state taxes.[33] This was a highly questionable decision, but at least political harmony between East and West was not disturbed.

CONFEDERATE CURRENCY

Practically no coins, not even copper coins, were produced by the Confederacy,[34] though some patterns have been discovered. Instead, unbelievable chaos developed as a result of the mass and variety of paper money. "Treasury notes" were issued, not only by the Confederacy but by its states [35] and municipalities. Strangely enough, while the Confederacy's notes were not legal tender, the state notes were made so by state legislatures, even though the Confederate Constitution had adopted the prohibition that states could not make anything but gold and silver legal tender.

In addition, there was no bar to the issuance of bank notes. In fact, the banks at first were in an advantageous position because they had gold from pre-wartime reserves; in the course of the war, however, these reserves were exchanged chiefly for Confederate bonds or simply confiscated by the Confederate government. Postage stamps were circulated, too, and shinplasters abounded, even more than in the North. Counterfeiting flourished as never before. Inevitably, strange phenomena were to be found in this medley, such as a Confederate issue of monetary notes in 1861 which promised payment after ratification of the peace with the North, a condition which at least made nonredemption legal. Some of the Confederate notes possessed a military feature absent in the greenbacks, indicative perhaps of the spirit of the Southern aristocracy. There were notes showing an artillery charge or a general on horseback in a commanding gesture; [36] others displayed the pictures of Generals Lee and Stonewall Jackson.

The issuance of paper money, to a much greater extent than in the North, was the means of war financing. There was less resort to taxation; and duties laid on imports and exports were widely made nugatory by the Northern blockade.

As a result of all these conditions, heavy inflation of the Confederate dollar developed soon and, after 1864, took on a pernicious character. A Southern journalist [37] told this story:

> The prices which obtained were almost fabulous, and singularly enough there seemed to be no sort of ratio existing between the values of different articles. I bought coffee at forty dollars and tea at thirty dollars a pound on the same day. . . .
>
> My dinner at a hotel cost me twenty dollars, while five dollars gained me a seat in the dress circle of the theatre. I paid one dollar the next morning for a copy of the Examiner, but I might have got the Whig, Dispatch, Enquirer, or Sentinel, for half that sum. For some wretched tallow candles I paid ten dollars a pound. The utter absence of proportion between these several prices is apparent. . . . A facetious friend said . . . "Before the war . . . I went to market with the money in my pocket, and brought

back my purchases in a basket; now I take the money in the basket, and bring the things home in my pocket." . . . Towards the last . . . bartering, or "payment in kind," as it was called, became common. . . . To fix a price for the future in Confederate money when it was daily becoming more and more exaggeratedly worthless, would have been sheer folly.

Smuggling and blockade-running brought some relief, primarily, of course, to the wealthy class, and with great profit to the transgressors. United States notes were among the smuggled objects; others were hoarded as a precious residue of past times. More important, the invading Northern troops spent their money in the South (a strange analogy to the payments in British money by the British army during the Revolutionary War). Greenbacks were publicly quoted by Richmond brokers until public opinion forced them to discontinue this practice. The Confederate government itself had to make use of United States money. By the end of the war some Confederate soldiers could be kept under arms only if they were paid in greenbacks.

After the war was ended the Confederate dollar had lost any value whatsoever and no "honorable burial" ever took place. It was the worst case of inflation in American history.

The grave problems of Reconstruction with which the United States was confronted after the war have often been described. In the monetary field the main question was presented by the debts contracted in Confederate dollars. Declaring them entirely worthless would have been another heavy blow to the paralyzed Southern economy, though it would have been easy to justify such a ruling juridically.

However, the Supreme Court of the United States held that contracts made in terms of Confederate dollars could not per se be regarded as made in aid of the insurrection; the Court deemed them valid, that is, the debtor had to pay in United States dollars the actual value of Confederate dollars as it existed at the place and time of contracting.[38]

As mentioned above, the engraving of the wartime notes of the United States lacked any military features. But, late in the 1880's and particularly in the "Treasury notes of 1890," [39] President Grant and some of his generals were pictured. However, General Sherman, though more successful and famous (or, to Southerners, notorious) than some of the portrayed heroes, was not included on any one of the notes. When a small fractional note of 15 cents had been prepared with the heads of Grant and Sherman, it was on second thought not placed in circulation.[40] And in 1925 the United States issued a commemorative half-dollar piece showing the images of Lee and Stonewall Jackson. It might be difficult to find anywhere in the world a counterpart to such honor conferred upon defeated "rebels."

The Struggle against the Gold Standard 1865-1900

DESPITE THE slump of the dollar during the Civil War, the gold ratio laid down by the laws of 1834 and 1837 had not been changed. Nor was there any intention of undertaking such a change after the victory was won and brilliant opportunities opened up for the economic development of the United States.[1] In fact, an adjustment of the dollar's gold value to the statutory ratio finally succeeded, an extraordinary achievement.[2] By way of comparison, one is reminded of the restoration of the £'s or the guilder's gold value after World War I.

THE GREENBACKS

But the American situation was a much more difficult one. Not only did the dollar depreciate about twice as much as the £ was to depreciate half a century later, but the resistance to the reestablishment of the original value of the dollar, which had to be accomplished through redemption of the greenbacks, was much stronger, especially on the part of the economically most important and politically powerful farmers. They feared that the revalorization of the dollar would result in lower prices for their products and, at the same time, aggravate their debts; credits were a fundamental factor in agriculture. It was mainly for this reason that it took more than thirteen years to restore the gold value of the dollar. Immediately after the end of the Civil War the atmosphere was favorable for starting the restoration of the gold standard, and the Treasury, supported by Congress, began to reduce the greenbacks in circulation. But the situation changed in 1867 when the war boom began to fade. The Democrats, whose main strength was in the agricultural states, adopted an inflationist, or at least anti-deflationist attitude, which also found many followers among the Republicans. On February 4, 1868, Congress suspended the further withdrawal of the greenbacks, the circulation of which had been reduced by the Treasury from $450 to $356 million. The suspension inaugurated a period of further uncertainty. Speculation in gold, which had never ceased, received a new incentive.

In the months preceding Lee's surrender, the dollar had slowly moved up in terms of gold value from 45 to 70, but always subject to considerable fluctuation. It was only on September 24, 1869, "Black Friday," that the worst excesses of gold speculation occurred.[3] Jay Gould, one of the country's leading financial magnates, and his accomplice, James Fisk, had devised a plan to corner the gold supply so as to place the "short sellers" of gold at their mercy. These two men, notorious for their ruthlessness, succeeded within a few days in pushing up the price of gold from 130 to 162, but on September 24 the Federal government, which had so far shut its eyes to the maneuvers, ordered the sale of its gold. Thereupon the price of gold plunged within fifteen minutes to 133. A thorough Congressional investigation revealed the grave consequences brought about by the maneuver, mainly because of the importance which gold then had in the foreign trade. In the words of the report of the Senate committee, "a heavy blow was dealt to our credit abroad" and "for many weeks the business of the whole country was paralyzed." The minority report of the committee also censured the administration, even President Grant, for having allowed himself to be grossly misled by the sly Gould. Black Friday has remained a day of evil memory in American history; it did much to arouse popular animosity against the financial magnates of the day.

After Black Friday the gold rate of the dollar rose from 76 to 82 in the latter part of 1869; to 87 in 1870; to 89.5 in 1871; and in 1872 it amounted to 89. Congress and the government had contributed little to this improvement, which simply reflected the tremendous expansion of American population, industry, agriculture, and railroads. Large foreign investments were another favorable factor. Early in 1873, however, this development was interrupted by an economic depression which, though international in origin, was again deepened in this country as a result of overspeculation, especially in the stock market. The New York Stock Exchange had to close its doors for ten days, but a currency shortage was again averted through the issuance of clearinghouse loan certificates.

By a strange concatenation of political events, the depression, which lasted no less than four years, became the cause for the redemption of the greenbacks. The Republicans, long in power, were held responsible for the depression, and in the

Congressional elections of 1874 they were defeated by the Democrats. There was a feeling among the Republicans that they should do something to restore a sound currency. Hence, on January 14, 1875, during the last ("lame-duck") session under Republican majority, Congress adopted the Resumption Act: the Treasury had to stand ready on January 1, 1879, to redeem the greenbacks in coin and to bring about thereby the general resumption of specie payments. "Coin" was understood to mean gold; when the Resumption Act was passed, silver dollars, as will be seen, were not legal tender. In fact, the Resumption Act formed part of a definite gold standard policy. The Democrats had sufficient voting power to repeal the act but such a step would have required stronger determination than they possessed; moreover, in 1875 the international trade balance changed in favor of the United States and resulted in an ample influx of gold. This development greatly favored the redemption. Though much popular sentiment persisted against the enforcing of gold payments, the only pro-greenback measure carried through by the Democratic majority in Congress, in May, 1878, prohibited a further withdrawal of greenbacks, the maximum of circulation being fixed at $346,681,000. This amount has remained mandatory up to the present day.

It was a sign of the country's financial strength that even during the worst years of depression, 1873–75, the average gold value of the greenbacks was reduced in 1873 to no more than 87.9 cents and to 87 in 1875—the latter figure indicating that the Resumption Act had not yet offered much encouragement to bullish speculators in greenbacks. The credit for carrying through the redemption of the greenbacks goes chiefly to John Sherman, who early in 1877 was appointed Secretary of the Treasury by the new President, Rutherford B. Hayes, successor to Grant and likewise a Republican. Sherman was lucky in that since the end of 1876 the balance of trade had shifted further in favor of the United States, chiefly through increased exports of agricultural products. But Sherman also knew how to attract foreign investors and by the sale of treasury bonds piled up a large reserve in the Treasury. The gold value of the dollar, still 89.6 in 1876, rose to 95.5 in 1877. By the end of 1878 the gold premium had disappeared and on the first business day in January, 1879, the Treasury was faced with nothing like a gold rush. There was, in fact, more demand for greenbacks than for gold.

These events again illustrate the unique role of monetary problems in American politics. Not only was the Democratic, as well as the Republican, election program largely concerned with the redemption of the greenbacks—the Republicans being more in its favor—but in 1874–76 a new party, the Greenback party, made its appearance. It stood for repeal of the Resumption Act and for new issues of legal tender notes, that is, for "soft money," as opposed to "hard money." [4] Allied with certain labor groups, the Greenbackers, as the Greenback-Labor party, polled in the Congressional elections of 1878 more than 1 million votes.

They had a song which is noteworthy far beyond the greenback episode. It illustrates the sentimental feelings aroused in monetary political struggles; strange as this verse seems to us, it contributes to a better understanding of the dollar's history: [5]

Thou, Greenback, 'tis of thee,
Fair money of the free,
  Of thee we sing.
And through all coming time
Great bards in every clime
Will sing with joyful rhyme,
  Gold is not king.

Then smash old Shylock's bonds,
With all his gold coupons,
  The banks and rings.
Monopolies must fail,
Rich paupers work in jail,
The right will then prevail,
  Not money kings.

After 1878 the Greenback party declined rapidly, but it left its mark on the monetary system, since the retention of $346,681,000 in greenbacks must be traced back in part to its influence. Still, the retention did little real harm, in view of the then imminent convertibility of the greenbacks (and consequently also of the national bank notes).

The length of time consumed before the restoration of the value of the dollar was achieved had at least this advantage, that large purchases of gold and other artificial measures to raise the value of the dollar were avoided. On the whole, the restoration was the natural result of a vigorously growing economy.

CRISIS

Though the value of the dollar was again at par with the gold rate after January 1, 1879, this actual gold standard was obscured by the law and endangered by powerful counter-movements.[6] The silver dollar had remained outside the country after the war, exactly as during and before the war. It was practically forgotten, a fact which perhaps explains a strange occurrence. On February 12, 1873, a new Coinage Act was passed in which the silver dollar was not even mentioned. Instead, a "trade dollar" of 378 grains of silver fine (420 grains 9/10 fine), surpassing the silver dollar by 6¼ grains of fine silver, was declared legal tender in sums not exceeding $5; [7] free coinage of this new dollar was allowed.

"Trade coins," the foremost example of which is the (Austrian) Maria Theresa dollar of 1780, are designed for foreign trade. Prior to the act of 1873 silver dollars, we know, had been coined by the mint for exportation, especially to the Far East. There they had to compete with the Mexican silver dollar, a trade coin of 377¼ grains fine. The trade dollar was designed to displace the Mexican piece. It showed a sitting Minerva surrounded by the thirteen stars, and on the reverse, not very appropriately, the eagle with arrows and the olive branch.

Since the legal tender quality is necessarily a criterion of domestic circulation, its application to coins designated merely for foreign use was paradoxical, and all the more surprising as it had taken the Treasury several years to draft the bill. Behind this and other developments in monetary legislation preceding and following the Civil War there is a lack of scholarly knowledge and understanding.[8] The late development of monetary theory in this country may have been a contributing factor.

Aside from the creation of the trade dollar, the act of 1873 did not provide any notable innovation, although it was designed as a general revision of the coinage laws. But it may be mentioned that it introduced into the American coinage, in addition to "In God We Trust," the inscription "E Pluribus Unum," a legend, we remember, which was contained in the Great Seal and which was particularly appropriate after the reestablishment of national unity. The inscription had been employed in the half-eagle of 1796 but was dropped afterwards.

The trade dollar became the center of a famous controversy arising from a new development in the silver market. In 1873 silver prices began to decline to an extent never seen before. The main cause for this decline, in addition to the increase in the production of silver, was the transition of Germany and other European countries to the gold standard. The forgotten silver dollars started now to return to the United States and silver producers began to offer their silver to the Mint to have it converted into trade dollars. Hence, in 1876 the trade dollar was divested of its legal tender status and its free coinage was canceled. It was a hard blow to American silver producers, particularly since silver could no longer be exported with profit as before. Soon a powerful political movement emerged under the slogan of "free silver" (that is, free coinage of silver), supported, not only by the silver interests, but also by inflation-minded groups. The law of 1873 furnished other formidable slogans for the free-silver agitation: it had abolished, so it was alleged, "the dollar of the Fathers," it was "the Crime of 1873," etc. Actually, the bill had been examined by Congress and government in the customary way, no objection having been raised to the blunder of conferring a legal tender quality upon a trade coin; and no one could be blamed for not having forseen the heavy depreciation of silver.

The free-silver movement was closely related to the Greenbackers' program, but at the outset did not have so much the character of a party affair. It proved dominant in the Congressional Silver Commission of 1876 [9] and obtained on February 28, 1878, its first legislative success, over the veto of President Hayes, through the Bland-Allison Act, which reinstated the silver dollar of 371⅜ grains fine, the "standard silver dollar," with unlimited legal tender status. Free coinage, however, was not extended to the silver dollar, as demanded by the silverites, but remained confined to gold. Congress, instead, undertook to counteract the depreciation of silver, which in 1878 had reduced the bullion value of the dollar to 89 cents. The Bland-Allison Act authorized the Treasury to purchase $2 million to $4 million of silver per month at the market price to coin it into dollars; moreover, on deposits of silver dollars a new type of paper money, "silver certificates," was to be issued in amounts of no less than $10. The certificates were not legal tender but were receivable in payment of public duties including customs. By an enactment of August 4, 1886, Congress authorized the issuance of silver certificates in denominations of $1, $2, and $5, which gradually attained a large circulation to become finally, we know, an outstanding constituent of present-day circulation. But the reference to silver was originally no more than a formal gesture; the value of the certificates was never dependent on the value of silver.

A legislative measure of an apparently opposite course was undertaken on July 12, 1882, when Congress authorized the Treasury to issue gold certificates in amounts of $10, $20, $50, and upward to $10,000 on the basis of gold deposits received. Gold certificates had already been issued under an act of March 3, 1863, but were then placed on order only and not designed as paper money; they were chiefly used by banks and clearinghouses in large denominations. In 1882 their amount had dwindled to $6 million. But now the gold certificates were made paper money receivable in public payments, like the silver certificates. The act provided that the issuance of the notes had to be stopped if the Treasury's gold reserves for the United States notes, the greenbacks, were to fall below $100 million; apparently in such a case the holders of gold, especially the banks, were to be approached first of all to sell it to the government for replenishing the Fund. It was the first time that the law provided for such a reserve fund, whose actual standing became thereby a subject of much public attention; to that extent the new law was of great significance. The gold certificates themselves, however, did not attain much importance in this period because of serious disturbances in the gold and silver market.

The legislative support of the silver dollar proved entirely ineffective. The bullion value of the silver dollar declined further and in 1885 amounted to 82 cents. Thereafter it decreased more rapidly, slumping in 1889 to 72 cents and, after a brief recovery, to 48 cents in 1900, despite the fact that the Bland-Allison Act was replaced in 1890, as will be seen, by an even stronger pro-silver law.

At the same time the world-wide transition to the gold standard created a decline in prices which, in the United States, was aggravated by the inflexibility of the monetary system and by an unfavorable balance of trade. The decline became more pronounced after 1884. While the farmers, also under the pressure of crop surpluses, were affected most seriously, many business enterprises were ruined, to be followed by serious labor disturbances. The Middle West and the South were especially hit. The inflationary movement gathered new and formidable strength. The catchword was no longer expansion of the greenbacks but "bimetallism," which meant the unlimited coinage of silver dollars (or a corresponding increase in silver-backed notes). The undervalued gold would then be driven out of the country, in accordance with Gresham's law, but the emphasis was on the rise of prices, especially farm products, and a better balance of economic forces. Again, the movement was backed mainly by the farmers of the West and South and by labor groups. It had a broad program somewhat left of the Democratic party, demanding, for example, government ownership of railroads and financial reforms reminiscent of the later New Deal. In favoring bimetallism, the inflationary movement perhaps acted chiefly for reasons of political strategy.[10] Bimetallism was also supported by a large majority of the Democrats and by some Republicans.

On July 14, 1890, the so-called Sherman Silver Purchase Act was passed. (Sherman, then a prominent Senator, had succeeded in getting together a Senate majority for the act, although there were parts of it which he himself did not favor.) The Sherman Act obligated the Treasury to buy each month 4½ million ounces of silver, almost twice as much as under the Bland-Allison Act, and to use for this purchase a new type of "treasury notes." Their minimum amount was $1; they were legal tender and "redeemable in coin," that is, in gold or silver at the discretion of the Treasury. In this respect there was no difference between the "treasury notes of 1890" and the greenbacks, but Congress hesitated to increase the amount of the greenbacks. The implication was that the Treasury might decide to redeem the treasury notes in silver, but continue to redeem the greenbacks in gold. Actually, the Treasury stuck to gold redemption in both instances.

Even so, the effect of the Sherman Silver Purchase Act was serious enough. It compelled the Treasury to take over practically the entire output of the American silver mines. Inflationary pressure on the currency was thereby seriously aggravated. Uncertainty and fear spread in this country and abroad as to whether the United States would maintain its gold standard, and the result was a growing demand for the redemption of greenbacks and treasury notes. The Treasury's gold holdings decreased from $190 million yearly in 1890 to less than $100 million by April, 1893, that is, below the statutory level, a disturbing event. At the same time the market price of silver dropped steadily. In June, 1893, the mints of India, foremost area of silver currency, were closed to further minting of silver. Silver fell to 65 cents an ounce and gold exports rose sharply. The crisis became more and more severe. People began presenting paper notes for redemption and hoarding gold; by the end of the month the Panic of 1893 broke out and banks failed by the hundreds.

The Panic of 1893 possesses a particular interest from the monetary point of view. There was not so much a craving for gold, which, in fact, was held by the banks in their vaults. What the public wanted was all types of money, including paper money and fractional currency, not so much to hoard as to get the means of paying wages or discharging other obligations and for covering the expenses of living. Despite the large supply of money (almost $24 per capita), a "currency famine" developed, with premiums up to 4 per cent over bank deposits and checks.[11]

In the absence of a central bank, the clearinghouses again had to intervene by means of clearinghouse loan-certificates. This time, however, excesses occurred. In some sections of the country, especially in the Southeast (not in New York or New England), clearinghouse certificates of $10 or even $1, intended for circulation, made their appearance. In fact, the designation "clearinghouse certificate" was used in towns lacking any clearinghouse at all, the intention being to indicate that the town banks had formed an association for the guaranty of the certificates. In addition, miscellaneous other expedients turned up, "negotiable certificates of deposit," "certified checks," and "teachers' warrants," all denominated in round numbers for currency purposes. Issuers and users of such unauthorized "notes used for circulation" [12] were subject, under the "death tax" law protecting the national bank notes, to the "death tax" of 10 per cent. A few specimens were submitted to the Attorney General of the United States for examination. He decided, in a very brief opinion,[13] that these specimens were "promissory notes" and therefore not affected by the tax law—a highly questionable argument since "promissory notes" may very well constitute "notes" in the sense of the tax law. However, one can easily understand that the government wished to refrain from harsh measures. A contemporary writer could report that despite the grotesque assortment of money substitutes, "not a single dollar was lost." He adds that "no civilized nation has ever experienced such a currency famine; none has ever found itself so fettered by positive law in its efforts to rescue itself; none ever so promptly arose to the emergency." [14]

Certainly the strength of ingenious self-help even in the monetary field, including its feature of transgression, is characteristically American. Still, the chief credit in the gradual overcoming of the panic goes to Grover Cleveland, who had become President for the second time in 1893. Despite the inflationary attitude of most Democrats, he believed in strict adherence to the gold standard. After the gold reserve fund had dropped below the $100 million level he nevertheless ordered the Treasury to continue the gold redemption of its "1890" notes. When the panic broke out he immediately called Congress on June 30 to a special session to repeal the Sherman Silver Purchase Act. This step and the repeal voted by the House of Representatives on August 28 brought some relaxation of public tension. The Senate yielded only after strong resistance, hence the repeal of the act was not signed until November 1, 1893. It was a great achievement for the high-minded and courageous President. The panic gradually receded but unrest and danger to the gold standard remained.

In 1894 the government secured more than $100 million in gold by exchanging notes for gold from banks mainly in New York City, inasmuch as the banks were concerned with the maintenance of the gold standard. But this step proved to be insufficient and early in 1895 Cleveland, following the advice of J. P. Morgan, undertook to attract foreign gold by the emission of a special series of 4 per cent government bonds purchasable by gold; through an American-European syndicate [15] headed by Morgan 3¼ million ounces of gold equal to about $65 million were procured. Cleveland not only had to invoke a forgotten statute of 1862 which permitted such purchases, but also had to expect harsh criticism for negotiating with private banks which, in the old American tradition, were distrusted, especially by Cleveland's own party. But again he decided to take the risk, seeing no other way to maintain gold in circulation. He was sharply criticized, especially when it was found that Morgan had gained a handsome profit. But criticism died down because the gold transaction, expertly handled by Morgan and his associates, proved to be a temporary success. Still, soon afterwards foreign investments were withdrawn on a large scale due to Anglo-American tension over the Venezuelan Boundary Dispute, and early in 1896 $100 million in 4 per cent bonds were offered by the government to the public, this time without recourse to bankers; again payments had to be made in gold coin. The loan was heavily oversubscribed, evidencing the confidence now enjoyed by the government, and gold flowed anew into the vaults of the Treasury. Nevertheless, the Treasury's gold situation remained insecure and unstable, reflecting the fear aroused by the unabated silver campaign.

Recovery was also delayed by a crop failure in 1894 as well as by industrial setbacks leading to strikes and riots. While events took a turn for the better in 1896, the depreciation of silver continued (in 1894 the bullion value of the dollar had sunk to almost 50 cents). Strangely enough bimetallistic agitation persisted and control of the Democrats by free-silver advocates was even strengthened. In the presidential election of 1896 William Jennings Bryan of Nebraska, an extreme silverite, became their presidential candidate through his famous "Cross of Gold" speech to the Democratic national convention. He called the silver question the "paramount issue" confronting the convention and said the party had to decide whether it would fight "upon the side of the idle holders of idle capital" or upon the side of "the struggling masses." The speech reflects the popular feeling about gold. Bryan was nominated the Democratic candidate, though more than one hundred and fifty members at the convention abstained from voting. In the following election, in November, 1896, it was the Republican William McKinley who won. This meant, to all intents and purposes, the definite defeat of the "free-silver movement." From the viewpoint of party politics the outcome was a defeat also for Cleveland, but the monetary policy which he had endorsed in the interest of the country and in defiance of all party pressure did triumph and proved a solid basis for the continued economic rise of the country.

CURRENCY

After the Resumption Act had become effective gold coins were again employed as a medium of payment. The inconvenient $1 and $3 pieces were withdrawn by an enactment of 1890. Hence, only half eagles, eagles, and double eagles remained.

Silver dollars were coined in an annual amount of about $30 million from 1878 to 1890, as compared to the total money stock of $1.7 billion. And even this limited coinage did not meet the economic necessity. The public disliked the silver dollars as too heavy and cumbersome and returned them in large numbers to the Treasury; a somewhat different position taken in the West and South is partly explicable by the fact that illiterates such as the former slaves had difficulty with the paper money.

The trade dollar, we know, was deprived of its legal tender status in 1876 and used for export purposes. With the continued depreciation of silver, trade dollars flowed back from the Orient and finally became the object of a speculative trade. In 1887 Congress decided to redeem the trade dollars unless they were defaced and mutilated, a limitation excluding most of the pieces shipped to China where the pieces had been customarily "chopped." Only a third part of the trade dollars amounting to $8 million was redeemed.

The output of half dollars and smaller silver coins [16] rose considerably before the greenbacks had become redeemable, reaching a climax of $15 million in 1877; but the growing influx of these coins from abroad made new measures necessary. Their coining was practically stopped, and the poor condition of many of the old pieces caused Congress on June 9, 1879, to order the redemption in "lawful money" of such silver coins in amounts of $20 or multiples thereof. At the same time they were made legal tender up to $10. The coinage (or recoinage) of subsidiary silver pieces was resumed on a larger scale only after 1890 without ever reaching, prior to World War I, the peak of 1877.

The coins below the silver coin level were the cent (copper) and the 3 and 5 cents (mixture of copper and nickel). The need for them increased greatly after 1880, with the rise of mass production of low-priced commodities (cigars, beer, etc.), of 1-cent and 2-cent newspapers, of cheap transportation and of typically American standardized products. However, the 3-cent copper-nickel coins created in 1865, similar in appearance to the dime and disliked by the public, were withdrawn by the enactment of 1890. The 2-cent pieces introduced in 1864 had been abolished as unnecessary by the Coinage Act of 1873. The remaining fractional coins were those of 50, 25, 10, 5, and 1 cent, the same as we have today.

Turning to paper money, we may first look at the United States notes (greenbacks and silver certificates). Both circulated—the silver certificates, as was seen, after 1886—in convenient denominations of $1, $2, $5, $10, $20, $50, and $100.[17] Legally they were completely different. To summarize what was said before: the greenbacks were redeemable in "coin," that is, actually in gold coin, and they were legal tender except for customs and interest on the public debt; silver certificates were formally based on the silver holdings of the Treasury (originally they bore the imprint "Certificate of Deposit"), were redeemable in (depreciated) silver coins only, and were not legal tender, but they were receivable in public dues including customs. The people did not bother about these intricate differences nor were they deterred by a feature common to both specimens, namely, the lack of treasury reserves sufficient to cover the issues. The credit of the Federal government was strong enough throughout the country, and balances of American indebtedness to foreign creditors were not paid in these notes but in gold or foreign exchange. Since the greenbacks were restricted to a total of $347 million, their amount was soon surpassed by that of the silver certificates, $380 million in 1890 and $408 million in 1900.

The early silver certificates did not look like conventional paper money. They bore for the most part the portraits of persons not memorialized on other paper money, such as Robert Fulton, Samuel F. B. Morse, the Sioux Indian chief Onepapa, Robert Morris, Captain Stephen Decatur (War of 1812), and Martha Washington, the only woman accorded such honor. The predilection for feminity was marked by a number of allegorical females, particularly those contained in the three specimens of the "Educational Series," representing History, Steam (!), and Electricity, with companions. While the "educational" value of these notes may be questioned, their popularity cannot be. There has been such a persistent demand for them that they are expected to be very rare in time.[18] Their emphasis upon the bodies of allegorical figures, unusual for paper money, may be connected with a neo-classical trend in the American art of that period.

United States notes and silver certificates were not the only types of government paper money. There were also the "treasury notes of 1890." Their design sought to commemorate the Civil War by presenting pictures of the various military leaders and statesmen of that period (excluding, however, General Sherman). Because of the repeal of the Sherman Silver Purchase Act, they were shortlived. Their total had risen to $150 million but they were rapidly withdrawn.

"Gold certificates" were another kind of government paper currency.[19] They reached in 1893 a total of $141 million, but when the Treasury's gold fund fell below the $100 million level the issuance of the certificates was discontinued. Most of those already issued were withdrawn in the following years. Artistically they were generally on a high level, representing carefully prepared portraits of various presidents or some arbitrarily selected political figures. The reverses are presented in a vivid golden orange with rich and impressive design (eagle). They were colloquially called "yellowbacks."

The fractional notes of 3 to 50 cents of the Civil War period were removed from circulation by Congressional enactments in 1875 and 1876; (actually the Treasury had started their redemption some years before). Like the postage currency, they had proved to be utterly inadequate. The public had suffered from deterioration and loss of the notes, and the Treasury's task of sorting, redeeming, and reissuing new specimens was far too expensive. They were conveniently replaced by fractional coins.

In addition to government paper money there was an authorized private paper money, the national bank notes. The national banks had increased from 638 at the beginning of 1865 to 2,052 in 1880 and 3,326 in 1890. In 1872 the circulation of national bank notes exceeded, for the first time, the amount of $300 million. It fell below that level in 1885 and remained there from 1887 to 1889, and this despite the general increase of the money stock of the United States from $775 million in 1870 to $1,429 million in 1890. The main reason was that the banks could issue bank notes only on the basis of qualified Federal bonds and that these bonds had meanwhile attained a considerable premium due to the favorable development of the country. It proved more profitable for the national banks not to invest their money in Federal bonds for the issuance of notes but to use it in other ways. The lack of elasticity which had impaired the New York free banking system proved even more disturbing after that system had been placed on a national basis.

Taken altogether, the money circulation of the period suffered from an exaggerated variety and much confusion, but nevertheless showed a trend toward growth and strength. It advanced from $775 million in 1870 to $973 million in 1880, $1,429 million in 1890, and $1,602 million in 1895. The movement reflects the rise of the population: 1870, 40 million; 1880, 50 million; 1890, 62 million; and 1895, 70 million. Strangely enough, the silver dollars so greatly desired in the preceding periods were now repudiated. The inveterate American predilection for paper money prevailed.

The war with Spain (1898) affected the monetary structure of this country even less than did the Mexican War, and the victorious outcome only strengthened the trend toward consolidation of the gold standard.

INTERNATIONAL MONETARY CONFERENCES

It is in this period that an international trend made its appearance in the monetary field mainly through a number of international conferences.[20] Generally speaking, the 1860's of the last century opened a new era of international law, owing to the tremendous technological progress in transportation and communication the world over. Events such as the Postal Congress of 1863, the Statistical Congress of the same year, the Geneva Convention for the Protection of the Wounded in War, the Universal Telegraphic Union of 1865, raised fervent hopes for a progressive internationalization on a large scale, hopes that extended also to the monetary field. Early in 1866 the House of Representatives passed a resolution calling for preparatory measures toward a "uniform coinage between the United States and foreign countries." [21] The voting majority was not impressive and the Senate did not join the House, but the resolution illustrated a trend which found a historically more important expression in 1867, when Napoleon III invited a great number of countries, among them the United States, to an international monetary conference in Paris.[22] In 1865 he had concluded the Latin Monetary Union with Italy, Belgium, Switzerland, and Greece, in an effort to extend the essential features of the French monetary system to those relatively weak countries. By way of the new conference, Napoleon expected to expand the area of French monetary supremacy through the establishment of a universal monetary system based on the French unit. The French even suggested somewhat naively that the dollar should be rebuilt as an equivalent to the 5-franc piece, basic unit of the Latin Union, and be represented bimetallistically by a tiny gold piece as well as by a silver coin. At the conference the opinion prevailed, however, that bimetallism had to be replaced by the gold standard; a resolution in favor of a common standard to have the weight of gold coin "9/10 fine" was unanimously adopted. But this declaration, which left the weight undefined, remained completely ineffective except for a curious postlude on the American scene. In 1868 the Parliament of the newly established Dominion of Canada, with express reference to the Paris conference, passed an act contemplating that the United States would render its half-eagle equivalent to the French 25-franc piece and adjust its other coins correspondingly; in such a case, the government of the Dominion was authorized to issue a proclamation adopting on the same basis a complicated mixture of the American and English monetary system.[23] The Canadian enactment had no effect whatsoever and no attention has been paid to it in historical and monetary literature.

Another reverberation of the Paris conference occurred in the enactment of the Coinage Act of 1873 when, on John Sherman's advice, Congress undertook some adaptation of the subsidiary silver coins to the 5-franc piece of the Latin Union, the weight of which was 25 grams, equal to 385.8 grains.[24] The statute of 1873 therefore expressed the weight of the half dollar and the smaller silver coins in "grams (grammes)" rather than in grains, as was customary. But the practical effect was chiefly that the fine weight of the half dollar had to be increased from 172.8 to 173.61 grains. This step was considered a kind of approximation to the Latin monetary unit and thereby of a possible universal coinage. Actually, it was an entirely ineffective and rather naive obeisance to France and to the idea of internationalization. A truly international approach obviously would require the accommodation of the basic monetary units. The metal contents of *subsidiary* coins are unimportant, even apart from the fact that they are subject to frequent changes of minor significance. In 1926 the subsidiary silver coins were redefined in the U.S. Code in terms of grains without further ado. The entire affair was soon forgotten.

We may mention also a rather fanciful "international" step undertaken by the United States Mint, which in 1874 produced a pattern of a gold coin with the inscription of "$10 £2.1.1 Marken 41.90 Kronen 37.33 Gulden 20.73 Francs 51.81."[25] The experiment remained, of course, without practical consequences. Nor have there been serious attempts anywhere else to create a wide international system of coins as resolved by the Paris conference of 1867.

An international monetary conference of a somewhat different type, namely, for the establishment of a common monetary ratio between gold and silver, was initiated in 1878 by the United States under a provision of the Bland-Allison Act. A solution to this problem was sought through a conference of delegates, mainly of European powers, to be convoked by the American government. The primary purpose was to present a new hope to the silverites who were dissatisfied by the Bland-Allison Act. The conference again took place in Paris.[26] Germany, which had just successfully introduced the gold standard, courteously declined the invitation, and England accepted it only with strong reservations. Since an agreement among the delegates could not be attained, the conference "adjourned."

In 1881 another conference was convoked on the joint invitation of the United States and France,[27] which suffered from a "limping" gold standard even more than this country. She had lost much gold through an unfavorable balance of trade, especially to the United States, and had been inundated with silver. This time the German Empire took part in the conference, since the powerful landowners, the junkers, had become heavily interested in bimetallism, with the difference, however, that there was not a "populist" movement behind them. Still, the incessant unrest resulting from the steady decline of the silver prices, together with the divergence of interest among the governments, once more made an agreement impossible. Nevertheless, in 1892 the United States government made a last attempt to establish a basis for bimetallism through international agreement. The conference which met, this time at Brussels,[28] was a hopeless enterprise from the beginning. Resistance to bimetallism was stronger than before and there seems to have been a feeling of resentment among the delegates that the United States government called the conference. Its failure meant practically the end of bimetallism. Even in Germany the government in this matter withstood the pressure of the powerful rightist groups which it was eager to satisfy in most other fields.

The conferences illustrate the fact that the United States after the Civil War had become a great power, the first one outside Europe. The reluctance of the other governments to decline the invitation of the hopeless Brussels conference in 1892 can be considered significant in this respect. On the other hand, it was a sign of the esteem enjoyed abroad by this country's currency that the eagle was made legal tender in Canada in 1871[29] and about the same time in Mexico.[30] In Switzerland the dollar was temporarily made legal tender in 1870[31] and it is possible that similar measures were taken elsewhere. It was a kind of reversal of the part played in earlier times by foreign coins in this country.

Apart from these American aspects, the international efforts of the period were in some way a contribution to the old idea of "world money." This was originally a Utopian conception of some imaginative writers, but it found its strongest and semi-realistic approach under the neo-internationalist atmosphere of the period discussed.[32] There was never again a similar official move toward "world money." In an entirely different sense an evolution toward a kind of world money appeared more recently, as will be discussed below.

Looking back one receives the impression that there has been hardly a period of American monetary history more colorful and perhaps more illustrative of favorable and unfavorable features of American political psychology. That is why it has aroused much interest in foreign countries, as evidenced by pertinent publications.[33]

The Gold Standard Consolidated

THE MONETARY development of this period was on the whole under a rather conservative spirit not common in American monetary history, but some exciting and depressing disturbances resulting from speculation intervened. Moreover, the country was not yet strong enough economically to resist concussions which came from abroad. And until 1914, the absence of a central banking system presented another harmful factor.

THE GOLD STANDARD ACT

Bryan's defeat and McKinley's victory led to the official elimination of bimetallism through what is known as the Gold Standard Act of March 14, 1900. It declared the gold dollar consisting of 25.8 grains 9/10 fine to be "the standard unit of value." Practically, this was no revision. Free coinage of silver dollars, we know, had been abolished in 1878. Hence silver coins had remained subsidiary since that time. However, the new act brought a striking change in emphasis. The enactment of 1837, still basic to this country's coining, had merely altered the weight of the "eagle" to 25.8 grains 9/10 fine of gold coined. The new reference to that dollar was one of principle and its designation as the "standard unit of value" was entirely abstract. Such an expression was not only new to American (and English) law but was unknown also to the laws of other countries. The term "unit of account," it is true, appears as early as the Coinage Act of 1792, but only with special reference to accounting. As a fundamental conception in the monetary structure it appears only in German legislation (*Rechnungseinheit*). Generally speaking, there had been much discussion of basic monetary conceptions in Continental economic literature.[1] Actually, in the American situation of 1900 the term "unit of value" hits the mark better than the more popular term "unit of account." The addition of the word "standard," though theoretically dispensable, had a political significance; it told the silverites, who were very strong in the Senate, that henceforth they would have to submit to the gold standard.

Though the theoretical formula should not have been expected to impress the silverites, the majority felt that some sedatives had to be offered to them. The title of the act reads: "An Act to define and fix the standard of value, to maintain the parity of all forms of money issued or coined by the United States to refund the public debt, and for other purposes." The long-winded character of the title is common to the United States legislation and needs no discussion, but the phrase "all forms of money" includes, of course, first of all the silver coins. This seemed to indicate "parity" for silver, and the act has actually been called, even by courts of law, the "Parity Act." In reality, nothing more was set forth than that the circulation of nongold specimens had to be maintained at their nominal value—a self-evident necessity for any gold standard and, in a broader sense, for any monetary system. In the American situation of 1900 "parity" implied a restriction rather than an expansion of the use of silver.

But there were also several other though unimportant concessions to the silverites. First the act provided that it was "not intended" to preclude the accomplishment of *international* bimetallism by way of international agreements. A provision closer to reality ordered the withdrawal of the treasury notes of 1890 and their replacement by silver dollars. The resulting increase in silver dollars, so little desired by the public, was not worth mentioning, but at least one of the all-too-numerous types of circulating media was eliminated.

Paper currency as a whole, however, was by no means reduced. The elimination of the treasury notes of 1890 was more than compensated for through a lessening of the requirements for the issuance of national bank notes, mainly through a reduction of the minimum banking capital, again a measure favoring the establishment of new banks in small cities. Also, banks were permitted to issue notes up to the full amount of their reserves. As a result, the circulation of these notes rose from $300 million in 1900 to $716 million in 1913. In 1905 they even constituted the largest part of the circulating media, amounting to $548 million; up to 1905, the highest amount was represented by silver certificates, and after 1905, as will be seen, mostly by gold certificates.

The principal effect of the Gold Standard Act was psychological. It proclaimed to the world the definitive American resolution to maintain the gold standard; domestic, as well as foreign, confidence was reestablished. Generally speaking, the political and economic situation of the country was prosperous. An impressive expansion started about the time the agreement with Colombia over the Panama Canal in 1903 was concluded. The New York banks entered into broad international lending activities. In the monetary field proper this growth was symbolized by a tremendous increase in gold certificates (yellowbacks). Their amount rose at once to $201 million in 1900 and climbed steadily to $803 million in 1910 and $1 billion in 1913. Actually the notes were employed to a large extent as bank reserves, but they were also widely used by the public, especially after the minimum denomination had been reduced from $20 to $10 by an enactment of 1907.[2]

THE RISE OF THE FEDERAL RESERVE SYSTEM

Nevertheless, the nonexistence of a central bank and the inelasticity of the currency found drastic expression in the Panic of 1907.[3] Again, the collapse of unwholesome speculation was the cause of the panic. Runs on banks and trust companies affiliated with speculative enterprises soon developed. Loans were called in, deposits withdrawn, and private hoarding of money developed; in New York cash went at a premium of 4 per cent above certified checks. The increase in small national banks brought about by the Gold Standard Act only intensified the panic because these local institutions were especially dependent on cash. The panic was overcome by extensive issuance of clearinghouse certificates and a favorable turn in the country's balance of trade, which was chiefly brought about by a good crop. However, much criticism was voiced against the New York banks, symbolized by J. P. Morgan and Company. These banks were accused of having shown too little concern during the panic for the national interest and public welfare. The catchword "Wall Street" signified in the popular mind a dangerous type of financial hegemony. A committee of investigation, the Pujo Committee, was appointed in 1912 by the House of Representatives and did a thorough job.[4] This so-called Money Trust Investigation confirmed the fact of the unsound financial supremacy of the "interlocked" leading banks and bankers.

In fact, the necessity for reform was everywhere felt as a result of the Crisis of 1907. A first step was taken on May 30, 1908, by the Aldrich-Vreeland Act, an amendment to the National Bank Act, which permitted the issuance of "emergency currency" on an elastic basis, including commercial paper. The National Currency Associations, a new type of organization to be formed voluntarily by groups of at least ten national banks, were authorized to issue emergency notes through their member banks with the consent of the Treasury. Actually, this device was used only once, and then transitorily. But there was little doubt among the experts [5] that a fundamental change in the monetary and banking system was necessary. As a preparation for the reform the Aldrich-Vreeland Act itself provided for the establishment of a National Monetary Commission consisting of members of Congress. After the Commission had published an immense number of studies encompassing more than twenty volumes, Nelson W. Aldrich himself, a Republican Senator of great distinction and expert knowledge, submitted a bill in 1912 proposing the creation of a new type of banks of issue centralized in the "National Reserve Association." [6] The association was to be based on a number of regional associations and to be controlled primarily by bankers. But in 1912 the Democrats won the election and Woodrow Wilson became President. Under Wilson's leadership the Federal Reserve Act,[7] which took over in large measure the structure of the Aldrich plan, was passed by Congress and signed by the President on December 23, 1913.

The Federal Reserve Act provided for the establishment of twelve large regional banks, the "Federal Reserve Banks" (district banks) to be headed by a Federal Reserve Board in Washington. The Board was to consist of the Secretary of the Treasury, the Comptroller of the Currency, and five other members to be appointed by the President. All the national banks had to join the Federal Reserve Bank of their district; state banks were permitted to do so. The member banks, national or state, had to subscribe to the capital stock of the district banks a share varying in amount according to statutory provision. The Federal Reserve Banks themselves were authorized—and this is the core of the matter—to issue a new type of money, the Federal Reserve notes. The notes were to be a direct obligation of the United States government, in addition to the liability of the issuing bank, on whose assets they would have a first and paramount lien. They were to be endowed with public receivability and to be engraved by the Comptroller of the Currency. Issued in denominations of $5 and above, they were designed to replace gradually the national bank notes; the government bonds required as security for the national bank notes were to be withdrawn gradually. The new notes were to be secured fully by commercial (or other qualified) paper acquired by the district banks through rediscounting, perhaps the most important feature taken from the Aldrich-Vreeland Act. It made feasible the automatic adaptation of available currency to the changing needs of the national economy. However, in addition to the commercial paper, a reserve of not less than 40 per cent in gold (or, under a later amendment, in gold certificates) was required from each district bank for its notes—an excessive restriction.

The simplicity of this currency device was somewhat disturbed by the fact that still another type of note was authorized to be issued by the Federal Reserve Banks, namely, the "circulating notes" (the legislative name for them) or the "Federal Reserve Bank notes" as they were commonly called. They were supposed to make it easier for the national banks to get rid of bonds serving as security for their own notes. For this purpose the Federal Reserve Banks were authorized to buy such bonds from their member banks and to issue on the basis of these bonds, without any gold or further securities, Federal Reserve Bank notes at the par nominal value of the bonds. By virtue of amendments to the act, Federal Reserve Bank notes were also circulated to a limited extent during World War I, the depression of 1929, and World War II as emergency currency. But, on the whole, this type of Federal paper money remained insignificant.

Other provisions of the Federal Reserve Act were designed to improve American banking practices in the public interest. Outstanding among these were stringent requirements for reserves against demand deposits with member banks. For "country banks" they amounted to 12 per cent; for "city banks" they were 15 to 18 per cent; and for district banks themselves, no less than 35 per cent. Also, and this comes closer to the subject of currency, provisions were made to secure the "par" collection of checks throughout the country, that is, the collection without cost to the payee or to the payer, an undertaking which, as will be seen, led to a sharp conflict.

A striking difference between the Federal Reserve Act and the Aldrich plan consisted in the attempt by the act to entrust financial leadership and direction to the Federal government, which had to appoint the Board of Governors, rather than to private bankers. However, under the law of 1913 the power of the Board was still limited. It was to appoint only a third of the directors of each district bank as representatives of the public at large. The remaining two thirds were elected by the member banks, which were therefore in a position to pick the heads (governors) of the Federal Reserve Banks, and it was the governors who actually became the dominant figures in the system. The liability of the Federal government, a feature far removed from the Aldrich plan, further emphasized the public rather than the private character of the system. Aside from the unforeseen development in the status of the governors, it may well be said that the differences between the Federal Reserve Act and the Aldrich plan illustrate a basic difference between Democratic and Republican policies. The American Bankers Association declared in a public statement that it was very hard for those who did not believe in socialism to accept the new system.

The creation of the Federal Reserve System was an event

of fundamental significance in the monetary field. This substitute for a central bank constituted a superb invention adapted to the wide range of the country and to the diversity of its many regions. There developed in it creative capacities exceeding those of a typical central bank.

The first district banks started business in September, 1914, that is, more than a month after the beginning of World War I in Europe. Although it was to take some time to build up the new organization, yet the United States was most fortunate in having the support of the Federal Reserve System during most of the war and the following critical years.

WORLD WAR I AND ITS AFTERMATH

At the outbreak of the war [8] foreign assets in this country, primarily bonds and other securities, exceeded American assets abroad by at least $3.7 billion. Shortly before the outbreak of war in July, 1914, a panic developed in Europe. It soon led to the sale of American bonds amounting to several hundred million dollars, and their equivalent in gold had to be shipped to Europe. But for several weeks shipping was paralyzed by the fear that cargoes might be sunk. An informal embargo on gold was therefore urged in this country. As a result the dollar rate dropped more than 40 per cent in terms of the European currencies. Before long, however, arrangements were made for gold to be transported to a depository which the Bank of England had established in Ottawa. Furthermore, the situation was improved through increasing war orders which flowed in from Europe. By October the sterling-dollar rate returned to normal and soon the picture changed completely in favor of the United States. This country became the outstanding source of military supplies and other commodities needed by the belligerent powers. The yearly balance of American exports over imports rose so rapidly that in 1916 and 1917 it exceeded $3 billion; the United States was soon transformed from a debtor into a towering creditor with surplus assets of more than $3 billion.

There was a run on currency by bank depositors in the panic following the outbreak of the war; but it soon came to an end. In 1914 the government ordered the issuance of $364 million in Aldrich-Vreeland "emergency notes." These notes were framed exactly like national bank notes, the only difference being that in a very narrow margin the words "Secured by United States notes deposited with the Treasury of the United States" were replaced by "Secured by United States bonds and other securities." [9] The close similarity of the Aldrich-Vreeland notes to national bank notes was somewhat objectionable. However, the notes were withdrawn in 1915 after the Federal Reserve System came into operation. This was the first and last issuance of Aldrich-Vreeland notes.

The efficiency of the Federal Reserve System was increased by an amendment of June 21, 1917. It eased and simplified the requirements for the issuance of Federal Reserve notes by the district banks. The gold security of at least 40 per cent had merely to be supplemented by 60 per cent or less of commercial paper provided the total security amounted to 100 per cent. At the same time the member banks were ordered to keep at their district bank gold and "lawful money" as reserves against their deposits. Though the minimum reserves were reduced, the measure led to a considerable increase in the gold holdings of the Federal Reserve System. In fact, gold had flowed into the United States to an extent unprecedented in history, reaching in 1915 the amount of $499,000,000 and in 1916, $531,900,000.[10] However, at that time the outcome of the war was uncertain, and the government felt the necessity to keep its hands on the nation's gold as far as possible.

On April 6, 1917, when this country entered the war against Germany, the situation changed. Aid to the Allies was now granted in the form of loans which amounted to about $10 billion and further consolidated the creditor position of the United States. At the same time, however, the gold situation took a turn for the worse. The Allies were no longer required to make payments in gold to the United States. Instead, the United States now had to make gold payments to the neutrals. The exports of gold began to exceed the imports considerably and the gold reserves of the Treasury and the Federal Reserve System were shrinking. Hence, in September, 1917, President Wilson prohibited the export of gold from the United States except under license from the Federal Reserve Board.[11] Licenses were granted in only a very few cases, though domestic redemption of notes by gold remained legal. As a result, the dollar depreciated again in terms of gold standard currencies of neutral countries. Their premiums ranged from 7 per cent to 10 per cent, and in some instances were even higher. For example, the premium of the Dutch guilder reached 29⅜ per cent and that of the Swedish crown, 69¼ per cent. These figures certainly did not reflect a corresponding weakness of the dollar. The currencies of

England, France, and other belligerent countries receded even more and had to be "pegged" to the dollar by the United States. In fact, the gold stock of the United States declined only a little, while the gold holdings of the Federal Reserve System increased until June, 1919, when they amounted to $850 million, due chiefly to the 1917 amendment to the Federal Reserve Act. By the end of 1918 the country's stock of gold equaled 40 per cent of the world's known gold reserves. The restriction on the export of gold was removed on June 9, 1918. This removal was first followed by a large flow of gold to neutral countries whose claims had greatly increased during the embargo period, but after May, 1920, gold imports again brought about a growing surplus amounting in the fiscal year from June, 1920 to June, 1921 to $511 million. The dollar's discount against neutral currencies disappeared, of course, after the resumption of gold payments.

All things considered, the dollar had not only preserved its gold value despite the pressure of the war, in contrast to the currencies of all the other belligerent countries, but it had become the leading monetary unit through the large reserves behind it and the strong credit position which the United States had attained.

Expansion of business and employment during the war and the necessity of facilitating the government's war loans resulted in an extremely heavy demand for currency. That demand was met in the first place by Federal Reserve notes, which increased from $507 million in 1917 to $1.7 billion in

1918 and $3 billion in 1920, representing the foremost circulating medium; in September, 1918, denominations up to $10,000 were permitted. The increase was all the more striking inasmuch as the planned withdrawal of national bank notes was not accomplished; the amount in 1914, $750 million, remained practically unchanged in the following years. The gold certificates maintained the high circulation they had reached in 1913, but in 1918 the circulation dropped sharply to $510 million and reached a nadir in 1920 with $260 million. The cause was technical only—the certificates were transferred from the member banks to the Federal Reserve Banks where they served as security for the issuance of Federal Reserve Bank notes, but were no longer part of the circulating media. The circulation of greenbacks, which amounted to $340 million in 1914, declined, for no important reason, by about 10 per cent during the war.

Silver certificates met a peculiar fate. As the British government needed silver to cover expenses in India, the United States on Congressional authority (Pittman Act of 1918) sold more than 200,000,000 ounces of silver somewhat above the market price to the British government. This price in any event was high because of the exigencies of war. Remarkably enough, the act obligated the Treasury to repurchase the silver, at the same rate it was sold to the British, from American silver producers, who made a handsome profit when silver prices dropped after the war. The transfer of the silver led to a heavy reduction of silver certificates, from $470 million in 1917 to $98 million in 1920. The gap was filled for the most part by the provisional issuance of Federal Reserve Bank notes, an action facilitated by the Pittman Act. This was emergency paper money like the Aldrich-Vreeland notes of 1914. Whereas the name of the issuing bank on the Federal Reserve notes is not easy to discover (it is found on the rim of the small circle left of the portrait), the name dominates the obverse of the Federal Reserve Bank notes, indicating thereby the obligor; and like national bank notes, they carry the inscription "national currency." The entire issuance was unimportant and transitory; the amount circulating reached its peak in 1920 with $185 million, but the notes were thereafter withdrawn so fast that in 1923 only $20 million remained. Soon after they disappeared almost entirely.

While paper money went through much confusion and experimentation, there was little disturbance in the matter of coins. Gold, coined or uncoined, was stockpiled as much as possible by the Federal Reserve System, as mentioned above. Hence, the circulation of gold coins declined from $612 million in 1914 to $475 million in 1920. But a demand for fractional currency developed through rising prices as well as through "sumptuary" taxes of one to several cents for cigarettes and other small articles, transportation, etc.[12] In 1917 and 1918 the mints had to produce more than 25 million fractional coins annually as compared with a little more than 3 million in 1913. In the fall of 1917 there had been a serious shortage of one-cent copper coins but gradually the deficiency was overcome without legislative measures.

Some difficulties arose also in the field of checks. The Federal Reserve Act, we know, envisaged the generalization of "par" collection. All members of the Federal Reserve

System had to accept this important principle, but the Federal Reserve Banks also tried to impose it upon the nonmember banks which were ordinarily "country banks." A conflict arose reminiscent somewhat of the efforts a century earlier of the Second Bank of the United States to secure full redemption of notes of other banks. The country banks refused par collection and were partly supported in this respect by their state governments. Again the Supreme Court had to decide. Surprisingly enough, it held for the country banks, calling the efforts of the Federal Reserve System for the par collection "a sort of warfare upon legitimate creations of the states." [13] The opinion was written by no less an authority than Mr. Justice Holmes. It must be said, however, that an understanding of economic developments was not one of the great achievements of this celebrated judge. Two years later the Supreme Court, while avoiding a direct conflict with Justice Holmes's line of reasoning, reached a decision in favor of the Federal Reserve System in a decision written by Mr. Justice Brandeis.[14]

Prices started to rise after the outbreak of the war. When this country entered the war prices were bound to rise considerably because of the large increase in war production, the decline in gold imports, and the premium on neutral currencies. Still, during the period of hostilities the government succeeded in restraining the people from avoidable purchases through appeal to patriotic duty and by an increasingly courageous tax policy. There was also some official price control. However, after victory was won in the fall of 1918 the repressed desire for enjoying the new opportunities for spending money broke out with irresistible force. The available facilities of banking credit improved through the reorganization of the Federal Reserve System. Currency circulation rose from $4 billion in 1917 to $4.9 billion in 1919 and $5.5 billion in 1920. The cost of living, if the figures for 1913 are taken as 100, mounted to 183 in 1919 and 208 in 1920 and reached a climax of 247 in May, 1920. The public eventually reacted to this pressure by refraining from purchases and even organized a fight against the profiteers. A downward movement started and was strengthened when by a postwar commercial crisis in Japan and other foreign countries imports from the United States were sharply reduced. After May, 1920, prices dropped within one year more than 40 per cent. Still, they remained more than 50 per cent above the prewar level, though the dollar had preserved its full gold content and ranked foremost in international finance.

The responsibility for this "inflationary" development has been placed in part upon the Federal Reserve Board which, on the Treasury's demand, had considerably lowered the rediscount rate in order to offer credit facilities for the purchase of the government's war (Liberty) bonds. But the effect of this complacency, if any, can have been transitional only. We are confronted here with the beginning of an evolution which became more evident after World War II and may therefore be discussed later in the light of a wider experience. It is sufficient to state at this point that despite all the extreme deflections of the dollar quotations the monetary events of the war did not affect the country too seriously. One need only think of the experiences encountered in the Revolutionary War, the War of 1812, or the Civil War. It is almost symbolic that in 1920 the Independent Treasury System, that awkward remnant of monetary disorder, definitely disappeared.

"PROSPERITY" AND THE GREAT DEPRESSION

The recession of 1920–21 was followed by a period of apparent prosperity characterized by a definite restraint of the government to interfere with business (President Harding's "normalcy"). It was a time of wide business expansion in the national as well as the international field. Still, rediscounts by the Federal Reserve System declined due to the end of the government war financing. Since gold continued to flow into its coffers the System decided to utilize it for the issuance of gold certificates rather than employing it together with rediscounted commercial paper on a large scale for the issuance of Federal Reserve Bank notes. Designed to counteract an inflationary overexpansion of credit, the measure was reflected in actual circulation by a heavy increase of gold certificates, which were gladly accepted by the public at home as well as abroad. From $259 million in 1920 they rose to $1 billion in 1925 and remained at that level for the rest of the period.

In 1929 the size of American paper money was reduced from 7⅜ by 3⅛ inches to the present size of 6 by 2⅝ inches.[15] The change, which saved the Treasury millions of dollars, indicated the expansion of the daily use of dollar bills and multiples thereof by the general public.

The period of "prosperity" was followed by the Great Depression of 1929–33, the most severe and, certainly in the monetary field, the most serious of all the crises which have afflicted the United States. There had been flaws in the "prosperity," such as a decline in agricultural exports and, more important, a typically American overspeculation in the stock market by large numbers of the population. The first phase of the breakdown occurred in October, 1929, with the collapse of the value of stocks listed on the New York Stock Exchange. The decline extended throughout the entire field of business and resulted in increasing unemployment. There was a certain amount of recovery in 1931, but then the second and most shocking blow fell in the latter part of the year. It came from abroad and was monetary, hence, fundamental in character. Mainly as a result of the stoppage of American investments, European countries, first Austria and Germany and then England and France, were no longer able to discharge their debts; the exportation of gold and payments in general to other countries were placed under "exchange control" by these European governments. The gold standard was abandoned and all the currencies involved broke down. This led to a ruinous depreciation of the almost $2 billion of American investments which had been made, often carelessly, in European enterprises during and before the prosperity period.

Among the existing 24,079 banks, 1,352 (including 161 national banks) had to suspend their payments in 1930. In 1931 the number of bank failures rose to 2,294, to be followed in 1932 by an additional 1,456. From the beginning of January, 1933, until March, 1933, when the government intervened, no less than 408 new failures occurred. The stock market dropped down to about one sixth of its late 1929 level.

The breakdown of 1931 had entirely reversed the psychological attitude of the people. The spirit of overconfidence turned more and more into a deep pessimism, if not despair, a feeling aggravated by the presidential elections held in the fall of 1932. The campaign was dominated by the general distress and the resultant resentment of the people, the Democrats attacking the Republicans for the failures of the Hoover administration and the Republicans accusing the Democrats of ineptitude.

The danger resulting from the depression and threatening the monetary system itself consisted, first, in the shrinking of commercial paper eligible for the issuance of Federal Reserve notes; more and more, the notes had to be backed by gold. Since the demand for currency was increasing due to the growing distrust in investment, the Glass-Steagall Act passed under the Hoover administration in February, 1932, authorized the Federal Reserve Banks to use—for one year—government bonds instead of commercial paper as collateral for Federal Reserve notes, though the 40 per cent gold reserve was maintained.

But the act offered no protection against a far greater distress. Owing to the bank failures, the confidence of the depositors in the banks began to fade. In 1932, at first slowly and then with increasing speed and pressure, a depositors' run started all over the country. Soon the depositors were no longer satisfied with Federal Reserve notes or other "lawful money"; gold coin, or at least gold certificates, were demanded. Foreign creditors and investors also joined the alarmed crowd. For the people at home hundreds of "barter" organizations were created and as in the crisis of 1897 various scrips were circulated by municipalities as local substitutes for legal currency; [16] such a measure was prepared even by New York state at the end of the crisis. The state governments tried to protect the banks within their borders by banking moratoria (Nevada, in October, 1932, was first), which were called banking holidays after the English precedent of 1914. When such holidays were ordered on February 14, 1933, by the governor of Michigan for eight days, the excitement grew feverish. Everywhere banking holidays were proclaimed, sometimes even by the banks themselves. New York resisted the movement, but early on March 4, the day of Franklin D. Roosevelt's inauguration as President, Governor Lehman in agreement with the Federal authorities, closed the doors of the New York banks. Suddenly and by one of the most dramatic events in monetary history, to which we shall turn in the following chapter, the tempest calmed and confidence returned. But during February and until March 4, $624 million in gold had been withdrawn, partly for export, from the Treasury and the Federal Reserve Banks, and circulation of currency had grown by about $1,800,000,000.

The New Deal

ON SATURDAY, March 4, 1933, Franklin D. Roosevelt became President. On Sunday, March 5, he called Congress into extraordinary session. The next day, March 6, at one o'clock in the morning, he proclaimed a national bank holiday to last until Thursday, March 9, inclusive. During this period banks were forbidden to transact any business whatsoever, and especially prohibited from paying out coin or bullion or currency, except with the permission of the Secretary of the Treasury. The proclamation was based on the Trading-with-the-Enemy Act of October 5, 1917, a wartime statute; its use was therefore somewhat questionable in time of peace. But the presidential action definitely had the full support of public opinion.[1]

The question of legality lost its practical significance when Congress on March 9 adopted an Emergency Banking Act. The statute confirmed the action taken by the President and declared the presidential power granted by the act of 1917 applicable in any emergency. In addition, new ways to meet the calamity were provided by the Emergency Banking Act, which authorized (*a*) the issuance of Federal Reserve Bank notes up to 90 per cent of the value of eligible commercial paper acquired by the Federal Reserve Banks (hence the issuance of an emergency currency); (*b*) the Secretary of the

Treasury to require from every person the delivery of gold coin, gold bullion, and gold certificates for an "equivalent amount" of money; (*c*) the regulation, by license or otherwise, of the entire banking business of the nation. On March 9 the President extended the bank holiday to Sunday, March 12. The next day, Monday, 4,507 national banks and 567 state member banks—altogether 76 per cent of the member banks of the Federal Reserve System—were permitted to open their doors. Thereafter 2,301 member banks and 2,733 nonmember state banks were in one way or another gradually liquidated.[2]

THE RECOVERY OF BANKING

After the bank holidays public confidence in banking was soon restored. Bank deposits, including gold, were to a large extent returned to the banks. Calmness of mind was greatly furthered by the President's first "fireside chat," a masterpiece, delivered on March 12.[3]

> I want to talk for a few minutes with the people of the United States about banking,—with the comparatively few who understand the mechanics of banking but more particularly with the overwhelming majority who use banks for the making of deposits and the drawing of checks. I want to tell you what has been done in the last few days, why it was done, and what the next steps are going to be. . . . I know that when you understand what we in Washington have been about I shall continue to have your cooperation as fully as I have had your sympathy and help during the past week.

The President described in simple words how a bank invests most of its deposits "to keep the wheels of industry and agriculture turning around" and withholds only a comparatively small amount in currency.

What, then, happened during the last few days of February and the first few days of March? Because of undermined confidence on the part of the public, there was a general rush by a large portion of our population to turn back deposits into currency or gold,—a rush so great that the soundest banks could not get enough currency to meet the demand. The reason for this was that on the spur of the moment it was, of course, impossible to sell perfectly sound assets of a bank and convert them into cash except at panic prices far below their real value.

By the afternoon of March 3d scarcely a bank in the country was open to do business. Proclamations temporarily closing them in whole or in part had been issued by the Governors in almost all the States. It was then that I issued the proclamation providing for the nationwide bank holiday, and this was the first step in the Government's reconstruction of our financial and economic fabric.

The President went on to tell how the Congress, Republicans and Democrats alike, in devotion to public welfare and in realization of the emergency, instantly enacted the necessary laws, and he showed how the bank holidays were essential to supply the banks with the needed currency.

Let me make it clear to you that if your bank does not open the first day you are by no means justified in believing that it will not open. A bank that opens on one of the subsequent days is in exactly the same status as the bank that opens tomorrow. . . .

It is possible that when the banks resume a very few people who have not recovered from their fear may again begin withdrawals. Let me make it clear that the banks will take care of all needs,—and it is my belief that hoarding during the past week has become an exceedingly unfashionable pastime. It needs no prophet to tell you that when the people find that they can get their money,—that they can get it when they want it for all legitimate purposes,—the phantom of fear will soon be laid. People will again be glad to have their money where it will be safely taken care of and where they can use it conveniently at any time. I can assure you that it is safer to keep your money in a reopened bank than under the mattress.

The success of our whole great national program depends, of course, upon the cooperation of the public,—on its intelligent support and use of a reliable system.

Remember that the essential accomplishment of the new legislation is that it makes it possible for banks more readily to convert their assets into cash than was the case before. More liberal provision has been made for banks to borrow on these assets at the Reserve Banks and more liberal provision has also been made for issuing currency on the security of these good assets. This currency is not fiat currency. It is issued only on adequate security, and every good bank has an abundance of such security.

One more point before I close. There will be, of course, some banks unable to reopen without being reorganized. The new law allows the Government to assist in making these reorganizations quickly and effectively and even allows the Government to subscribe to at least a part of new capital which may be required.

I hope you can see from this elemental recital of what your Government is doing that there is nothing complex, or radical, in the process.

We had a bad banking situation. Some of our bankers had shown themselves either incompetent or dishonest in their handling of the people's funds. They had used the money entrusted to them in speculations and unwise loans. This was, of course, not true in the vast majority of our banks, but it was true in enough of them to shock the people for a time into a sense of insecurity and to put them in a frame of mind where they did not differentiate, but seemed to assume that the acts of a comparative few had tainted them all. It was the Government's job to straighten out this situation and do it as quickly as possible. And the job is being performed.

I do not promise you that every bank will be reopened or that individual losses will not be suffered, but there will be no losses that possibly could be avoided; and there would have been more and greater losses had we continued to drift. I can even promise you salvation for some at least of the sorely pressed banks. We shall be engaged not merely in reopening sound banks but in the creation of sound banks through reorganization. . . .

After all, there is an element in the readjustment of our financial system more important than currency, more important than gold, and that is the confidence of the people. Confidence and courage are the essentials of success in carrying out our plan. You people must have faith; you must not be stampeded by rumors or guesses. Let us unite in banishing fear. We have provided the machinery to restore our financial system; it is up to you to support and make it work.

It is your problem no less than it is mine. Together we cannot fail.

Money in circulation, which amounted to $7.5 billion in the last days of the crisis, decreased by $1.25 billion until the end of March and $2 billion more until the end of April; and from March 4 to April 5 Federal Reserve notes in the amount of $1,225 million were returned to the Reserve Banks, while $630 million in gold coins and certificates were returned to the Reserve Banks and the Treasury by the end of March. It was thus not necessary to make much use of the Federal Reserve Bank notes; they reached their peak, $206 million, in December, 1933, representing less than 4 per cent of the circulating currency. The introduction of Federal Deposit Insurance by the Banking Act of June, 1933, further strengthened the position of the banks even before January 1, 1934, when the insurance became effective.

THE NATIONALIZATION OF GOLD

The reopening of banking and the restoration of regular money circulation were accompanied by another and more challenging measure, the nationalization of gold. On March 10, at the end of the bank holiday, the President, relying on the Emergency Banking Act, prohibited by executive order the export of gold and gold certificates as well as any payment in such media by banks, except under license by the Secretary of the Treasury. Moreover, business transactions in foreign exchange were limited to "legitimate and normal business requirements and for travelling and other personal contracts." The latter part of the order is remarkable—leaving aside the abortive act of 1867—as the only American instance of "exchange control," which, however, through its lack of precision, differed widely from the exchange control measures taken by other countries. Also, it did not last long. It was abrogated to all intents and purposes in November, 1934, through a "general license" granted by the Secretary of the Treasury.[4] Not much was to become known about the application and effect of that exchange control; its restoration, though legally permitted, was never undertaken. In any case, the question of abrogating the exchange control soon proved insignificant because foreign currency became less and less attractive to the American people. The nationalization of gold was far more important. The pertinent provisions of the executive order of March 10 met with some legal objections from the judiciary and had to be revamped several times. But the only significant change was the elimination of a clause permitting the individual to keep $100 in gold coin or bullion; only "gold scraps or gold sweepings" were permitted to be kept up to the value of $100. It was also made clear that gold held in this country by foreigners likewise had to be surrendered to the government. However, the government was never given the power held by the British and other governments to seize objects made of gold other than coin or bullion.

It took many years before the nationalization of gold was completed.[5] But there is no doubt that the provisions of the law were finally obeyed. It was a memorable achievement, especially when one considers that it was accomplished in peace time. France was unable to carry through the nationalization of gold even under the pressure of war and countries such as Italy or Spain never even attempted it. It may be that the apparently less intense American craving for gold was a factor in this achievement.

The nation was now protected against another flight of gold and against the possible danger of destroying or seriously harming the country's monetary structure. Of course, the fact that the dollar creditor was no longer entitled to payment in gold was expected to reduce the value of the dollar, especially in the foreign markets. However, until the middle of April there was little change in the exchange rate of the dollar. Thereafter a decline began, but mainly because it was favored by the government. At this point a complex, enigmatic, and dramatic situation arose which finally led to a stringent legal debasement of the dollar.

FORCING DOWN THE GOLD PRICE OF THE DOLLAR

Aside from the critical but temporary banking paralysis, two great problems were foremost in the President's mind: the wide unemployment throughout the country and the deep depression in agriculture. Early in 1933 there were about 13 million unemployed as compared with the 4.6 million in October of 1930; and the prices of farm products (taking the 1914 figures as 100) had slipped to 55 in March, 1933, in line with a world-wide downward movement. Depreciation of the dollar was expected to raise prices and improve business with a corresponding increase in employment.

The agricultural crisis led on May 12, 1933, to the adoption of the Agricultural Adjustment Act. Its primary purpose was to provide improvements in the situation of the farmers. But the inflationists, who were powerful in the Democratic Party, succeeded under the leadership of Senator Elmer Thomas of Oklahoma in passing an amendment to the act in May, 1933, that was of a monetary and banking nature. Parts of this "Thomas Amendment" were of lasting significance in this respect: all U.S. coins and currencies were declared legal tender with no limitation for silver coins or baser metals. Furthermore, the President was granted the unprecedented power of reducing the gold content of the dollar 50 per cent or less if, in the President's opinion, such a measure was necessary for the stabilization of domestic prices or for protection against depreciation of foreign currencies. More particularly, the President was authorized to establish a ratio for gold on the basis of a forthcoming international agreement. Other novel discretionary powers were entrusted to the President but expired without being used. They included the establishment of bimetallism with unlimited coinage on a gold-silver ratio to be determined by him or by an international agreement, and the issuance of no less than $3 billion in greenbacks for the purchase of securities of the government or of government corporations. Among relatively minor powers which were actually used by him, we might mention an authorization to accept payments in silver from foreign governments for a period of six months; the rate was to be no more than 50 cents an ounce, whereas the market price was about 36 cents. The President chose the 50-cent rate. The main beneficiary was England, which thereby received some easement of her war debt, but Mussolini's Italy also reaped some advantage from it. Of course, the measure was too insignificant to influence the general price level of silver, let alone the prices of farm products. It was no more than a somewhat expensive sport on the part of an administration which could afford it.

The Thomas proposal to overcome the monetary crisis through an international agreement was not merely the expression of familiar bimetallistic theory; it had a more convincing reason in the truly international nature of the monetary distress which had come about since 1931 through the abandonment of the gold standard by England, Germany, and other important countries. The result was the World Economic and Monetary Conference under the leadership of the United States and Great Britain, which convened at London in June, 1933.[6] But the policies of the participating governments soon proved to be too far apart to permit agreement on monetary matters. The European countries, whose exports had gained from the depreciation of their own currencies, were now losing this advantage by the depreciation of the dollar; they certainly would have welcomed an international and immediate stabilization. In fact, in anticipation of such an arrangement, the decline of the dollar slowed down in the foreign exchange market and domestic prices stopped rising. This development definitely ran counter to New Deal policies and on July 2 President Roosevelt issued a message rejecting an immediate stabilization. As a result, the Conference came to an end. It had a somewhat strange postlude, however, through a subcommittee of the Conference which remained in session and brought about a limited international arrangement between the United States and other silver-producing countries to the effect that silver should not be dumped but rather be bought from the respective domestic producers. Figures specifying the amount of purchases were provided for in the agreement. Actually, as will be shown later, a burden was placed on only one country, the United States, for the benefit of the American silver producers.

Meanwhile, the dollar had depreciated in foreign markets by more than 30 per cent and wholesale prices, especially of farm products, had risen considerably. But in July the dollar once more gained strength and the increase in prices subsided; the price of farm products even suffered a setback. The President now felt that he had to employ his powers in a firm and well-planned manner in order to create a more satisfactory situation. He turned for advice to Professor G. F. Warren of Cornell University, a noted agricultural economist, but less experienced in the field of general economics. Warren was definitely in favor of raising the price of gold by purchasing gold bullion in sufficient quantities at high prices. The dollar could then depreciate and the price level rise proportionately. Following this advice and yielding to the pressure of the inflationists, Roosevelt authorized the Treasury at the end of August, 1933, to purchase gold from domestic producers at the market price of $29.62 an ounce, while the value of an ounce would have been $20.67 according to the statutory weight of the gold dollar. The new regulation meant, in the first place, a profit to domestic gold producers. Two months later, the purchasing was expanded to foreign markets; on October 25 the administration took the initiative by purchasing foreign gold at $31.36 an ounce, or $0.27 above the London market rate. Gradually, though by no means uniformly, the price of gold was raised. In December the market price of gold in terms of dollars remained considerably below the prices paid by the United States government, certainly a strange phenomenon. This situation continued into January, 1934, but now a final decision on the gold ratio of the dollar could no longer be postponed.

THE DEVALUATION OF THE DOLLAR

Following a presidential message of January 15, 1934, Congress passed on January 30 the Gold Reserve Act, which created a new basis for the American monetary system. Coining of gold was discontinued; all gold was to be kept in bars;

the gold held by the Federal Reserve Banks was to be vested in the United States for dollars constituting the value of the gold according to the new weight of the dollar as proclaimed by the President; that weight was to be no more than 60 per cent of its previous statutory weight.

The next day, January 31, 1934, the President issued his proclamation: the "weight of the gold dollar" was fixed at 15 5/21 grains, 9/10 fine. There was, we know, no "gold dollar." It would have been more exact to fix the "standard unit of value" at 15 5/21 grains of gold 9/10 fine, and this is the real meaning of the proclamation. The choice of 15 5/21 grains is explained by the fact that 9/10 of this, namely 13 5/7 grains of gold fine, multiplied by 35, represented the market price of an ounce of gold fine. This ratio, $35 = 1 ounce of gold fine, is the gist of the presidential proclamation. The depreciation amounted to 40.94 per cent; that is, $1.69 was now the equivalent of the 1932 dollar.

But, as was seen, no eagle or other gold coin had to be produced at the new level and no paper money was to be redeemed in gold. Hence, the gold *coin* standard was abandoned. Nor was the gold *bullion* standard adopted under which, up to 1931, the Bank of England had to sell bars of gold for a certain minimum amount of Bank notes. But the gold standard as such, that is, the exclusive definition of the monetary unit in terms of gold, was upheld. Henceforth, the gold value of the dollar had to be maintained through management by the Treasury, that is, primarily through transactions with foreign central banks and governments. But this management also included the regulation of the domestic use of gold for industrial, artistic, and other legitimate purposes—a complex administrative affair.[7] The gold coin standard has thereby been turned into a "gold management standard."

This devaluation of the dollar is a unique event in monetary history. Throughout the centuries and particularly during the first decades of our century, there have been numberless devaluations of monetary units, but they were the result of inflation—that is, of an unsound increase of available cash, mainly paper money—and of a resulting depreciation of the unit. In such a case the devaluation through legislative action tries to escape the pressing inflation by the establishment on a lower level of a new and stable "standard unit of value." The devaluation of the dollar was of an entirely different character. It was not the result of irresistible monetary pressure but of freely working domestic policies. No other country has even ventured or could have ventured such an arbitrary "marking" of its monetary unit.

The peculiarity of the occurrence is increased by the fact that the Warren theory [8] on which the monetary policies of the New Deal had been based was refuted by economic developments. To be sure, heavy devaluation will in the long run lead to a broadly proportional increase in prices. But there are numerous other factors in the formation of prices—political, physical, technical, etc.—in the domestic as well as in the international field. Hence, an expected increase may be delayed for years, eliminating it more or less from the area of practical politics. As a matter of fact, it was only in

World War II that the wholesale price index reached a level equalizing the devaluation of the dollar. Farm prices first recovered faster, but a drought not confined to this country was an important cause for this development. Indeed, the late thirties brought again a decline in prices which was only overcome by wartime exigencies.

The English economist Roy Harrod has recently asserted that the effect of the Gold Reserve Act was "null" until the outbreak of World War II.[9] This was due, he asserts, to the operation of the free market for gold bullion in London; "any individual holder of the dollar" could obtain gold there at the official rate "via sterling." "It would not be an exaggeration," he adds, "to say that we in Britain maintained the U.S. gold standard for them during this period."

This is a puzzling statement. The gold-value standard of the dollar as established by the presidential proclamation of 1934 was maintained by the United States itself, whose gold reserves amounted to four or five times those held by the United Kingdom. Hence, the Gold Reserve Act was fully effective. Whether the holder of the dollar could also get a corresponding quantity of gold was of little importance, since the effectiveness of the act secured to him the full gold value of the dollar.

If gold bullion actually was freely available in London at the official rate, this would have been true not only for the holder of the dollar but also for the holder of any other foreign currency. The gold bullion standard would have been upheld for the entire world by the United Kingdom, which had to struggle so hard to maintain the value of its own pound sterling. We do not need to delve any further into the details because there is no indication, and none is given by Harrod, that the supposed private sales of dollars for gold have occurred at London to any extent worth mentioning.

THE GOLD CLAUSES

Though devaluation had been achieved, a number of dollar creditors claimed that their rights had not been affected by it.

Since the Middle Ages, when an economy based on monetary exchange developed, creditors have tried to protect themselves against harmful changes in the medium of payment by clauses which were designed to prevent the debtor from making use of such changes. The most frequent type of these protective agreements were the "gold clauses" [10] by which the debtor obligates himself to make payment in a specified amount of contractually defined gold coins irrespective of later changes in the law or the currency circulation. The use of such clauses spread from the latter part of the nineteenth century, particularly in this country as a reaction to the bimetallist agitation. It became a matter of routine to insert in bonds and mortgage deeds a phrase such as this "to pay dollars in gold coin of the United States of the standard and fineness existing on [date of contracting]." Most bonds of the Federal government, especially the Liberty bonds, contained such a promise. Estimates of the total amounts included in these clauses in this country vary from $75 billion to $123 billion.

Important changes in the monetary system are generally

caused by serious national emergencies. It was the great French jurist Molineaus (1500–1556) who first developed the theory that private individuals cannot by agreement exclude the sovereign's determination of the weight, fineness, and nominal value of coins. As a matter of fact, the French courts in modern times have consistently held invalid gold clauses concluded between French nationals. In this century numerous countries abrogated gold clauses by legislative action, particularly under the pressure of the monetary disturbances following World War I; many more did so after the abandonment of the gold standard following the monetary crisis of 1931. On June 5, 1933, Congress passed a joint resolution declaring gold clauses to be contrary to public policy and providing that the gold dollar's obligation "shall be discharged upon payment, dollar for dollar, in any coin or currency" being legal tender and covering the nominal amount of the debt.

The constitutionality of the joint resolution, denied by a number of gold-clause creditors, was recognized by the Supreme Court of the United States in February, 1935. These "Gold Clause Cases" are among the most dramatic in the history of the Supreme Court. Negating the constitutionality of the act would have brought about a catastrophe, especially to the United States government; the President, it became known, had decided to go before the people in such a contingency and declare the execution of the decision to be impossible. Recognition of the joint resolution's constitutionality was attained only by a compromise among four of the justices. In an opinion written by Chief Justice Hughes they dismissed the claims of the suing creditors. Nevertheless, the opinion declared the joint resolution to be unconstitutional with respect to government obligations since Congress could not "disregard the obligations of the Government at its discretion." The claims of the government's creditors were dismissed only on the ground that owing to the nationalization of gold they were no longer entitled to gold as such. Merely a loss in domestic purchasing power would have given them a right to compensation, and such a loss had not been proved or even asserted. Actually, the gold clause legally has nothing to do with purchasing power, and Justice Stone, later the Chief Justice, joined the group led by Chief Justice Hughes in a lucid and impressive separate opinion holding the joint resolution constitutional also with respect to government obligations. Hence, the claims of the gold creditors were rejected by a vote of five to four. Warren's mistake regarding the time of the rise in the price level had proved a blessing in disguise for the Federal government.

This is not the place to undertake a closer juridical inquiry into the legal aspects of the gold clauses. From a historical and political point of view, however, the opinion of the minority written by Justice McReynolds deserves attention. While entirely condemning the joint resolution, it stated, with a look at the majority opinion, that "loss of reputation for honorable dealing will bring us unending humiliation; the impending legal and moral chaos is appalling." In an impulsive exclamation from the bench, Justice McReynolds asserted that "it is not too much to say that the Constitution is gone," and somewhat obscurely he referred to Nero as a precursor of Congress. In a later case, along with two other justices, he stigmatized the attitude of the government when it started to pay the Liberty bonds at their nominal dollar values "as a dishonest effort to defeat the contract and to defraud the creditors." He even recommended that dissenters should "reverently fix their gaze on the Eighth Commandment" (thou shalt not steal). Apparently, Justice McReynolds and the other members of the minority (the "steady four") were influenced by a "grim" anti-New Deal attitude. In any case, we are here confronted with an outburst of political passion which in an embarrassing way illustrates the fact that the Supreme Court of the United States is burdened with a task which, for inescapable historical reasons, may exceed the juridical sphere.

Further litigation against the government on the grounds of abrogated gold clauses was cut off by a joint resolution of Congress of August 27, 1935. Otherwise the purchasing power theory of Chief Justice Hughes might have created a great danger to the nation. As in the case of the gold metal standard, the American abrogation of the gold standard seems to constitute the finale of a world-wide development. Gold clauses have been abandoned almost everywhere and a wide search for substitutes has begun.

THE SILVER ISSUE REVIVED

The revival, under the New Deal, of the silver issue [11] has already been touched upon. While the Thomas Amendment was chiefly domestic in nature, it also contained a minor section, as we have seen, which was international in character.

On the other hand, the silver agreement of the London Conference was on the surface international in character; intrinsically, however, it was a result of American domestic policies. This feature found full expression in a "ratifying" presidential proclamation of December 31, 1933. The London agreement had "obligated" the United States to buy from the domestic producers 24,400,000 ounces of silver (an amount equal to the total 1932 production), but no similar obligation had been laid upon the other parties to the agreement. Now the President, under the broad power granted him by the Thomas Amendment, directed the mints to buy all the domestically produced silver whose amount was soon to grow, at the rate of 64½ cents an ounce, as contrasted with the world market price of about 45 cents. This rate equaled one half of $1.29, the statutory evaluation of the dollar-silver. The deduction of 50 per cent was justified officially as "seigniorage," a strange explanation, since seigniorage in modern times has always meant the deduction of a very small percentage covering the expenses of the government and perhaps a moderate fee. The real point was the continuing of the large profit for the silver producers.

The economic strain upon the farmers led to a renewal of bimetallistic-inflationist agitation, of which the silver producers were natural supporters. As a result, Congress passed on June 19, 1934, the Silver Purchase Act, authorizing the President to order free coinage of silver dollars at a rate chosen by him, thereby creating real bimetallism. The President never made use of this power. Still, Congress had established by the act a new policy according to which the proportion of silver to gold in the monetary stocks of the United States should be increased; the ultimate objective was to have one quarter of the monetary value of the stocks in silver. That goal was to be attained under the act by purchase here and abroad until the market price of $1.29 an ounce was reached! These formulae, though sounding formidable, left it to the discretion of the Treasury as to the time and amount of purchase. The rate of 64½ cents applied to newly produced silver, but other silver in the United States on May 1, 1934, was to be bought by the government at 50 cents an ounce. These and other restrictions and, more important, the discretion left to the administration, made it possible for the President to comply with the Silver Purchase Act. Also, a few days after its passage, the Treasury issued, on the basis of the act, an embargo on silver which would make it impossible for American residents to ship their silver abroad and then present it to the Treasury as "foreign silver" at a higher price. In August, 1934, the embargo was replaced by a presidential order, again based on the act, providing the general delivery of domestic silver to the mints at the price of 50 cents an ounce.[12] Hence, silver, too, was "nationalized." Through many exceptions, nationalization was limited to silver bullion only. Senator Pittman, leader of the silverites, called the "nationalization" the proper way for settling the silver question forever.

As a result of all these measures, but chiefly of the Treasury's continued purchases in the London open market, the price of silver rose considerably, reaching a peak of 81 cents on April 26, 1935. This was mainly the result of maneuvers undertaken by speculators in the market where the Treasury appeared as the invariable buyer. Then the Treasury decided to change its purchasing methods by fixing the price at which it was willing to buy and by gradually lowering the price. The market yielded at once. In the last months of 1935 the price of 65⅝ cents was upheld by the Treasury. But then one day the Treasury refrained from bidding altogether. No quotations proved possible. It was a kind of collapse. Afterwards the price fell in December, 1935 and January, 1936, to 45 cents, where it stayed with slight fluctuations, until the end of this period—again, partly with the help of the Treasury.

The President, however, could not avoid raising the price for domestic silver in April, 1935, to 77.57 cents (a seigniorage of 40 per cent), but in 1937 the price of 64½ cents was restored, to become effective January 1, 1938, and remained in force until June 30, 1939. Thereafter the silver bloc forced upon the President, by a law of July 6, 1939, a price for domestic silver of 71.11 cents per ounce (seigniorage of 55 per cent); but the war soon created new conditions.

On the whole this country's economy was little affected by the Silver Purchase Act and the ups and downs in the price of silver which it caused. Other countries suffered far greater damage, especially China, which was on the silver standard. The silverites, and particularly Senator Pittman, had strongly emphasized the great advantages which China, a good customer of ours, would draw from an increase in the value of silver. What actually happened was a rise in the export of silver coins from China, with a resulting decrease in domestic prices (deflation) in that country, due to the scarcity of money; trade shrank rapidly there and business enterprises and banks collapsed. In November, 1935, the Chinese government decided to abandon the silver standard and in its stead rely on paper money partly backed by gold made available by the United States.

All in all, the new bimetallistic eruption had led to a complete anticlimax. The 25 per cent silver quota of the Silver Purchase Act remained on the statute books, and the American silver producers received extra profits from the government as before, but despite some unrelenting counterpropaganda, silver was now definitely eliminated as a possible basis of the monetary system. The revival of bimetallism during the New Deal period must be explained to a large extent by a peculiarity of the American constitutional system. In the Senate, definitely the more powerful part of Congress, the leading silver states—Idaho, Utah, Montana, Arizona, Nevada, and Colorado—had twelve representatives, that is, six times as many as New York state, which then had four times as many inhabitants as those six states combined. Since nearly all of the Senators concerned were Democrats, at that time the majority party, their disproportionate power was further enhanced. Here monetary history illustrates a striking weakness of American political life. In the silver question it was chiefly due to President Roosevelt that this country was spared a bimetallistic disaster. Despite his inflationist leanings in favor of agriculture, he was not silver-minded, and while avoiding a clash with the silver bloc, he proved far superior to the silverites in defending the national interest.

THE COMPONENTS OF THE MODIFIED MONETARY SYSTEM

First, we have to turn to the Federal Reserve notes, because of their importance as well as because of the remarkable changes which they underwent.

The entire Federal Reserve Board was remodeled by the Banking Act of August 23, 1935, which replaced the former "Federal Reserve Board" by the "Board of Governors," whose members were to be appointed by the President for fourteen years. The regulative power of the Board of Governors was considerably broadened beyond that wielded by the old Board; and the heads of the district banks, whose title was now transformed from "governor" to "president," found themselves in a secondary position. The expansion of the prerogatives of the Federal Reserve System had started with the Banking Act of 1933 and the Thomas Amendment. Now, under the Banking Act of 1935 the Board of Governors received a dominant position, first of all, in the field of credit control. For instance, the Board was authorized to regulate the rediscounting rates of the district banks—rates on which those charged by the member banks to their customers practically depend. Further, the Board was granted the power to expand or restrict, within certain limits, the reserve requirements for bank deposits and to prescribe interest rates for time deposits (interest for demand deposits had already been prohibited by the act of 1933). As a result, the Federal Reserve System received more legal authority than that held by the European central banks.[13] However, the Federal Reserve System has no power over such state banks that have not decided to become members of the System, and these nonmember banks are more numerous than member banks. In 1933 the nonmember commercial state banks amounted to 8,300 and in 1939 to 8,000, as compared with 5,600 and 6,300 member banks respectively, but the nonmember banks are financially far less important.

But there were also innovations of a technically monetary character. The general extension of the legal tender quality included, of course, the Federal Reserve notes. Other changes were related to the reserves and securities underlying the issuance of the notes. First of all, there was no longer any security in gold bullion or gold coin owing to the transfer of all gold to the Treasury. While the 40 per cent minimum rate of "gold" reserves was maintained, the gold metal was replaced under the Gold Reserve Act by "gold certificates"; but these certificates are completely different from the "yellowbacks" of old. They are no longer money and do not circulate among the public. They are issued exclusively in large denominations and are to be held by the Federal Reserve Banks which do not have even a formal legal claim to the metal; the Secretary of the Treasury has to redeem the certificates only at such times and in such amounts as in his judgment are necessary to maintain the purchasing power of the dollar. Moreover, not even the certificates are much used for this purpose; their place has been widely taken by "gold certificate credits" of the Treasury, that is, by ledger transactions of the Treasury.[14]

Another change in the collateral securities of the notes

had, we know, already been brought about for one year by the Glass-Steagall Act, namely, the use of government bonds instead of commercial paper. This provision was renewed by the New Deal legislation and became permanent in 1945. Actually, not much use has been made of this provision which, apparently, is more intended for emergency situations. A monetary character in the strict sense of the word may also be attributed to the power of the Federal Reserve Board to regulate rediscounting rates since such regulation is bound to affect the amount of redeemable commercial and other paper acceptable as collateral security.

The monetary significance of these changes should not be overrated, however. The main point remains that the full strength of the United States is behind the Federal Reserve notes, and it may be added that the extra reserves of the district and member banks for notes and deposits—no separate figures are available—mounted from 63–68 per cent in 1933 to 84–87 per cent in 1939, aside from a temporary slump in March, 1933; since the Korean War the level has been between 40 and 50 per cent. In fact, the circulation of the Federal Reserve notes rose from $3 billion in 1933 to $4.5 billion in 1935, whereas the total monetary circulation rose during the same period from $5.7 billion to $7 billion.

The Federal Reserve notes are denominated in amounts of $5 to $10,000. They still contain the inscription, as before the Gold Reserve Act, that "the United States will pay to the bearer on demand . . . dollars" and that the notes are "redeemable in lawful money at the United States Treasury or at any Federal Reserve Bank." But an exchange for any other United States money, say, silver certificates or U.S. notes, would not make sense. The government probably feared that a change in inscription might cause unnecessary alarm among the lay public.

Since the New Deal legislation the needs of the public for small, especially for $1 and $2, notes have been taken care of by means of silver certificates and U.S. notes. Higher amounts of the certificates up to $1,000 were originally provided for and issued. However, only the $1, $2, $5, and $10 notes are in actual circulation. In view of the growing silver holdings, the Silver Purchase Act obligated the Treasury to issue silver certificates in an amount not less than the cost of all the silver purchased by it. Hence, their circulation rose from $361 million in 1933 to $705 million in 1935 and $1,230 million in 1938. In daily transactions they have become the commonest type of paper money. They still give the bearer a claim against the Treasury for an equal amount in silver which is actually deposited with the Treasury. However, despite the heavy devaluation of the dollar, the value of the metal contained in the silver dollar equals only a fraction of the dollar in this period (in 1939, 30 cents). Strangely enough, the inscription on the silver certificates permits the Treasury to make payment in fractional silver coins representing about 6½ per cent less silver than the dollar, though the Silver Purchase Act provided that it be made in the *standard silver dollar*.[15]

No more than $347 million in United States notes (greenbacks) were permitted, we know, by the law of 1878. Actually, a lesser amount was in circulation during the period under discussion, $279 million in 1934 and $266 million in 1939. Apparently the Treasury was little interested in this inelastic type of currency. Under the Gold Reserve Act the Treasury, however, has to keep a reserve gold fund of $150 million for the redemption of the greenbacks as well as of the treasury notes of 1890. The latter had practically disappeared but gold redemption, we know, was discarded. The Treasury maintained the reserve, however, but this is no more than a ledger transaction. The inscription on the greenbacks regarding the bearer's right to payment is just as meaningless as the similar inscription on the Federal Reserve notes.

National bank notes in this period finally met the fate that had so long been planned for them. They could be issued only on the basis of certain government bonds. These bonds were now redeemed by the government through a fund of $675 million, which was apportioned for this purpose from the devaluation profit. The circulation of these notes shrank from $902 million in 1934 to $186 million in 1939, and later disappeared, to all intents and purposes. Federal Reserve Bank notes, as an emergency expedient, were not employed to the extent expected by the government in the banking crisis of 1933–34. In 1934, $142 million of these notes circulated, but no more than $26 million in 1939. The former gold certificates, the "yellowbacks," were for the most part delivered to the government as required by the law, but a considerable amount—in 1939 still $72 million—were withheld, probably for the most part by foreigners who did not know about the nationalization of these certificates. Actually, prior to the Gold Reserve Act, the yellowbacks had a world-wide reputation as the pinnacle of security.

Silver dollars and the various types of fractional coins remained unchanged. The metallic value of the silver coins was, of course, proportionately increased by the 40.94 per cent devaluation of the dollar, but it still remained far below the monetary denomination. After 1935, when the value was 50 cents, it went down to 35 cents in 1936 and 30 cents in 1939. The Gold Purchase Act mentioned among the uses of the newly acquired silver the coinage of standard silver dollars in the first place, but the public's aversion to them persisted. The circulation of silver dollars rose from $30 million in 1934 to $39 million in 1938, but the subsidiary coins grew from $280 million in 1934 to $342 million in 1938 and $361 million in 1939. The figures reflected an improvement in the living standards of the people resulting in an increase in their daily expenditures.

Minor coins were and still are unlimited legal tender. A man owing $1,000 may discharge his debt by dumping upon his creditor 100,000 copper cents, that is, according to the letter of the law.

The American monetary system was definitely simplified and improved through the elimination from regular circulation of the national bank notes, the Federal Reserve Bank notes, and the yellowbacks. The question remains as to why U.S. notes were not exchanged for Federal Reserve notes;

the gold holdings were broad enough to cover the notes. A sentimental desire on the part of the government to preserve the notes of the Civil War may have been a factor.

As a curiosity it might be mentioned that during the early New Deal period a number of states began to issue "sales tax tokens" for the payment of state sales taxes.[16] While some of the tokens were made of cardboard, many others were made of aluminum and other metals. Because these taxes were levied also upon very small sales, some tokens were denominated in terms of "milles," the unit of 1792 which had never been used. It is reported that in 1937 the Treasury, rightly, protested the issuance of such "sales tax tokens," but apparently it took quite a number of years before the states yielded. In the last decade or so the tokens apparently have disappeared.

Inasmuch as the Federal types of circulating media have remained the same up to the present day, a word may be added here about the impact of counterfeiting. In this respect, conditions have vastly improved since the end of the Civil War and particularly during this century. The importance of the matter is indicated by the fact that the investigation of counterfeiting is entrusted to the Secret Service, which has only one other important task, namely, guarding the President of the United States. Counterfeiting still exists and has been improved technically and, so to speak, organizationally. A careful study published in 1944 with the support of the authorities [17] reports about counterfeiting "syndicates" found, in the thirties, it seems, especially in New York. Italian immigrants led in the committing of this crime.[18] Fortunately, the methods for detecting the counterfeiters improved far more than counterfeiting methods, and under the insistence of the government, the courts have become more severe in the punishment of the criminals.[19] Counterfeiting still exists, but it can be said that for several decades it has no longer constituted the common danger to the people that it sometimes used to be. Following the colonial tradition, national bank notes and the greenbacks up to 1917 contained an inscription threatening counterfeiters with severe punishment. The fact that the phrase has disappeared and has never been engraved upon the silver certificates and Federal Reserve notes may be taken as a gratifying omen.

THE DOLLAR AND GOLD INTERNATIONALLY

The Stabilization Fund was designed to protect the dollar against depreciation and generally against heavy fluctuation, but it soon appeared that there was no need for such an endeavor. Everywhere people were aware that the reduction of the dollar standard had been largely an artificial action and that under the robust American financial and economic system there was, so far as human judgment went, not the least danger of further depreciation in the markets of gold and foreign exchange. Rather, it was in the opposite direction that a new problem evolved. Owing chiefly to the rise of Hitler and fascism, a serious political and economic unrest developed. No area of safety seemed available to the European capitalist except the United States. At the same time, Americans shrank more and more from investing in Europe.

While in 1932 the gold exports from this country had surpassed the imports by $446 million, a surplus of gold imports of $1,132 million appeared in 1934 and grew every year until in 1939 it amounted to no less than $3,574 million. The gold stock had then climbed to $16 billion.

While the tremendous increase in wealth stimulated the American economy, the authorities developed the feeling that the United States could not react fast enough and that the use of the inflowing gold collateral and reserve for the issuance of Federal Reserve notes might lead to an unsound broadening of monetary circulation and of credit facilities. In December, 1936, the Treasury therefore decided no longer to turn the incoming gold to the Federal Reserve Banks, adding to their collaterals and making payment with the reserve notes; instead, the Treasury proceeded to keep the gold in "inactive" accounts. This "sterilization" of gold made it necessary for the Treasury to obtain the purchase price through the sale of government securities in the market, resulting in payment of interest. Still, the government's action proved fruitless. As early as 1937 a business recession took place; sterilization was curtailed and in April, 1938, abandoned altogether.

The stabilization of the dollar which the Stabilization Fund had to provide was interpreted by the Treasury in a very broad sense. Since the vicissitudes which important foreign currencies were undergoing might have repercussions upon the dollar—perhaps causing an undesirable increase of the dollar rate in the foreign markets—the Treasury decided to use the Fund for the support of the imperiled French franc, a new policy not officially disclosed. In September, 1936, however, the Tripartite Monetary Agreement was officially concluded between the United States, Great Britain, and France. It was a gentlemen's agreement, rather than a formal treaty, proclaiming the inauguration of a common monetary policy. It excluded exchange control and further currency devaluation except the pending devaluation of the franc. Shortly afterwards, the Secretary of the Treasury declared his willingness to buy gold from or sell it to the British and French governments at the statutory rate of $35 an ounce, subject to a handling charge of ¼ of one per cent and with the right of revoking the offer on twenty-four hours' notice. Corresponding facilities were offered to the United States by the two other governments mainly, it seems, to demonstrate complete equality. Actually, ostensible results of the agreement were not spectacular; however, it established a basis for the cooperation of the three governments in the monetary market. Soon joined by Belgium, the Netherlands, and Switzerland, the agreement was in fact an official demonstration of willingness to cooperate among the democratic nations in the light of the Hitler menace. Soviet Russia was not yet considered dangerous at this time; when the Tripartite Monetary Agreement was arranged, the Treasury made a transaction in pounds —a minor one, it is true—with Soviet Russia.[20]

How different were these international repercussions from those we have observed in the past. Although foreign trade and foreign investment, especially English, were always crucial factors in this country's financial history, the people did not look much beyond the frontiers or the oceans in monetary matters. The participation in Napoleon's international monetary conference was a kind of courtesy to France; and in the later conferences the United States was seeking aid for bimetallism. In the London Conference the United States was still looking for support, or rather, all parties were looking for support. Since 1934, however, the situation changed through the shift in the policies of the Stabilization Fund and more definitely in 1936 through the Tripartite Monetary Agreement. The United States appears as an assistant to friendly nations. It is the beginning of a great evolution which became more distinct in the next period.

This chapter is concerned with a period of something under six years. But never before was the American monetary system so drastically altered as in this short span of time. The statutory value of the dollar, untouched for 142 years (aside from the slight changes of 1834 and 1837), was now heavily debased. The gold coin standard was abandoned and gold was nationalized. It was a revolution, the effects of which far exceeded the confines of this period and the boundaries of the country.

Only to a limited extent can the monetary events be considered as typically New Deal measures. A characteristic feature of the New Deal was an expansion of the Federal government's functions and powers in the social interest while at the same time upholding true democracy. Roosevelt's monetary reforms culminating in the Gold Reserve Act were widely motivated by social considerations favoring the farmers and workers. But fundamentally reforms had become inevitable because of the Great Depression and its critical point in 1933. Nationalization of gold was more closely related to the spirit of the New Deal. The same is definitely true of the broadening of the monetary powers of the Federal Reserve System and the Treasury. The shift of power to the administration had the effect, among others, that the monetary subjects in the U.S. Statutes at Large were considerably reduced, a phenomenon not without general interest. From a comparative point of view the mass of monetary legislation piled up since 1792 has been amazing.[21] The explanation is to be found, at least in part, in the unwillingness of Congress to grant much leeway to the administration, which might be or might become of a different political party from that of the enacting majority, an attitude less apparent in the other, even democratic, countries.

Still, the New Deal aspects of the monetary developments are overshadowed by the international significance inherent in the American abandonment of the gold coin standard. The United States was the most important and the last country clinging to it. The Gold Reserve Act of 1934 meant, therefore, the end of the gold coin (or gold bullion) standard the world over. The introduction of this standard had been a great improvement over the previous confusion and had been helpful particularly in foreign trade. And the emphasis upon the personal gold holdings of the individual was much in accord with the old type of liberalism as cultivated particularly in England. But the tremendous progress in communication shattered this system. International movements of private gold, especially gold flight, proved destructive or utterly perilous to any national system based on a gold coin or gold bullion standard. Other weaknesses of the dominant system were revealed by World War I. Inseparable adherence of the monetary unit to the gold metal led, it was seen, to financial confusion and disturbance of the foreign exchange rate as a result of the devastating new methods and range of hostilities. Obviously the gold coin standard linked the value of the monetary unit too closely to the individual's give and take of the metal. We need not go into the theories set forth by Keynes which were opposed to the maintenance of a strict gold standard as such. In fact, the act of 1934 was intended to uphold the strict gold standard; only the rate of the dollar was to be maintained by the more subtle method of management; and this was in itself a measure of world-wide significance.

The nationalization of gold, too, though for a different reason, proved of utmost importance far beyond the area of the United States. The Treasury's gold stock rose from $8 billion in 1934 to $18 billion in 1939. Hence, the international position of this country was greatly strengthened—and though this was not yet envisaged by the New Dealers—a favorable monetary position was created for this country with regard to the approaching war.

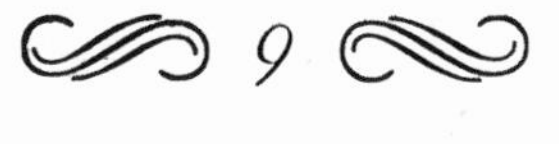

World War II and After

THE INITIAL monetary disturbances which had appeared in World War I, and had been more or less connected with the gold coin standard, were absent in World War II. The gold stock of the country grew in 1939 by $3.1 billion and in 1940 by $4.4 billion, the sharpest increase ever experienced; in the comparable years 1915 and 1916, the figures had been $499 million and $531 million, respectively. Since the years 1939 and 1940 preceded this country's active participation in the military operations, the transfer of the gold must be attributed in the first place to the grave developments in the countries threatened or attacked by Hitler.

INTERNAL DEVELOPMENTS

The monetary and financial vigor of the United States was fully demonstrated in the years after its actual entrance into the war, from December, 1941 to August, 1945. This period was twice as long as that of American participation in World War I, and the government's wartime expenses reached the stupendous figure of $281 billion, as contrasted with $35.5 billion (equal to about 50 billion of the devaluated dollar) of World War I. Prices only rose 33 per cent during the war, whereas during the much shorter World War I, prices rose 60 per cent. The more favorable figure of World War II is explained not only by an effective governmental price control and heavy taxation, but by a stupendous rise in domestic production. Although the increase in gold turned into a decrease amounting in 1944 to $1.3 billion (in World War I the increase never came to a full stop), the circulating currency rose from $6 billion in 1939 to $27 billion in 1945, of which no less than $23 billion consisted of Federal Reserve notes. But there were no serious disturbances. Only toward the end of the war did the reserves of the district banks come close to the 40 per cent minimum of gold reserves. Hence, in June, 1945, near the end of the war, an amendment to the Federal Reserve Act reduced the minimum of gold reserve to 25 per cent, permitting the rest ("collateral") to be covered by qualified commercial paper or government securities. Actually, the gold reserve for the Federal Reserve notes invariably remained above 40 per cent. The amendment further provided for the withdrawal of Federal Reserve Bank notes, thereby simplifying the monetary system. Finally, it canceled the long outdated presidential power to issue greenbacks up to the amount of $3 billion.

Silver remained, of course, an element in the monetary structure because of the silver dollars, the circulation of which rose from $46 million in 1940 to $125 million in 1945. Subsidiary silver coins grew in amount from $384 million in 1940 to $788 million in 1945; [1] there was less change with regard to the silver certificates (about $1.6 billion in 1945). But bimetallism, we know, was dead. In 1956 the gold stock of the United States amounted to 22 billion and the silver stock to 2.2 billion, but no one worried about the ultimate goal of having silver equal 25 per cent of the whole stock as envisaged by the Silver Purchase Act.

However, an unexpected demand arose for silver out of the needs of the war. Hence, the Treasury was authorized by Congress to sell or lease silver, at first for military purposes, and on July 31, 1946, following the war, for manufacturing use. The latter enactment also raised the price to be paid for domestic silver to 90.5 cents an ounce, corresponding to a seigniorage of 30 per cent. In the market silver prices had risen in 1946 to 80.2 an ounce and climbed in 1951 to 89.4 cents; in 1956, after a decline, it reached 91.4 cents. From a monetary point of view it is strange that under the act of 1946 silver "leased" by the Treasury is permitted to serve as reserve for silver certificates, provided it remains under the Treasury's "control." But this regulation only demonstrates that the monetary value of the silver certificates is actually based more upon the credit of the United States than upon the silver bullion itself. From a more general point of view, it may be added that the rise of the silver market, which came as a surprise to every one, offers, of course, no argument in favor of bimetallism. The new movement illustrates rather the fact that the instability of silver prices has grown under modern technical conditions. Up to 1956 Congressional attempts to abolish the bounty for the silver producers have failed and have been opposed by the administration. However, the tremendous rise in the market price of silver might lead to an unexpected solution of the problem, and the losses suffered by the Treasury through the silver subsidies have been quietly reduced.

The strength of the American monetary system is illustrated by the fact that during the war and the preceding period of tension no danger of capital flight from this country ever appeared and therefore no "exchange control" proved necessary. Instead, in March, 1940, after the German invasion of Norway, the President decreed a "freezing order" based on the power granted him by the Emergency Banking Act of March 9, 1933. The purpose of this order and later supplementary decrees [2] was not the protection of the monetary structure but economic warfare against the Axis powers. In broadest terms, private monetary transactions were prohibited with countries dominated or influenced by the Axis. Transactions with people of other countries, for example, Great Britain and her allies and Latin America, remained lawful except with specific persons mentioned in a remarkable government blacklist. Importation of money from Axis territories was likewise forbidden. After the war all these restrictions were gradually abolished up to the end of 1948.

Emergency Federal Reserve notes and emergency silver certificates were issued in Hawaii after Pearl Harbor and later as "spearhead currencies" in occupied African and Italian territories.[3] To avoid confusion, they had a brown or yellow seal instead of the green or blue seal of regular notes. They were later replaced by an Allied military currency denominated in the monetary units of the occupied countries.

In one important respect the monetary development of the United States following World War II resembles the events of the years after World War I: increase of prices became a serious problem. The purchasing power of the dollar—taking 100 as the base for 1947–49—amounted to 97.3 in 1948 and 1950.[4] A price control established after the outbreak of fighting in Korea in June, 1950, became effective late in 1951, but did not prevent a further decline of the dollar's purchasing power to 90.1. This process slowed down in 1952 (88.1). The advent of the Eisenhower administration led to the complete abrogation of price control, but no further tangible rise in the price level occurred until the second half of 1956. In March, 1957, the purchasing power of the dollar fell to 84.6. But the increase in prices has been counterbalanced to some degree by rising production, employment, and wages, by an increase in leisure time, by expansion of consumer credit, and by a qualitative improvement of goods and services, as well as by better social care—factors that cannot always be represented in terms of economic statistics. In other words, the inflation was offset more successfully than the one following World War I. Currency circulation did not change much; in 1952 it rose to $29 billion and in 1956 to $30.7 billion, of which no less than $25.8 billion and $27.7 billion, respectively, were Federal Reserve notes.[5]

Control of the currency was improved by strengthening the position of the Federal Reserve Board. Following the war the Board opposed the Treasury's policy of trading government bonds at "pegged" prices, a practice which the Board considered as a way of transforming such bonds into money. In March, 1951, the controversy led to a formal and publicized agreement aimed at "minimizing monetization of the public debt."[6] The agreement is historically noteworthy beyond the particular question involved. It confirms to the authority of the Board of Governors, which is in a position to negotiate with the Treasury on terms of equality, a status in the public interest, inasmuch as the Board is less exposed to political pressure than the Treasury. Still, economic and political factors may tax the efficiency of the Board and the Treasury.

The monetary systems of civilized nations have been subject to fundamental changes everywhere during the last thirty or forty years, the rise of the living standard of the working class being probably the main factor, apart from international disturbances. Perhaps a brief reference to recent Soviet monetary policies will luminate the essence of the recent American evolution. Again and again the rulers of the countries under Soviet domination have tried to combat inflation by brutal and sudden measures seriously damaging large groups of the populace, including the workers.[7] In April, 1957, the Soviet government itself resorted to such a measure; it "froze" for twenty years all payments on its interest-bearing 260 billion ruble bonds acquired mainly by workers and farmers under government pressure, in the case of workers mainly through payroll deductions. These bonds were an official type of savings bonds. No countermovement or even protest against the government's action is possible under the Soviet regime. We are not concerned with the consequences of such a measure, but with its comparative implications. The economic position of labor has improved strikingly in this country, but historical perspective strengthens the view that the United States will never go through similar experiences.

While dissent and struggles between government, business, and labor in monetary problems are inevitable, final conformance to gradual adjustment of the monetary standard can be expected. And as things have developed more recently, international factors may also be helpful in the solution of our monetary problems.

INTERNATIONAL DEVELOPMENTS: THE INTERNATIONAL MONETARY FUND

As indicated in the preceding chapter the international position of the dollar had grown considerably under the New Deal. This evolution became striking and definitive in the present period. Even before the charter of the United Nations was adopted at San Francisco, the conception favored by Roosevelt and Churchill of a world-wide political organization first led, in the monetary and financial field, to the Bretton Woods Conference of July, 1944. There the foundation was laid for the International Monetary Fund and the International Bank for Reconstruction and Development. We are only concerned here with the Fund, and even this inquiry has to be confined to the impact of the Fund upon the position of the dollar.[8]

The agreement which established the Fund became effective on December 17, 1946. The Fund, with its central office in Washington, D.C., constitutes a stabilization fund on the widest scale. In the spirit of "international monetary cooperation," the Fund has "to promote exchange stability, to maintain orderly exchange arrangements and to avoid competitive exchange depreciation." Membership in the Fund is based on "quotas" resembling shares in a joint-stock company, except that the various quotas are diverse in amounts and are neither divisible nor transferable. The quotas determine the voting rights of the members and thereby their share in the Fund's administration.

A fundamental question presented to this organization was the choice of the monetary unit which would serve as the basis for the quotas. The Fund Agreement chose the dollar of the weight and fineness in effect on July 1, 1945, that is, the dollar of 15 5/21 grains, 9/10 fine. A "par value" defining the relation to this gold dollar had to be determined for the monetary unit of each member country. For example, in the beginning the par value of the English £ was determined as $4.03, of the French franc as 0.84 cents and the Belgian franc as 2.3 cents. The par value was not only the basis for the calculation of the quota but, more important, it had to be observed in all exchange transactions by the member states and in all transactions whatever carried on by the participants within their own territories. The vast majority of the countries outside the Soviet bloc, and even Yugoslavia, have joined the Fund, which now has fifty-eight members.[9] Switzerland, Argentina, Spain, and Portugal, the main exceptions, have established par values to the dollar on a gold basis.[10] Also, under the European Payments' Union the debtor country may pay at its choice in dollars or gold at $35 the ounce. Hence, the dollar has become in an unprecedented way the central monetary unit of the non-Soviet world.

Nevertheless, the pound sterling, leading internationally prior to World War I, still holds in the new system a far-reaching position through the British establishment of the Sterling Area.[11] Apart from British Colonies and Protectorates, independent nations as important as India, Pakistan, the Union of South Africa, and Australia belong to it. Current sterling payments among the territories of the area (called the "scheduled territories") are on the whole free of mutual exchange restrictions. On the other hand, the British government holds a dollar and gold pool for the whole area, serving thereby its members as a kind of banker in transactions outside those territories. Therefore, and because of the pound's allegiance to the dollar, the large sterling area is fundamentally dependent on the dollar, illustrating again the dollar's international leadership.

Regarding the financial structure of the Fund, the "quota" has a dual significance. The quota of the United States amounts to $2,750 million, 35.61 per cent of the whole stock when the Fund was established. $687 million thereof was paid in gold, representing more than half of the total gold then received by the Fund ($1,344,000,000).[12] The United Kingdom took second place with a quota of $1,300 million (16.84 per cent of the total), a payment of $210 million in gold and $130,000 in dollars. France, with a quota of $525 million (6.8 per cent) paid $79.5 million in gold and $52,000 in dollars. (Payment of balance was everywhere deferred in various ways.) The later devaluation of most currencies—of the £ from $4.03 to $2.80 in 1949, for example—obligated the nations concerned to pay to the Fund the difference in their own currencies without further contributions in gold. The percentages of the total of the quotas were of course affected by the increase of membership; in 1956 the percentage of the United States had receded to 31.45.

Another no less important aspect of the quota is the right of member countries to purchase from the Fund foreign currency —in actuality, quite preponderantly dollars—by their own currencies within limits related to their quotas. The highest amount would be the equivalent of twice the quota, but the actual amounts are considerably lower, due to the charges and special prerequisites relating to the extent of the purchase. Assistance to weak or endangered members has further been promoted by the introduction in 1953 of "standby agreements" through which the Fund grants a member, first for six months, the assurance of transactions necessary for the maintenance of the par value, the official rate of exchange of the member's monetary unit—a tremendous expansion of the Fund's functions, creating a new opportunity for the consignment of dollars.

The operation of the Fund was soon confronted with considerable obstacles. As early as 1948 France, one of the first members of the Fund, revolted against the par value of her franc and abandoned it, creating in Paris a business market for gold. In 1949 Canada dropped the par value of her dollar. Formosa-China, Greece, Indonesia, Israel, Italy, Syria, Thailand, and Uruguay have "not yet" established a par value, although Greece, Italy, Syria, and Uruguay were among the first members of the Fund.

Moreover, the law, and particularly international law, may be a weak factor in private transactions in gold and to some extent in foreign currency. Effectiveness of the restrictive regulations will depend on the spirit and efficiency of the governments concerned, and there will always be "loopholes" for evasion.[13] Where the restrictions are contrary to popular feeling or tradition, enforcement may be ostensible only.

Difficulties in international gold transactions are increased by the fact that, in addition to Paris, there are some free gold markets independent of the Fund, for example, in Hong Kong, Beirut, Macao, and (now fading) Tangier.[14] After the establishment of the Fund, gold prices in the free markets reached a peak of $55 an ounce of fine gold in May, 1949; the chief reason for this seems to have been a hedging against the British and other devaluations, which were generally expected. After the devaluations had actually occurred in 1949, gold prices dropped; they stood at $36 when the Korean War began in June, 1950. Thereupon a new gold boom started, culminating at $44 in January, 1951. There was growing pressure upon the United States to have the dollar devaluated again, thereby increasing the gold price, in accord with the developments in the free markets. Strong support for this movement came from the Union of South Africa, the foremost gold-producing country of the West, and from countries suffering from "dollar shortage." Such a reduction, it was strongly asserted, would restore the desirable international liquidity in the common interest of the free nations.[15] The United States resisted the pressure. In this country, it was felt, devaluation would have caused serious inflationary troubles without offering a lasting help to other nations. But in September, 1951, the Executive Board of the Fund yielded by leaving its members "the practical operating decisions" involved in their gold trade. Canada as well as Belgium-Luxembourg removed the restriction on gold transactions in 1956.

In 1954 the London gold market, closed since the outbreak of World War II, was reopened with the consent of the Fund after the British government had given assurances that the "par value" rules would be strictly observed in the market. But the permissible "margin" for such transactions—originally amounting to only ¼ per cent above and below the par value—was expanded by the Board to 1 per cent above and below, or a total of 2 per cent. London has now become a new center of gold trade. Trading is done there partly in £, to be converted into U.S. dollars at the current sterling-dollar rate.

Still, the lessening of international legal control has had no bad effects at all. Since the end of 1951 the market price of gold has been declining. By the end of 1953 it came close to the $35 rate, at times dropping below; and remarkably enough, neither the Formosa nor the Suez troubles have thus far disturbed this development; the par values have been preserved to the present time.

This favorable development is to a great extent certainly the merit of the Fund. Governments frightened by inflationary trends are no longer compelled to rush into the gold markets and cause new troubles. They now enjoy the assistance of the Fund getting their dollars or other currency on the quota basis or support of future maintenance by standby agreements. And the situation is not purely financial but contains political and psychological aspects. The nation which needs support applies to the Fund as one of its members. The United States may be behind major Fund transactions, but approaching the United States government or any other government for help might be embarrassing and may raise difficult questions even of a constitutional nature. The arrangements of the Fund with Great Britain and France after the Suez Canal disturbance are typical. Great Britain received on its quota basis $560 million for £ paid on the par value ratio and a standby quota of $738 million, likewise favorably computed with consideration of the quota. The Fund calling in noninterest bearing U.S. Treasury notes got the $561 million from the U.S. Treasury, but the Treasury had to raise a part of the amount mainly from banks by 90-day bills, delaying thereby the reduction of cash.[16] There was no constitutional difficulty; Congress did not need to be approached and sensational public statements were avoided. International cooperation in the monetary field proved to be at its best. France met with similar support to a more limited extent.

The experience shows that what the member nations need are dollars rather than gold. Generally speaking, gold seems to have lost somewhat its prominence. Gold production has decreased. In 1956 the output of gold was 8 million ounces (22 per cent below the output of the record year 1940).[17] Gold offered its members by the Fund sometimes exceeded their demands.[18] The most striking phenomenon is that the United States as well as other countries suffering from inflation seem not to give much thought to devaluation, which in the past has been widely resorted to as a final solution. In other words, there is less inclination to lower the gold equivalent of the unit in order to adapt it to the rising price level.

Little attention has been paid so far to this phenomenon. An attempt at explanation will necessarily be speculative. It may be that the multimillennial craving for gold is somewhat abating. Everywhere the gold coin standard has been abandoned; [19] a generation has grown up which has never seen gold coins except in museums and collections, and even the financiers are no longer plagued by gold clauses. People may instinctively feel that in the environment of the atomic age gold is no longer a reliable instrumentality of salvation. Perhaps it is significant that in jewelry genuineness of gold seems to have become less important. One is reminded of the unexpected depreciation of silver which started in 1873. That depreciation could be measured easily by the equivalent of gold; today one depends on conjectures.

In any case, the dollar which now has preserved its value for more than twenty years has become the outstanding unit, pushing aside gold in international relations. Even the Soviets and their satellites cannot help concluding trade agreements in terms of dollars.[20] Maybe the value of gold depends now more on the value of the dollar than vice versa.[21] A kind of international dollar-gold standard seems to have emerged.

In the light of these experiences it is easier to form an opinion about the different American and English approaches and the resulting controversy at Bretton Woods. The project for the United States had been worked out by Harry Dexter White, Assistant to the Secretary of the Treasury, and is commonly called the White Plan; [22] the other, prepared for the

United Kingdom under the strong influence of Lord Keynes, is generally known as the Keynes Plan.[23] In contrast to the White Plan, which was essentially an international expansion of the U.S. Stabilization Fund, the Keynes Plan envisaged an international super-bank entitling the member states to drawings on the largest scale and endowing it with powers which would have seriously affected the commercial and financial independence of the member states. We are concerned especially with the monetary unit proposed in the Keynes Plan, called the "bancor." This device, a *moneta imaginaria*, was merely a new accounting unit to be used in and limited to transactions within the planned "International Clearing Union" and for settling the international balances of its members. The value of bancors was not to be determined by the Plan itself but by the Union's powerful Governing Board in terms of gold—on what basis was not indicated—and the Board would have authority to alter it. Members were prohibited from purchasing gold above the gold parity of the bancor, but no machinery was planned to coordinate the value of the bancor with the gold market. One can imagine the differences which would have arisen among the members of the Governing Board in connection with developments in the free gold market, as well as the resulting uncertainties, speculations, and disturbances in the financial world. One has to assume that Lord Keynes was probably aware of the weakness of the pound sterling but was unwilling to accept a non-British unit as the international yardstick. Other features of his plan likewise indicate such sentiments. The "quotas" of the Clearing Union, which would have given access to tremendous credits, were not to be based on present conditions (no "Fund" was planned by Keynes), but on the happier past, namely, the average foreign trade of the last three *prewar* years; and the offices of the Union would have to be in London and New York, with *alternating meetings of the Board in London and Washington.*

The Keynes Plan had little chance of acceptance. The British government itself had called it "a preliminary contribution to the solution" of the problem involved, declining any commitments to the principles or details of the plan. Proposals submitted by Canadian experts were much closer to the American than to the British project; the accounting unit was to be the value of gold fine contained in ten dollars (137 1/7 grains). The final agreement, on the whole, follows the lines set by the White Plan, and this is especially true of the key position of the dollar. Obviously, White himself played an important role in the various negotiations which, partly preceding Bretton Woods, finally led to the defeat of the bancor. The protocols of these negotiations have not been published, but Roy Harrod of Oxford who obviously possesses inside information about the discussions, calls White "a distinguished and eminent and hard fighting American"; he ascribes to him, in the first place, the American success regarding the International Monetary Fund.[24]

There was no disagreement between the White Plan and the Keynes Plan on the elimination of the individual as holder and master of the crucial gold coin. But Keynes' broader theories, which permit a manipulation of the money value in the social interest, were not accepted; such functions certainly cannot be entrusted to international agencies. The price of gold resulting from actual trade and international cooperation in terms of the dollar was finally considered the best available basis for determining the value of monetary units. It is remarkable that after the Suez disaster the Fund worked so helpfully for Great Britain and the Sterling Area. A disaster which would have affected the non-Soviet World was averted. The strength of the dollar proved effective.

Conclusion

AMERICAN monetary history is truly spectacular. We have seen how the early settlers in this country, while by no means lacking in moral strength, were first of all driven by a desire to acquire property, and this tradition was quite naturally espoused by later immigrants who brought no wealth with them. Human concentration on material improvement was for a long time not too much disturbed by any great interest in higher learning or art; and where such trends appeared they did not have much effect upon the cultural pattern, except perhaps in some centers of New England. The early elaboration of credit facilities could only strengthen the pecuniary preoccupation. Inevitably this attitude became the source of a fundamental social and political antagonism—the conflict between the moneyed and the inpecunious, or more generally, between the financially well settled and the common man. That conflict is, of course, a serious cause of political clashes everywhere, but outside the United States it is far more interwoven with other political and social factors of antagonism. Hence, the monetary element operated in this country with greater distinctiveness. Moreover, its significance was enhanced by factors originating in the political structure of this country. During the colonial period the purely prohibitive attitude of the mother country in monetary matters aroused bitter resentment and worked rather as a monetary stimulus. After the establishment of the United States a different problem arose, in fact, one of fundamental significance, which again seriously affected the monetary interests of the individual. We refer to the antagonism between the Federal government and the state governments. Nothing of this kind appeared, or could have appeared, in any other confederation, say, Germany, Switzerland, or Australia. This dangerous antagonism did great harm to the nation, but fortunately has finally been overcome in the monetary field.

Concerning the presidency, our discussion has shown that the President of the United States has more power in monetary affairs than a monarch in the Western democracies. We have seen the important role played in this field by Jefferson, Jackson, Cleveland, Wilson, and Franklin D. Roosevelt; Van Buren, Grant, and Hayes had also to be mentioned. This aspect of the history of the dollar is perhaps not the most felicitous. It so happens that the most venerable of them all, Jefferson, pursued a most unfortunate policy in this matter. Nor were Jackson's pertinent actions any more propitious, on the whole. Grant's tactics actually present a black spot. It is, we believe, Cleveland to whom the highest admiration is to be paid within the orbit of our inquiry. Wilson, too, served the nation well, and Franklin D. Roosevelt certainly deserves high praise for most of his transactions in this field. However, we do not think that monetary subjects are the proper test for presidential greatness.

A specifically American phenomenon is also exemplified by the Supreme Court. True, the strong impact of the judiciary is in accord with the common-law tradition which has worked so much to promote fairness, equality, and freedom. However, in Great Britain the development of the monetary system rested invariably first with the Crown and later with Parliament. In the United States it was the Supreme Court which made Federal paper money and Federal banking possible. Such creative power would not have been tolerated without the common-law tradition, but nevertheless it represents a unique and typically American phenomenon. It illustrates not only the spiritual forces behind the monetary evolution, but also the drawbacks which are inevitably connected with such a semipolitical function of the judiciary. In general, it may be said that because of the Supreme Court's position, as well as because of the circumstantial elaboration of monetary legislation, the history of the dollar is more closely related to legal history than is the case with the history of the monetary units of other countries.

Other remarkable features of American monetary history are psychological in nature. In the first place, we must refer to the characteristic American adaptability and resourcefulness. While these qualities have proved more enduring and efficient in other fields, they are clearly recognizable in the monetary area as well. As colonial examples we cite the issuance of bills of credit, the first real paper money. Other instances are the standardization of wampum, the tobacco notes of Virginia and Maryland, and the "depreciation" bills of Massachusetts. In the era of the United States the "free-banking" system, the Independent Treasury System, and the ingenious Federal Reserve System are among the characteristic accomplishments. Also, private coinage, including the manufacture of the California gold pieces up to $50, the paper money tokens, and perhaps "encased postal stamps" of the Civil War, is worth mentioning. The people's adjustment in the early nineteenth century to the circulation of nonredeemable bank notes may likewise be included in this list.

Of course, strong individualism has something to do with the democratic spirit of American life.[1] This spirit is a factor in the phenomenon that the predominance of the moneyed classes never led to revolution, except for Shays's Rebellion which, however, lacked real force and ended in a remarkably human way. And the democratic-socialist creation, connected with Franklin's name, of a public-credit organization offers a remarkable counterpart.

But there are also in the American mind features detrimental to monetary progress. This is true especially of the gambling spirit. That spirit is responsible for the serious crises which again and again shook this country's monetary structure; the inflationary trend, so difficult to subdue, is likewise connected with that spirit. And freedom is bound to degenerate where authorities are too weak to bar excesses. That is why in the first half of the nineteenth century lawlessness and corruption reached such shocking dimensions. On the whole, however, these disturbances were minor and transitory. Common sense finally prevailed.

The recent internationalization of the dollar is probably the most important event in its history. That evolution was not brought about by any kind of American imperialism but by an inevitable development serving all nations concerned. It has created a monetary alliance among the non-Soviet nations. They all are profiting from it.

Looking back at the domestic and international history of the dollar, one is confronted with a story whose dramatic course has been ever ascendant. The many obstacles and setbacks on the way certainly reveal weaknesses, but they were finally overcome, and the basic trend upwards justifies confidence for the future.

Notes

CHAPTER I: THE COLONIAL ERA

1. See Nettels, *The Money Supply of the American Colonies before 1720*, p. 208; Dewey, *Financial History of the United States* (12th ed., 1934), ch. I; Bullock, *Essays on the Monetary History of the United States*, p. 7; McLeod, "The History of Fiat Money and Currency Inflation in New England from 1620 to 1789," *Annals of the American Academy of Political and Social Science*, XII (1898), 57.

2. Especially in Virginia. See Ripley, *The Financial History of Virginia, 1609–1776*, p. 110; Royall, "Virginia Colonial Money," *Virginia Law Journal*, I (1877), 455.

3. This complication is illustrated by Madam Knight's report. See p. 13.

4. Chalmers, *A History of Currency in the British Colonies*, p. 6 n., referring to Hankey, *History of Banking in America*, tells a story about "young and uncorrupted girls imported in Virginia in 1620 and 1621 as wives for the colonists" and "rated originally at 100 pounds of tobacco (£15) but subsequently at the increased price of 150 pounds (£22, 10s)." Actually, it seems, the prices were paid on the basis of some official arrangement for the transportation of English women, the purpose being the establishment of an orderly family life in Virginia. See Willis and Saunders, *The Story of Virginia*, p. 61.

5. See p. 21.

6. John Winthrop, *A History of New England from 1630 to 1642*, ed. by James Savage (2 vols., Boston, 1825–26), II, 220.

7. G. F. Willison, *Saints and Strangers* (New York, 1945), p. 409.

8. Quiggin, *A Survey of Primitive Money*, p. 31 (a reproduction of a wampum "purse"); Einzig, *Primitive Money in Its Ethnological and Economic Aspects*, p. 177; Crosby, *The Early Coins of America*, p. 25; Rosendale, "Wampum Currency" in 3 *Sound Currency* (1896), 483 (confined to the New Netherlands). Some ornamental types of wampum are copied by Dickeson, *The American Numismatic Manual*, Plate V.

9. See the studies by Quiggin and Einzig and also Laum, *Heiliges Geld; eine historische Untersuchung über den sakralen Ursprung des Geldes.*

10. The early American coins have attracted much numismatic interest. See Raymond, *The Standard Catalogue of United States Coins* (17th ed. 1954), pp. 1 ff., with reproductions; Crosby, *The Early Coins of America*, pp. 25–122; Snowden, *A Description of Ancient and Modern Coins*, p. 83, with plates; Dickeson, *The American Numismatic Manual,* with plates and much documentation; *Encyclopedia Americana*, "Numismatics," Plate III.

11. Noe, *The Pine Tree Shilling of Massachusetts;* Felt, *An Historical Account of Massachusetts Currency*, p. 31; Sumner, "The Coin Shilling of the Massachusetts Bay," *Yale Review*, VII (1898), 247, 405; Nettels, *The Money Supply of the American Colonies before 1720*, pp. 171, 174. Reproductions of these famous coins are found, e.g., in Noe's study and in the numismatic works cited in n. 10.

12. Raymond, *The Standard Catalogue of United States Coins*, p. 5; Crosby, *The Early Coins of America*, p. 128 and Plate III; Dickeson, *The American Numismatic Manual,* Plate IV; Charles A. White, "The Archaic Monetary Terms of the United States," *Smithsonian Miscellaneous Collections*, L (1908), 93. Cf. also U.S. Bureau of the Mint, *Catalogue of Coins of the United States*, p. 3.

13. Raymond, *The Standard Catalogue of United States Coins*,

p. 3; Crosby, *The Early Coins of America*, p. 128 and Plate III; Dickeson, *The American Numismatic Manual*, Plate IV; Charles A. White, "The Archaic Monetary Terms of the United States," *Smithsonian Miscellaneous Collections*, L (1908), 95; U.S. Bureau of the Mint, *Catalogue of Coins of the United States*, p. 2.

14. Mexico City was the site of the first mint established in the Western Hemisphere; see Nesmith, *Coinage of the First Mint of the Americas at Mexico City, 1536–1572*. On the Spanish and the smugglers, cf. Roscher, *The Spanish Colonial System* (tr. from the German by Bourne), p. 37.

15. Laughlin, *A New Exposition of Money, Credit and Prices*, I, 199; Shaw, *The History of Currency, 1252 to 1894* (2d ed., 1896), pp. 107, 319; Chalmers, *A History of the Currency in the British Colonies*, p. 390; Sumner, "The Spanish Dollar and the Colonial Shilling," *American Historical Review*, III (1898), 607. Del Mar, *The History of Money in America from the Earliest Times to the Establishment of the Constitution*, is mainly concerned with the Spanish conquest.

16. For reproductions of the various Spanish coins, see Charles A. White, "The Archaic Monetary Terms of the United States," *Smithsonian Miscellaneous Collections*, L (1908), 93. A pillar dollar is reproduced by Laughlin, *A New Exposition of Money, Credit and Prices*, I, 204.

17. Analyzing monetary conditions of the eighteenth century, Michel Chevalier, the great French economist, stated: "Spanish money has long been considered the first money of the world, recognized as such both by the philosopher and by the merchant." Chevalier, *La monnaie* (2d ed., 1866), p. 183.

18. Feavearyear, *The Pound Sterling*, p. 174.

19. *Ibid.*, pp. 157, 192, 296.

20. Nussbaum, *Money in the Law, National and International* (rev. ed., 1950), p. 55. The term "lawful money" was used, however, in a different sense by Locke; see Feavearyear, *The Pound Sterling*, p. 124, n. 2.

21. Nettels, *The Money Supply of the American Colonies before 1720*, p. 242; Bullock, *Essays on the Monetary History of the United States*, p. 20; Nussbaum, *Money in the Law*, p. 538.

22. Nettels, *The Money Supply of the American Colonies before 1720*, p. 246, n. 34.

23. Hart, *American History Told by Contemporaries*, II, 228. See also Bronson, *A Historical Account of Connecticut Currency, Continental Money, and the Finances of the Revolution.*

24. Bronson, *A Historical Account of Connecticut Currency*, p. 22, thinks that "pay as money" and "pay" were identical.

25. Reproductions in Laughlin, *A New Exposition of Money, Credit and Prices*, II, 105; Shultz and Caine, *Financial Development of the United States*, p. 13.

26. Holland, *The London Bankers' Clearing House*, p. 267.

27. Sir Henry Yule, tr. and ed., *The Book of Ser Marco Polo* (3d ed., revised by Henri Cordier, 2 vols., New York, 1903), I, 423; Ramsden, *Chinese Paper Money*, p. 5; Vissering, *On Chinese Currency*. Lien-shêng Yang, *Money and Credit in China*, has accumulated a great many facts on Chinese monetary history without offering much elucidation.

28. Dorfman, *The Economic Mind in American Civilization, 1606–1865*, I, 93.

29. This value of the livre was equivalent to about 60 to 75 cents in today's money.

30. Lester, *Monetary Experiments, Early American and Recent Scandinavian*, p. 37; Shortt, ed., *Documents Relating to Canadian Currency, Exchange and Finance during the French Period*, I (1925), xlviii and 68; Laughlin, *A New Exposition of Money, Credit and Prices*, II, 82; all with reproductions.

31. Heckscher, *An Economic History of Sweden* (tr. from Swedish by Ohlin), p. 91; Clough and Cole, *Economic History of Europe* (3d ed., 1952), p. 276.

32. In medieval China, too, heaviness of coinage metal seems

to have contributed to the rise of paper money. Vissering, *On Chinese Currency*, p. 13.

33. The writings cited in notes 1, 2, and 4 are all concerned with this phenomenon. In addition, see Phillips, *Historical Sketches of the Paper Currency of the American Colonies*, Vol. I, where conditions in Pennsylvania, New Jersey, Rhode Island, and Vermont are discussed, and McLeod, "The History of Fiat Money and Currency Inflation in New England from 1620 to 1789," *Annals of the American Academy of Political and Social Science*, XII (1898), 57. An anonymous contemporary report on South Carolina's first paper money is reprinted in 5 *Sound Currency*, No. 4 (1898). The foreign interest in the subject is indicated by Gragnani, *La moneta nelle colonie inglesi del Nord America, 1607–1775*.

34. For reproductions of various types of bills, see Lester, *Monetary Experiments*, p. 132 (Delaware, 20 sh., 1758; Pennsylvania, 20 sh., 1756; New York, 10 sh., 1737; New Jersey, 15 sh., 1756). For numismatic material, with numerous facsimiles, see McKay, *Early American Currency*. Regarding New York, cf. p. 23 of the present book.

35. See pp. 20, 41–42.

36. *Works*, ed. by Charles F. Adams (10 vols., Boston, 1850–56), II, 420.

37. Lester, *Monetary Experiments*, p. 152; Fisher, "The Tabular Standard in Massachusetts History," *American Journal of Economics*, XXVII (1913), 417.

38. Shepherd, *History of Proprietary Government in Pennsylvania*, p. 401; MacFarlan, "Pennsylvania Paper Currency," *Annals of the American Academy of Political and Social Science*, VIII (1896), 50; Lester, *Monetary Experiments*, p. 56. On reproduction of notes, see n. 34.

39. See p. 18.

40. *The Works of Benjamin Franklin*, ed. by Sparks, II, 253.

41. See Franklin's remark on p. 27. Interest was 5 per cent (Shepherd, *History of Proprietary Government in Pennsylvania,* pp. 412, 414), a low rate under the conditions of the period. But considerable annual installments had to be paid.

42. Nussbaum, *Lehrbuch des Deutschen Hypothekenwesens* (2d ed., 1921), pp. 220, 222. Cf. also Hecht, "Les crédits fonciers en Europe," in *Congrès international des valeurs mobilières: Statistiques, Paris, 1900* (5 vols., Paris, 1901), III, Part 4. The organizational differences in the structure of public credit are not relevant to the above discussion.

43. Wyckoff, *Tobacco Regulations in Colonial Maryland,* including earlier English and Virginia regulations; Nussbaum, *Money in the Law,* p. 563.

44. Thayer, "The Land Bank System in American Colonies," *Journal of Economic History,* XIII (1953), 145; Davis, *Currency and Banking in the Province of Massachusetts-Bay* (1901) and *Colonial Currency Reprints* (4 vols., 1910–11).

45. Namely, through a retroactive extension of the Bubble Act; see p. 241, n. 19. A reproduction of a note of the Boston land bank is in Laughlin, *A New Exposition of Money, Credit and Prices,* II, 120.

46. In 1756 Virginia issued interest-bearing treasury notes as legal tender, but in 1757 she had to drop the promise of interest in the new notes in order to render them current. Ripley, *The Financial History of Virginia, 1609–1776,* pp. 154, 156. Connecticut went through a similar experience in 1755, Bronson, *A Historical Account of Connecticut Currency,* p. 82. Cf. also Martin, *The History of Louisiana,* II, 249; *Colonial Records of North Carolina,* VI (1888), 1309; VIII (1890), 5, 6, 9.

47. The main source is still Hickcox, *A History of the Bills of Credit or Paper Money Issued by New York,* giving a list of the New York emissions and enactments. See further, Fernow, "Coins and Currency of New York," in Wilson, ed., *Memorial History of the City of New York,* IV, 297, with numerous illustrations;

Horace White, "New York's Colonial Currency," in 5 *Sound Currency* (1898), 49; Flick, ed., *History of the State of New York*, II, 313; Lester, *Monetary Experiments*, p. 112. Nettels, *The Money Supply of the American Colonies before 1720* contains valuable remarks.

48. Copper coins, too, seem to have been of Dutch origin, Raymond, *The Standard Catalogue of United States Coins*, p. 5; Crosby, *The Early Coins of America*, p. 346.

49. Laurence D. Smith, *Counterfeiting, Crime against the People*, p. 54; McMaster, *A History of the People of the United States*, I, 191; Gillingham, *Counterfeiting in Colonial Pennsylvania* (the study is not limited to Pennsylvania); Scott, *Counterfeiting in Colonial New York*, *Counterfeiting in Colonial Pennsylvania*, and *Counterfeiting in Colonial America*; Bullock, *Essays on the Monetary History of the United States*, *passim*; and Nettels, *The Money Supply of the American Colonies before 1720*, *passim*. Counterfeiting has been a pressing problem for literary discussion since the Middle Ages, see, e.g., Tullio, Ascarelli, *La moneta*, p. 8, n. 1.

50. *The History of England from the Accession of James the Second* (5 vols., London, 1849–61), ch. XXI; cf. also Feavearyear, *The Pound Sterling*, pp. 5, 9, 43, 79, 84, 110.

51. *Bilder aus der deutschen Vergangenheit* (4 vols., Leipzig, 1876–77), III, ch. V.

52. Friedensburg, *Münzkunde und Geldgeschichte*, p. 150.

53. Scott, *Counterfeiting in Colonial New York*, p. 196.

54. Nussbaum, *Money in the Law*, p. 46.

55. Feavearyear, *The Pound Sterling*, p. 111.

56. Scott, *Counterfeiting in Colonial New York*, p. 6.

57. See p. 12. On the clipping of French overweight gold coins by American authorities during the Revolutionary War, see McMaster, *A History of the People of the United States*, II, 192.

58. *Political Essays on the Nature and Operation of Money*, p. 142.

59. Harlow, "Aspects of Revolutionary Finance," *American Historical Review,* XXXV (1929), 47.

60. *Works,* ed. by Sparks, II, 343.

61. The various pertinent utterances by Franklin have been collected in two attractive pamphlets by the Franklin Institute: *Benjamin Franklin on Industry, Frugality and Thrift* and *The Way to Wealth and Words of Wisdom from Benjamin Franklin* (1938). See also *Works,* ed. by Sparks, II, 87, 94.

62. As brilliantly shown by Max Weber, *Gesammelte Aufsätze zur Religionssoziologie* (3 vols., Tubingen, 1922–23), I, 31.

63. See pp. 132, 142. Thomas Hutchinson (1711–80), Governor of Massachusetts, stated that the common people regarded gold and silver coin, in contrast to paper money, as a privilege of the wealthy. McLeod, "The History of Fiat Money and Currency Inflation in New England from 1620 to 1789," *Annals of the American Academy of Political and Social Science,* XI (1898), 247.

64. *The Money Supply of the American Colonies before 1720,* p. 248.

65. For an excellent summary, see Faulkner, *American Economic History* (7th ed., 1954), pp. 107 ff.

66. Feis, *Europe, the World's Banker, 1890–1914,* p. 24.

67. There is more on this in Nussbaum, *Money in the Law,* p. 334 (with references).

68. Feavearyear, *The Pound Sterling,* p. 192.

69. This is, of course, no precedent to the modern subordination of the pound to the dollar. See Ch. IX.

70. *Works,* ed. by Sparks, III, 418.

71. Andrews, *The Colonial Background of the American Revolution,* p. 134.

72. Osgood, *The American Colonies in the Eighteenth Century,* III, 481; Bancroft, *History of the United States* (rev. ed., 1841), III, 65; William Wirt, *Sketches of the Life and Character of Patrick Henry* (2d ed., Philadelphia, 1818), p. 20.

CHAPTER 2: REVOLUTION AND REORGANIZATION

1. See Bolles, *The Financial History of the United States, from 1774 to 1789* (4th ed., 1896); Phillips, *Historical Sketches of the Paper Currency of the American Colonies*, Vol. II; Bronson, *A Historical Account of Connecticut Currency, Continental Money, and the Finances of the Revolution;* Dewey, *Financial History of the United States* (12th ed., 1934), p. 60; Watson, *History of American Coinage;* De Knight, *History of the Currency of the Country and of the Loans of the United States from the Earliest Period to June 30, 1900*, p. 12; Holt, "Continental Currency," in 5 *Sound Currency* (1898), 51; Harlow, "Aspects of Revolutionary Finance," *American Historical Review*, XXXV (1929), 46.

2. The term "continental" was originally used at the time of the colonies as an inoffensive designation of America in contrast to the British Isles.

3. There are reproductions of the continentals in Laughlin, *A New Exposition of Money, Credit and Prices*, II, 150, 151, and Holt, "Continental Currency," in 5 *Sound Currency* (1898), 51.

4. Harrod, *The Dollar*, p. 7.

5. Dewey, *Financial History of the United States*, p. 36; other writers, such as Hepburn, *A History of Currency in the United States* (rev. ed., 1924), p. 16, present even higher figures.

6. Details in Laurence D. Smith, *Counterfeiting, Crime against the People*, p. 67. Revolutionary periods offer special opportunities to counterfeiters. See Bouchary, *Les faux-monnayeurs sous la Révolution Française.*

7. Bullock, *Essays on the Monetary History of the United States*, p. 67; Horace White, *Money and Banking, Illustrated by American History* (5th ed., 1914), p. 96.

8. On North Carolina and New Hampshire, see Bullock, *Essays on the Monetary History of the United States,* pp. 184, 260; Rhode Island and Virginia: Phillips, *Historical Sketches of the Paper Currency of the American Colonies,* Vol. I; Connecticut: Bronson, *A Historical Account of Connecticut Currency.* The North Carolina bills of 1775 bear Masonic emblems, *American Journal of Numismatics,* XXVI (1892), 640. Reproductions of a Massachusetts bill of 1775 and a New Jersey bill of 1781 (1 sh. 6 d.) are in Charles A. White, "The Archaic Monetary Terms of the United States," *Smithsonian Miscellaneous Collections,* L (1908), 96, 98. See also Fiske, *The Critical Period of American History, 1783–1789* (4th ed., 1889), p. 168, and Harlow, "Aspects of Revolutionary Finance," *American Historical Review,* XXXV (1929), 46.

9. There is little reason, however, to praise the Massachusetts experiments as supporting Irving Fisher's "tabular standard," as Fisher ("The Tabular Standard in Massachusetts History," *American Journal of Economics,* Vol. XXVII, 1913) and Lester (*Monetary Experiments*) have done.

10. Marion L. Sharkey, *A Little Rebellion* (New York, 1955). See also Wildman, *Money Inflation in the United States,* p. 63. It was with an eye to Shays's Rebellion that Jefferson made the famous statement: "A little rebellion now and then is a good thing and as necessary in the political world as storms in the physical,—it is a medicine necessary for the sound health of government. The tree of liberty must be refreshed from time to time with the blood of patriots and tyrants. It is a natural manure."

11. McMaster, *A History of the People of the United States,* I, 330; Peleg W. Chandler, *American Criminal Trials* (2 vols., Boston, 1841–44), II, 267; James M. Varnum, *The Case, Trevett against Weeden* (Providence, 1787).

12. Korb, "Schenectady Church Money," *The Numismatist,* LII (1939), 853.

13. See McMaster, *A History of the People of the United*

States, I, 189, 191; Domett, *A History of the Bank of New York, 1784–1884*, p. 20.

There is much numismatic interest in the New York jeweler Ephraim Brasher, who, after the war, countermarked circulating gold coins with an E.B., certifying thereby, in the absence of an official authority, their full value. He himself produced a small amount of high quality "doubloons" of the Spanish type. His petition to the New York legislature for a license to coin copper cents was rejected. U.S. Bureau of the Mint, *Catalogue of Coins of the United States*, p. 6; Raymond, *The Standard Catalogue of United States Coins* (17th ed., 1954), p. 16; Edgar H. Adams, *Adams' Official Premium List of United States Private and Territorial Gold Coins Indicated by Prices Brought at Public Coin Sales* (New York, 1909), p. 11.

14. Mint Ordinance of Oct. 16, 1786, *Journal of the American Congress* of the same day. State legislatures, too, restricted the use of certain copper coins. Carothers, *Fractional Money*, p. 44.

15. A most laborious statistical study on *Prices and Inflation during the American Revolution, Pennsylvania, 1770–1790* (Wharton School, University of Pennsylvania Research Studies, XXXV, Philadelphia, 1951) was undertaken by Anne Bezanson. It represents a modern type of economic statistical research which raises doubts as to whether the result is worth the tremendous effort.

16. Lewis, *A History of the Bank of North America*, with reproduction of its notes; informative also about the Bank of Pennsylvania.

17. Gras, *The Massachusetts First National Bank of Boston, 1784–1934*.

18. Nevins, *History of the Bank of New York and Trust Company, 1784 to 1934;* Domett, *A History of the Bank of New York, 1784–1884;* Horace White, *Money and Banking*, p. 284.

19. See, e.g., Collins, *The History, Law and Practice of Banking*, pp. 67, 70, 254. The Bubble Act, which prescribed the incorporation by Crown or Parliament of joint-stock companies, was

of an uncertain range of application and was apparently not considered as doing away with the common-law rule. Du Bois, *The English Business Company after the Bubble Act, 1720–1800*, p. 4.

20. Laughlin, *A New Exposition of Money, Credit and Prices*, II, 244. Nevins, *History of the Bank of New York and Trust Company*, p. 32, reproduces a 1791 $1 note of the Bank, calling it one of the first notes of the institution. The correctness of this statement may be questioned. Nevins only touches upon the charterless period of the bank, and does not mention at all the common-law rule of banking. See also Horace White, *Money and Banking*, p. 248.

21. Main source for the monetary era preceding the adoption of the Constitution are the official documents in International Monetary Conference, Paris, 1878, *Proceedings and Exhibits*, pp. 417 ff. See also Preston, *History of the Monetary Legislation of the United States*, pp. 21 ff.

22. The report was to a great extent the work of Gouverneur Morris, an assistant (not a relative) of Robert Morris.

23. U.S. Bureau of the Mint, *Catalogue of Coins of the United States*, p. 32. In any case, Benjamin Franklin was interested in the coming experiment; see his somewhat jocose letter of October, 1779, reprinted by Watson, *History of American Coinage*, p. 25.

24. Crosby, *The Early Coins of America*, p. 297, Plate VII; Dickeson, *The American Numismatic Manual*, Plate XI; *Encyclopedia Americana*, "Numismatics," Plate III.

25. U.S. Bureau of the Mint, *Catalogue of Coins of the United States*, p. 4; Raymond, *The Standard Catalogue of United States Coins*, p. 31; Crosby, *The Early Coins of America*, pp. 177, 203, 225, with plates; Henry C. Miller and Hillyer Ryder on the state coinage of Connecticut, Vermont, and Massachusetts in *American Journal of Numismatics*, LIII (1919), Part I, with plates.

26. See the thorough discussion by I. L. Thompson in *Encyclopedia Americana*, "Great Seal of the United States," including numismatic aspects.

27. Charles A. Beard, *An Economic Interpretation of the Con-*

stitution (1935 ed.), p. 179, curiously enough, criticizes this provision as a favor to "money lenders and security holders."

28. Holdsworth and Dewey, *The First and Second Banks of the United States;* Bolles, *The Financial History of the United States, from 1789 to 1860* (4th ed., 1894), p. 127; Laughlin, *A New Exposition of Money, Credit and Prices,* II, 210; Hamilton's report "On the Subject of a National Bank" is reprinted in *American State Papers: Finance,* Vol. I, and in *The Works of Alexander Hamilton,* I, 59.

29. *A Treatise on Money,* I, 9.

30. See the reproduction in Laughlin, *A New Exposition of Money, Credit and Prices,* II, 220. A photostat of another note was kindly sent to me by the Chase Manhattan Bank, Museum of Moneys of the World.

31. *Annals of the Congress of the United States* (42 vols., Washington, D.C., 1834–56), II, 2112. It has often been reprinted, e.g., in *American State Papers; Finance,* Vol. I; *The Works of Alexander Hamilton,* I (1810), 275; and International Monetary Conference, Paris, 1878, *Proceedings and Exhibits,* p. 454.

32. Stewart, *History of the First United States Mint,* p. 50.

33. Since that time the cent pieces, needed in tremendous quantities, have become an ever-growing source of profit to the government. The early cent has also met with much numismatic interest. See Sheldon, *Early American Cents, 1793–1814;* Clapp and Newcomb, *The United States Cents of the Years 1795, 1796, 1797, and 1800; American Journal of Numismatics,* III (1869), 97.

34. Reproductions of the coins are found in Raymond, *The Standard Catalogue of United States Coins,* and reproductions of the "historic" fractional coins in Carothers, *Fractional Money,* frontispiece.

35. See pp. 143, 144, 250, n. 7, 259, n. 16. For details, cf. U.S. Bureau of the Mint, *Catalogue of Coins of the United States* and *Domestic Coin Manufactured by Mints of the United States;*

Raymond, *The Standard Catalogue of United States Coins;* and Carothers, *Fractional Money.* Coining half-cent pieces was discontinued in 1857.

We are not concerned with the commemorative coins of 1892–1946; U.S. Bureau of the Mint, *Domestic Coin Manufactured by Mints of the United States,* p. 34. There is more on these in Bullowa, *The Commemorative Coinage of the United States, 1892–1938.*

36. The literature on bimetallism is boundless. For this country, see primarily Laughlin, *The History of Bimetallism in the United States* (4th ed., 1897), and Hütter, *La question de la monnaie d'argent aux Etats-Unis des origines à 1900* (thesis, Paris, 1938; 493 pages, with ample bibliography).

37. By the Italian economist Cernuschi; cf. Conant, *The Principles of Money and Banking,* I, 27.

38. Strangely enough, "milles" recently appeared as sales tax "tokens." See p. 202.

39. For this information I am indebted to Mr. Philip A. Hazelton, Law Librarian of the New Hampshire State Library.

40. Cajori, *A History of Mathematical Notations,* II, 15. The symbol $, used everywhere else in the present book, is, of course, a different form of the original $.

41. There were a number of well-designed trial pieces showing Washington's image. Crosby, *The Early Coins of America,* p. 349, with plate.

42. U.S. Bureau of the Mint, *Catalogue of Coins of the United States,* p. 16.

43. Sédillot, *Le franc,* p. 168. The text of the law (tr. into English) is in Laughlin, *The History of Bimetallism in the United States,* p. 312.

44. Chalmers, *A History of Currency in the British Colonies,* pp. 390 and *passim* (see Index, under "dollar"); Nussbaum, *Money in the Law,* pp. 316, with further references.

CHAPTER 3: CONFUSION AND CRUDE ACTION

1. For general information on this period, see Dewey, *Financial History of the United States* (12th ed., 1934); Horace White, *Money and Banking, Illustrated by American History* (5th ed., 1914); Sumner, *A History of Banking in the United States,* ch. 2–12, and Hasenkamp, *Die Geldverfassung und das Notenbankwesen der Vereinigten Staaten,* a valuable study.

2. U.S. Dept. of Commerce, *Historical Statistics of the United States, 1789–1945,* p. 278.

3. Director of the Mint, *Annual Report* for 1940, pp. 66 ff., from which also the later statistical data on coinage have been taken.

4. In the beginning, as a result of technical difficulties, even more than the prescribed silver content was put into the dollars. Carothers, *Fractional Money,* p. 70.

5. 26th Congress, 1st Session, Senate Executive Document No. 19 (1830), p. 76. The report presents a comprehensive picture of the country's dismal monetary system.

6. Carothers, *Fractional Money,* p. 82. In 1814 the "Corporation of the City of New York" issued notes of 12½ cents. Fernow, "Coins and Currency in New York," in Wilson, *The Memorial History of the City of New York,* IV, 333, with reproductions. U.S. postage stamps followed the decimal system from the beginning (1847).

7. The "real" (12½ cents) was also called "shilling" or "Mexican shilling" and in New Jersey and Pennsylvania "levy." For the half real the denominations "fippeny" or "picayune" (creole) were in vogue. U.S. Bureau of the Mint, *Catalogue of Coins of the United States,* p. 7; Charles A. White, "The Archaic Monetary Terms of the United States," *Smithsonian Miscellaneous Collection,* L (1908), 101.

8. In 1818, as high as 4 to 7 per cent in New York. Catterall,

The Second Bank of the United States, p. 38. See also McMaster, *A History of the People of the United States*, I, 189.

9. Dewey, *State Banking before the Civil War;* Sumner, *A History of Banking in the United States*, ch. 4–13; Wildman, *Money Inflation in the United States*, pp. 67, 82, offering a remarkable psychological analysis of the abnormal conditions of the period; Gilbart, *The History of Banking in America;* Gouge, *A Short History of Paper Money and Banking in the United States;* McMaster, *A History of the People of the United States*, IV, 286, Numismatic: John A. Muscalus, *The Characters and Events Illustrated on State Bank Notes.*

10. Sumner, *A History of Banking in the United States*, p. 37.

11. In addition to the writings cited in n. 1, see Bullock, *Essays on the Monetary History of the United States*, p. 83; Dillistin, *Bank Note Reporters and Counterfeit Detectors, 1822–1866*, p. 59; McMaster, "Wildcat Banking in the Teens," *Atlantic Monthly*, LXXII (1893), 331.

12. Sumner, *A History of Banking in the United States*, p. 107, quoting Hezekiah Niles, a noted journalist and editor of the period.

13. See Wismer, "Notes Issued by Cities and Towns in the United States from 1775 to 1866," *Coin Collectors Journal*, N.S., VI (1939), 31.

14. I, 46, in the 2d ed., 1835.

15. Moore, "The Labor Exchange Movement," *The Numismatist*, XLV (1932), 495, with illustrations.

16. Root, "New England Currency," in 2 *Sound Currency* (1895), No. 10, p. 25; Whitney, *The Suffolk Bank;* Horace White, *Money and Banking*, p. 291; and Lake, "End of the Suffolk System," *Journal of Economic History*, VII (1947), 183, giving a full history of the system. It sheds some light on the narrowness of prevailing conditions that the notes of the out-of-town banks were called "foreign notes." Whitney, *The Suffolk Bank*, p. 7.

17. Chaddock, *The Safety Fund Banking System in New York, 1829–1866*, pp. 227 ff.; Root, "New York Bank Currency," in 2 *Sound Currency* (1895), No. 5, p. 4; Horace White, *Money and Banking*, p. 303.

18. Statutes of Canada, Bank Act, 8 *Geo. VI* (1944), ch. 30, sec. 64 ("Bank Circulation Redemption Fund").

19. Horace White, *Money and Banking*, p. 328.

20. Such a table, in the New York *Sun*, Sept. 3, 1833, is reprinted by Shultz and Caine, *Financial Development of the United States*, p. 187.

21. For a discussion of the controversy from the opposite point of view (in favor of a "national bank" and even a "bank of banks"), see Erick Bollmann, M.D., *Plan of an Improved System of the Money Concerns of the Union* (Philadelphia, 1811).

22. De Knight, *History of the Currency of the Country*, p. 53; more instructive is Knox, *United States Notes* (3d ed., revised, 1899), p. 33; see also Dewey, *Financial History of the United States* (12th ed., 1934), p. 137. The Chase Manhattan Bank, Museum of Moneys of the World, very kindly let me have a photostat of a ten-dollar specimen.

23. Catterall, *The Second Bank of the United States;* Dewey, *The Second Bank of the United States;* Walter B. Smith, *Economic Aspects of the Second Bank of the United States.* For the official documents, see *American State Papers: Finance,* III, 306 ff.

24. As done by Dewey, *Financial History of the United States*, p. 156, whose figures differ from those in U.S. Department of Commerce, *Historical Statistics*, p. 261. In 1836 more than $23 million were in circulation, but this was part of the process of liquidation. Dewey does not assert that there was a rise in the general price level.

25. A specimen of 1819 ($5) is reproduced in Laughlin, *A New Exposition of Money, Credit and Prices*, II, 231; photostats of some other specimens were placed at my disposal by the Chase

Manhattan Bank, Museum of Moneys of the World. The notes of 1819 show a rather clumsy picture of a landing operation by Lawrence Kearny, one of the naval heroes of the War of 1812. Later notes present a seated Minerva, the head surrounded by 13 stars.

26. 17 U.S. 316.

27. Osborn v. Bank of the United States, 22 U.S. 738 (1824).

28. In addition to the writings cited in notes 1 and 23, see Bassett, *The Life of Andrew Jackson* (new ed., 1916), pp. 584, 610, 631; Hammond, "Jackson, Biddle and the Bank of the United States," *Journal of Economic History*, VII (1947), 1.

29. Cf. Hammond, "The Chestnut Street Raid on Wall Street," *Quarterly Journal of Economics*, LXI (1947), 605, 613.

30. A similar action had been taken by Massachusetts in 1712, Nettels, *The Money Supply of the American Colonies before 1720*, p. 264, and by Tennessee in 1820, Sumner, *A History of Banking in the United States*, p. 147. During and after the Napoleonic Wars England employed analogous procedural devices to force the notes of the Bank of England, though they were not legal tender, upon unwilling creditors. Cf. Nussbaum, *Money in the Law*, p. 47. (It seems that under common law civil-procedural legislation is not infrequently employed for eluding substantive law.)

31. Sumner, *A History of Banking in the United States*, p. 144; on pp. 125 ff. he presents an extensive discussion of the entire affair.

32. Briscoe v. The Bank of the Commonwealth of Kentucky, 36 U.S. 257 (1837).

33. The Indiana State Bank was an exception. Hepburn, *A History of Currency in the United States*, p. 246. For the problem in general, see Root, "States as Bankers," in 5 *Sound Currency* (1895), No. 10.

34. See International Monetary Conference, Paris, 1878, *Proceedings and Exhibits*, p. 502 (Lowndes's Report).

35. The enactments of 1834 and 1837 are analyzed by Laugh-

lin, *The History of Bimetallism in the United States* (4th ed., 1897), ch. IV, and Carothers, *Fractional Money*, pp. 88 ff.

36. Charges were again provided by the act of March 3, 1853, 10 *Stat.* 181, sec. 3, and the Revised Statutes, sec. 3524, but abolished again by the act of Jan. 14, 1875, 18 *Stat.*, Part 3, p. 296, sec. 3.

CHAPTER 4: THE STRENGTHENING OF THE DOLLAR, 1837–61

1. A scholarly survey of gold production in California and in the United States generally is presented by Quiring, *Geschichte des Goldes*, pp. 225 ff.

2. Manufacturing of this coin reached a climax in 1853 with $4.4 million dollars, to decline sharply in 1857 ($801,000). From 1863, for the most part, only insignificant amounts ($3,000 to $7,000) were coined, with some increase since 1902. From 1854 until 1889 a three-dollar gold piece was likewise produced, but on the whole in insignificant amounts. U.S. Bureau of the Mint, *Domestic Coin Manufactured by Mints of the United States*, pp. 9, 10. With respect to the engravings of the various coins, see *Domestic Coin*, p. 12 ff., 38 ff.

3. Feavearyear, *The Pound Sterling*, p. 349, lists an English "double sovereign" of 1489 (480.0 grains of gold fine) and a "treble sovereign" of 1549 (508.2 grains), but no modern gold coins beyond the sovereign. The double and treble sovereigns are not even mentioned by Shaw, *The History of the Currency, 1252 to 1894* (2d ed., 1896). We are not concerned with commemorative pieces.

4. On California private coinage, see p. 84.

5. Statistical data in U.S. Bureau of the Mint, *Domestic Coin Manufactured by Mints of the United States*, pp. 11, 63.

6. The act of 1851 does not make it clear whether free coinage should apply to the three-cent pieces. Actually these coins were

exclusively manufactured from government bullion. Carothers, *Fractional Money*, p. 109. Regarding the charges for free coinage under the act of 1853, see p. 249, n. 36.

7. The half-cents of 1792 were abolished by the act of 1857.

8. It was manufactured—for export purposes, it seems—in minimal amounts; only in 1859 and 1860 was there a greater production of pieces, 636,000 and 734,000 dollars respectively. U.S. Bureau of the Mint, *Domestic Coin Manufactured by the Mints of the United States*, p. 11.

9. U.S. Bureau of the Mint, *Catalogue of Coins of the United States*, p. 99 (gold coins); Edgar H. Adams, "Private Gold Coins," *American Journal of Numismatics*, XLV (1911), 11, 46, 129; XLVI (1912), 1, 57, 135, 165; Bullowa, *The Commemorative Coinage of the United States, 1892–1938*, pp. 112 ff.; Raymond, *The Standard Catalogue of United States Coins*, p. 185; Horace White, *Money and Banking*, p. 8 and frontispiece, all with reproductions.

10. Low, "Hard Times Tokens," *American Journal of Numismatics*, XXXIII (1899), 15, 48, 91, 118; XXXIV (1900), 17, 47; XXXV (1901), 23, with comments on 27, 105.

11. Emerich de Vattel, *Le droit des gens*, I, 10, sec. 107. The situation was different in antiquity; see Nussbaum, *Money in the Law*, p. 32.

12. Not, for instance, in Adolf Wagner's most comprehensive *Sozialökonomische Theorie des Geldes und Geldwesens*. John Stuart Mill, in his *Principles of Political Economy*, Bk. V, ch. I, p. 82, takes the view that the coining of money by the government is no more than a matter of "genuine convenience," but he does not refer to the American situation which would have offered some support to this theory.

13. Zerbe, "Private Silver Coins Issued in the United States," *American Journal of Numismatics*, LI (1918), 153, with reproductions. The action of the Oregon man was probably not illegal since punishment is required only for those privately issued coins

above 5 cents which bear "resemblance and similitude" to the corresponding official coins. 18 *U.S. Code*, secs. 489, 491.

14. 28th Congress, 1st Session (1843), House Report No. 379, *Congressional Globe*, 1843, pp. 454, 460; De Knight, *History of the Currency of the Country and of the Loans of the United States*, p. 68; Knox, *United States Notes* (3d ed., 1899), p. 52, with extract from the report of the committee.

15. Knox, *United States Notes*, p. 63.

16. Sumner, *A History of Banking in the United States*, pp. 310, 414 (copious, but not very careful); Dewey, *State Banking before the Civil War*, not historical; Horace White, *Money and Banking*, pp. 328 ff.; an excellent survey with numerous tables is in U.S. Comptroller of the Currency, *Annual Report*, 1876, especially in preliminary pp. xxxviii ff.

17. Statistics starting with 1834 are given by U.S. Comptroller of the Currency, *Annual Report*, 1905, p. 355.

18. Root, "New York Bank Currency," in 2 *Sound Currency* (1895), No. 5; Horace White, *Money and Banking*, p. 311.

19. Oddly enough, in the evaluation of real estate the buildings were not counted, which indicates certain misgivings about the general quality of these structures.

20. In addition to Sumner, *A History of Banking in the United States*, see Hammond, "The Louisiana Banking Act of Feb. 5, 1842," in Federal Reserve Bank of Atlanta, *Monthly Review*, XXVI (1942), 1; Caldwell, *A Banking History of Louisiana*, pp. 71 ff.; Fortier, *A History of Louisiana*, II, 391; and Hooper, *An Examination of the Theory and the Effect of Laws Relating to the Amount of Specie in Banks*, pp. 8 ff. The 1842 banking law and its authorship and sources deserve special investigation. The writer of an article concerning the Banking Act of 1842 published in the *Bankers' Magazine* (New York), XXXIII (1877), 342 ff., mentions having been informed that the New Orleans banker Edward J. Forstall was "the person most influential in the framing of the Act" (p. 352). But despite the kind assistance of Dean

J. B. Trant of the Louisiana State University College of Commerce, I was unable to find out more about the creators and sources of the act.

21. Lawrence D. Smith, *Counterfeiting, Crime Against the People*, pp. 78 ff.; see also Sumner, *A History of Banking in the United States*, p. 437.

22. Shultz and Caine, *Financial Development of the United States*, p. 248.

23. The history of checks has been very little investigated. Conant, "Development of the Check," *Bankers' Magazine*, LXXXIII (1911), 581, is unsatisfactory. Gustav Cohn, "Zur Geschichte des Schecks," *Zeitschrift für Vergleichende Rechtswissenschaft*, I (1878), 117, gives some information about Italian and Dutch precursors of the check.

24. The text of such a note is reproduced by Holdsworth, *Money and Banking* (5th ed., 1928), p. 6.

25. Feavearyear, *The Pound Sterling*, p. 289.

26. L. M. Mitchell, *Le chèque dans les pays Anglo-Saxons*, p. 2.

27. See the caricature reproduced by Gibbons, *Banks of New York . . . and the Panic of 1857*, p. 294.

28. On clearinghouse institutions, see Cannon, *Clearing Houses*; "Clearing Houses," *Encyclopaedia of the Social Sciences*, III, 546–48; "Clearing System," in Robert H. I. Palgrave, *The Dictionary of Political Economy* (3 vols., 1894–99); Zollman, *The Law of Banks and Banking*, ch. 133. Here, too, an investigation especially of the American developments would seem highly desirable.

29. Holland, *The London Bankers' Clearing House.*

30. *Suggestions on the Banks and Currency of the Several United States*, p. 63.

31. Cannon, *Clearing Houses*, p. 75; Horace White, *Money and Banking*, p. 224; Zollman, *The Law of Banks and Banking*, sec. 3985.

32. E.g., the Revised Statutes of 1874, sec. 5192, admit as reserve for national banks only certificates "representing specie or lawful money."

33. See Yeardley v. Philler, 167 U.S. 344 (1897).

34. Kinley, *The History, Organization and Influence of the Independent Treasury of the United States* (1893) and *The Independent Treasury of the United States* (1910).

35. His comment is found in Report of the Secretary of the Treasury, Senate Executive Doc. No. 2, 33rd Congress, 2d Session (1855), p. 257. On Gouge, see pp. 66–67 of the present book.

36. Masters, "The Establishment of the Decimal Currency in Canada," *Canadian Historical Review*, XXXIII (1952), 129, is the main source for this discussion. See also Chalmers, *A History of Currency in the British Colonies*, ch. xv. McLachlan, "Money of Canada from the Historical Standpoint," *Proceedings and Transactions of the Royal Society of Canada*, IX (1915), 57, offers little help. Cf. also Canadian Archives, *Le change et les finances*, II (1925), 26.

37. *Statutes of Canada*, 1857, ch. 18.

38. The title of Professor Master's article must be explained, it seems, by his doubt whether the adoption of the term "dollar" was fortunate. Perhaps something like "royal" would have been preferable, he believes. However, he is not opposed to the term "cent," which is more American than "dollar."

39. Gibbons, *The Banks of New York . . . and the Panic of 1857*; Sumner, *A History of American Currency*, p. 180; Hepburn, *A History of Currency in the United States* (rev. ed., 1924), p. 168.

CHAPTER 5: THE CIVIL WAR

1. On greenbacks, we have the classic work of Wesley C. Mitchell, *A History of the Greenbacks*, covering the years 1862–65. Mitchell's *Gold, Prices and Wages under the Greenback*

Standard, covering the postwar period, is, in the author's words, no more than "the statistical apparatus for a book still to be written." See also Don C. Barrett, *The Greenback and Resumption of Specie Payments, 1862–1879* and Horace White, *Money and Banking, Illustrated by American History* (5th ed., 1914), p. 100.

2. Namely $500, $1,000 and since 1878, $5,000 and $10,000, but the latter notes seem to have been placed on order.

3. Hart, *Salmon P. Chase.* There are excellent short biographies by J. G. Randall in the *Dictionary of American Biography* and by J. R. Rines in the *Encyclopedia Americana.*

4. The inventor of the greenbacks was Elbridge G. Spaulding, a member of the House of Representatives. See Don C. Barrett, *The Greenback and Resumption of Specie Payments, 1862–1879,* p. 16 and Spaulding, *History of Legal Tender Paper Issued during the Great Rebellion* (1869; 2d ed., with "extra sheets," 1879).

5. Nussbaum, "The Meaning of Inflation," *Political Science Quarterly,* LVIII (1943), 86.

6. Mitchell, *A History of the Greenbacks,* pp. 26, 91, 174; J. J. Knox, *United States Notes* (3d ed., 1899), pp. 80, 110, with the text of notes; Bolles, *The Financial History of the United States, from 1861 to 1885* (2d ed., 1894), p. 51; Breckinridge, "The Demand Notes of 1861," 5 *Sound Currency* (1898), No. 20.

7. U.S. Secretary of the Treasury, *Annual Report,* 1864, p. 18. See, however, Mitchell, *A History of the Greenbacks,* pp. 174, 176.

8. Mitchell, *A History of the Greenbacks,* p. 177, asserts that two more types of government obligations, not being legal tender, passed freely from hand to hand as current funds. However, *Hunt's Merchants' Magazine,* LII, 382, to which he refers, confirms his statement only for "large transactions." This means something fundamentally different from a monetary point of view.

9. For the following, see Friedberg, *Paper Money of the United States,* with excellent reproductions.

10. A. Davis, *The Origin of the National Banking System* and

A. D. Noyes, *History of the National Bank Currency*. The *Annual Reports* of the U.S. Comptroller of the Currency offer important data on the national banks up to the present day.

11. Friedberg, *Paper Money of the United States*, pp. 71 ff.; Dillistin, "National Bank Notes in the Early Years," *The Numismatist*, LXI (1948), 791. In 1882 the showy vignettes were abandoned.

12. Zollman, *The Law of Banks and Banking*, sec. 302.

13. Their last year was 1878, U.S. Department of Commerce, *Historical Statistics of the United States, 1789–1945*, p. 275. See also Hepburn, *A History of the Currency of the United States* (rev. ed., 1924), pp. 310, 311, 320.

14. 75 U.S. 533 (1869).

15. On these state banks, cf. George E. Barrett, *State Banks and Trust Companies since the Passage of the National Bank Act*. See also Carothers, *Fractional Money*, p. 163.

16. For the following, see Faulkner, "The Private Issue of Token Coins," *Political Science Quarterly*, XII (1901), 321.

17. Carothers, *Fractional Money*, p. 166.

18. According to Carothers, *Fractional Money*, p. 168, the Supreme Court of the state of New York had declared that act unconstitutional, but Carothers gives no citation, and I have been unable to find a pertinent case.

19. Knox, *United States Notes*, p. 104, with reproductions; Mitchell, *A History of the Greenbacks*, pp. 98, 161; Carothers, *Fractional Money*, pp. 170, 180.

20. Carothers, *Fractional Money*, p. 180; Friedberg, *Paper Money of the United States*, pp. 17 and 198 (reproductions).

21. Carothers, *Fractional Money*, p. 187.

22. On the West, see Lester, *Monetary Experiments*, p. 161; Horace White, *Money and Banking*, p. 130; Moses, "Legal Tender Notes in California," *Quarterly Journal of Economics*, VII (1892), 1.

23. Simpkins v. Low, 54 N.Y. 179, 181 (1873).

24. Philpott, "National Gold Bank Notes," *The Numismatist*, XLVII (1934), 717; Friedberg, *Paper Money of the United States*, p. 101.

25. Lester, *Monetary Experiments*, p. 68.

26. Nussbaum, *Money in the Law*, pp. 586 ff. where the references are listed.

27. It is a strange fact that in the controversy on Chase's attitude in the Legal Tender Cases this action, which expresses more than an approval, has never been mentioned.

28. 72 U.S. 603.

29. Knox v. Lee and Parker v. Davis, 79 U.S. 457.

30. Meaning the greenbacks. Since the colonial "bills of credit" had been stigmatized by the Constitution, the greenbacks were sometimes, and even officially, titled "treasury notes," especially the issue of 1869, the last one preceding the decision. Later on, the term "United States notes" was exclusively employed.

31. Juilliard v. Greenman, 110 U.S. 421.

32. Bronson v. Rhodes, 74 U.S. 229 (1868).

33. Lane County v. State of Oregon, 74 U.S. 71 (1868).

34. Fuller, *Confederate Currency and Stamps*; Bradbeer, *Confederate and Southern State Currency*; Ernest A. Smith, *The History of the Confederate Treasury*; Lee, *The Currency of the Confederate States of America*; Dawson and Cooper, "The Effect of Inflation on Private Contracts: United States, 1861–1879: The Confederate Inflation," *Michigan Law Review*, XXXIII (1935), 706. See also *American Journal of Numismatics*, II (1867), 12, 36, 47; III (1869), 97; XII (1878) 99 and frontispiece. Bibliographical: *The Numismatist*, LXIV (1951), 513.

35. One note of the state of Florida is too curious to be left unmentioned. Instead of the customarily pictured goddesses such as Ceres, Minerva, etc., it shows the goddess Moneta (Bradley, *Confederate and Southern State Currency*, p. 116) which, one might say, belonged to another world indeed.

36. Splendidly reproduced in *American Journal of Numismat-*

ics, XII (1877), frontispiece. The specimen, made in England, had been intercepted. The general seems to be Washington.

37. George Cary Eggleston; see Hart, *American History Told by Contemporaries*, IV (1901), 247.

38. Thorington v. Smith, 75 U.S. 1 (1869).

39. See p. 146.

40. Friedberg, *Paper Money of the United States*, p. 111.

CHAPTER 6: THE STRUGGLE AGAINST THE GOLD STANDARD, 1865–1900

1. For general information, see Laughlin, *The History of Bimetallism in the United States*, pp. 92, 209; Hepburn, *A History of Currency in the United States* (rev. ed., 1924), ch. XII–XXI; Simiand, *Inflation et stabilization alternées: Le développement économique des Etats Unis des origines coloniales au temps présent* (1934), ch. III to V; Hasenkamp, *Die Geldverfassung und das Notenbankwesen der Vereinigten Staaten*, first part. The elaborate study by N. Prager, *Die Währungsfrage in den Vereinigten Staaten von Nordamerika* (Münchener Volkswirtschaftliche Studien, Vol. 23, 1897), pp. 125–447, offers little of substance.

2. Don C. Barrett, *The Greenback and Resumption of Specie Payments, 1862–1879*, p. 84; Wildman, *Money Inflation in the United States*, ch. IV and V.

3. Barrett, *The Greenback and Resumption of Specie Payments, 1862–1879*, p. 84; Horace White, *Money and Banking* (5th ed., 1914), p. 128; Henry Adams, "The New York Gold Conspiracy" (1870), reprinted in his *Historical Essays*, p. 318; 41st Congress, 2d Session, House Report No. 31 (1870), *Gold Panic Investigation*, p. 483. The articles by Allan Nevins on Gould and Fisk in the *Dictionary of American Biography* give a pungent picture of the two financiers and their environment. Regarding Gould, Hofstadter, *The American Political Tradition*, p. 165, states: "whose hand spoiled everything it touched."

4. F. E. Haynes, *Third Party Movements since the Civil War*, Part III; Wildman, *Money Inflation in the United States*, ch. I and V, presents a psychological analysis which is interesting even to those who would not accept his diagnosis of "social pathology." Further references in Dewey, *Financial History of the United States* (12th ed., 1934), p. 378.

5. Hicks, *The American Nation* (2d ed., 1949), p. 149.

6. Murad, *The Paradox of a Metal Standard;* Hütter, *La question de la monnaie d'argent aux Etats-Unis des origines à 1900* (thesis, Paris, 1938). Apart from an "Introduction" Hütter's impressive work (693 pp.) is devoted to the period discussed in this chapter. See also Young, *The International Economy* (3rd ed., 1953), p. 473.

7. Garnett, "History of the Trade Dollar," *American Economic Review*, VII (1917), 91; Carothers, *Fractional Money*, p. 275. Numismatic: U.S. Bureau of the Mint, *Catalogue of Coins of the United States*, p. 50 and Raymond, *Standard Catalogue of United States Coins* (17th ed., 1954), p. 112; reproductions of the trade dollar are also in Laughlin, *A New Exposition of Money, Credit and Prices*, I, 243. The act of 1873 has been defended by H. R. Linderman (Director of the Mint) in *Money and Legal Tender in the United States* (1877).

8. See, e.g., Wildman, *Money Inflation in the United States*, p. 163. A baffling letter was written by President Grant on Oct. 6, 1873, about eight months after the enactment; in it he recommends, apparently misunderstanding or forgetting about the act, a return to silver, "the standard value the world over," in order to supplement the circulating media. Dewey, *Financial History of the United States*, p. 405.

9. Senate Report No. 703, 44th Congress, 2d Session. The elaborate report was submitted in March, 1877.

10. An impressive analysis of this movement is offered by Hofstadter, *The Age of Reform* (1955), pp. 104 ff.

11. Sprague, *History of Crises under the National Banking*

System, p. 153; Warner, "The Currency Famine," 2 *Sound Currency* (1895), No. 6; Horace White, *Money and Banking* (5th ed., 1914), p. 177.

12. Numerous reproductions of such "notes" are in Warner, "The Currency Famine," 2 *Sound Currency* (1895), No. 6, 9 ff.

13. 20 Op. Att. Gen. 681 (1893).

14. Warner, "The Currency Famine," 2 *Sound Currency* (1895), No. 5, 6, and 8.

15. The text of the contract is found in Muhleman, *Monetary Systems of the World*, p. 190.

16. A small amount of 20-cent silver pieces was in circulation from 1875 to 1878.

17. Silver certificates of $500 and $1,000 were likewise produced, Friedberg, *Paper Money of the United States*, p. 12. Regarding higher denominations of other U.S. notes, see pp. 133, 166.

18. Friedberg, *Paper Money of the United States*, p. 6.

19. De Knight, *History of the Currency of the Country and of the Loans of the United States*, p. 92; Friedberg, *Paper Money of the United States*, p. 16, 103. Treasury certificates on gold deposits are also dealt with in an act of July 14, 1870, 18 *Stat. L.* 272, sec. 3, but bearing interest and lacking definitely any monetary character, they were not called "gold certificates." The history of gold certificates has been very little investigated.

20. Russell, *International Monetary Conferences* (1898; long winded and purely factual, though without references); Walker, *International Bimetallism* (1896; a brilliant study from the bimetallistic point of view); Laughlin, *The History of Bimetallism in the United States* (4th ed., 1897), *passim.*

21. 39th Congress, 1st Session, *Congressional Globe*, XXXII (2), 2654; (3) 3824. A special commissioner was to be appointed for that purpose.

22. International Monetary Conference, Paris, 1867, *Procès-verbaux.*

23. *Statutes of Canada,* 1868, ch. 45.

24. Carothers, *Fractional Money,* p. 237; Linderman, *Money and Legal Tender in the United States,* p. 44.

25. U.S. Bureau of the Mint, *Catalogue of Coins, Tokens and Medals,* pp. 19, 86 and Plate VII.

26. International Monetary Conference, Paris, 1878, *Proceedings and Exhibits;* with valuable Appendix by Dorton containing, among other things, a bibliography of American and foreign, particularly German, publications on monetary subjects until 1879 and a reprint of the *Proceedings* of the 1867 Conference held in Paris.

27. International Monetary Conference, Paris, 1881, *Proceedings.*

28. International Monetary Conference, Brussels, 1893, *Report of the Commissioners.*

29. By the "Act to establish uniform currency for the Dominion of Canada," *Statutes of Canada,* 1871, ch. 4, sec. 9.

30. Report of the Silver Commission, 44th Congress, 2d Session, Senate Report 703 (1876/77), I, 384 (actually the dollar commanded a premium). The dollar reappears as legal tender in Mexico, Decree of May 14, 1918, *Diario Oficial,* 1918, pp. 171, 172.

31. Proclamation of the Swiss *Bundesrat,* Aug. 10, 1870, *Amtliche Sammlung der Gesetze und Verordnungen,* X, 288.

32. "A Note on the Idea of World Money," 64 *Political Science Quarterly* (1946), 120, is a survey by the present writer. See also Knies, *Weltgeld und Weltmünzen* (Berlin, 1874).

33. Reference may be made particularly to the works of Hasenkamp, Hütter, and Simiand (see pp. 257, n. 1, 258, n. 6) and Dorton's Appendix, n. 26. English writers have shown less interest in these (and most other) aspects of American monetary history. We may mention, however, Agnes F. Dodd, *History of Money in the British Empire & the United States* (London, 1911), a helpful textbook for students.

CHAPTER 7: THE GOLD STANDARD CONSOLIDATED

1. The term "unit of value" as a basic monetary conception appears also in later Continental writings, though without reference to the American precedent. See, e.g., Knapp, *Die Staatliche Theorie des Geldes* (1905; English tr., *State Theory of Money*, by Lucas and Bonar, 1924).

2. Reproductions of gold certificates, including those of 1882 (see p. 136), are found in Friedberg, *Paper Money of the United States*, p. 103. The text of the certificate emphasizes that an equal amount of gold coin was deposited with the Treasury.

3. Sprague, *History of Crises under the National Banking System*, p. 216.

4. U.S. Congress, House of Representatives, *Money Trust Investigation.*

5. The New York banker Paul Warburg was outstanding among them. See his *The Federal Reserve System* (2 vols., New York, 1930).

6. The text of the Aldrich bill is found in Hepburn, *A History of Currency in the United States* (rev. ed., 1924), p. 500, and in Warburg, *The Federal Reserve System*, I, 178.

7. Robertson, *History of the American Economy*, p. 438; Laughlin, *The Federal Reserve Act; Its Origins and Problems;* S. E. Harris, *Twenty Years of Federal Reserve Policy;* Henry P. Willis, *The Federal Reserve System;* Hepburn, *A History of Currency in the United States* (rev. ed., 1924), ch. XXVIII. A recent analysis, brief but brilliant, is Roy Harrod, *The Dollar* (London, 1953), ch. II.

8. Noyes, *The War Period of American Finance, 1908–1925.* A general analysis of the effects of war on the gold standard is presented by Federici, *La moneta e l'oro* (rev. ed., 1948), ch. X.

9. See Friedberg, *Paper Money of the United States*, pp. 14,

84 ff. Only one of the issues referred in its text to the "National Banking Association."

10. Federal Reserve System: Board of Governors, *Banking and Monetary Statistics*, p. 637. It is perhaps symptomatic that in 1915 on the occasion of the Panama Pacific International Exposition in San Francisco a commemorative gold coin of $50 was issued. (A number of these were octagonal, "in remembrance of the products of the 'gold rush.' ") Raymond, *The Standard Catalogue of United States Coins* (17th ed., 1954), p. 154.

11. The prohibition was based on the Espionage Act of June 15, 1917, 40 *Stat.* 217, a questionable foundation, but the prohibition was affirmed by the Trading-with-the-Enemy Act of Oct. 5, 1917, 40 *Stat.* 411.

12. Carothers, *Fractional Money*, p. 287.

13. American Bank and Trust Company et al. v. Federal Reserve Bank of Atlanta, 258 U.S. 350 (1921).

14. 262 U.S. 643 (1923). Same parties as in preceding note.

15. Friedberg, *Paper Money of the United States*, p. 18.

16. Hector Lazo, *Scrip and Barter* (Bureau of Foreign and Domestic Commerce, mimeographed, 1933); *Commercial and Financial Chronicle*, March 11, 1934, pp. 1674, 1680.

CHAPTER 8: THE NEW DEAL

1. Crawford, *Monetary Management under the New Deal;* Johnson, *The Treasury and Monetary Policy, 1933–1938;* James F. T. O'Connor, former Comptroller of the Currency, *The Banking Crisis and Recovery under the Roosevelt Administration;* Paris, *Monetary Policies of the United States, 1932–1938;* Sussfeld, *La réorganisation bancaire aux Etats Unis et la crise du dollar* (a careful Paris thesis, 1935); Cassel, *The Downfall of the Gold Standard.* Cf. also Studenski and Kroos, *Financial History of the United States*, p. 382, and Goldenweiser, *American Monetary Policy*, p. 164.

2. More precisely: 2,122 were placed in liquidation and 179

were suspended until the end of 1936, *Federal Reserve Bulletin*, 1937, p. 867. O'Connor, *The Banking Crisis and Recovery under the Roosevelt Administration*, p. 52, analyzing the causes of the measures taken, lists the "failure" of 1,417 banks.

3. *The Public Papers and Addresses of Franklin D. Roosevelt*, compiled by Samuel I. Rosenman, II, 61; *Federal Reserve Bulletin*, 1933, p. 209.

4. Thus leaving the door open for a restoration of exchange control. Such restoration never happened. *Federal Reserve Bulletin*, 1934, p. 780.

5. The *Annual Reports* of the Treasury, under "Depositories of Public Funds," give information on the acquisition of "non current gold coin" at $20.67 an ounce (instead of $35). This seems to refer to coins not delivered in time. The Report for 1947, p. 9, still states for the year 1946–47 an amount of $116,000 in such coins.

6. On the London Conference, see Wheeler-Bennett and Heald, eds., *Documents on International Affairs, 1933–1934*, p. 1 ff.; Beyen, *Money in a Maelstrom*, p. 88.

7. Cf. the author's article, "The Legal Status of Gold," *American Journal of Comparative Law*, III (1954), 360, 365. The first regulation of this kind was the Treasury order of April 29, 1933, *Federal Reserve Bulletin*, 1933, p. 267.

8. For a critical appraisal of this theory, see Harris, *Exchange Depreciation, Its Theory and Its History, 1931–35*, pp. 254, 268; cf. Hardy, *The Warren-Pearson Price Theory* (Brookings Institution, Pamphlet Series No. 17; 1935).

9. *The Dollar*, p. 69.

10. Nussbaum, *Money in the Law*, ser. 15, with references.

11. Murad, *The Paradox of a Metal Standard; a Case History of Silver;* Carothers and Bradford, "Legal Aspects of Silver Policies of the United States in Recent Years," in *Money and the Law*, supplement to *New York University Law Quarterly Review* (1945); Westerfield, *Our Silver Debacle*. Cf. also Young, *The*

International Economy (3d ed., 1953), p. 476; Johnson, *The Treasury and Monetary Policy, 1933–1938,* ch. II; Paris, *Monetary Policies of the United States, 1932–1938,* p. 42.

12. *Federal Reserve Bulletin,* 1934, pp. 438, 440 (embargo by Treasury), and p. 564 ("nationalization" of silver by President).

13. Kisch and Elkin, *Central Banks* (4th ed., 1932), p. 115.

14. Federal Reserve System: Board of Governors, *The Federal Reserve System,* p. 99.

15. 31 U.S.C. 405a.

16. E. De Bella, "Sales Tax Tokens," *Numismatic Scrapbook Magazine,* X (1944), 169, 424; McKenney, "Sales Tax Tokens," *Numismatic Scrapbook Magazine,* III (1937), 217.

17. Lawrence D. Smith, *Counterfeiting, Crime Against the People.*

18. There seems to be a very old degeneration of Italian artistic talents in this respect; see p. 24.

19. Nussbaum, *Money in the Law,* p. 44. The statutory provisions against counterfeiting and forgery are very extensive, 18 U.S.C. Ch. XXV. An American peculiarity consists in the stringent prohibition of printing or photographing paper money, even though not for fraudulent purposes, 18 U.S.C. 474 (first in act of June 30, 1864, sec. XI; 13 *Stat.* 221). See Baughman (Chief, U.S. Secret Service), in *The Graphic Arts,* August, 1952, pp. 24 ff.

20. Johnson, *The Treasury and Monetary Policy, 1933–1938,* p. 107. Moreover, the Export-Import Bank was established by the government in 1934 for the trade with the just recognized Soviets.

21. See A. T. Huntington and R. Z. Mawhinney, *Laws of the United States Concerning Money, Banking and Loans, 1778–1909:* "Coinage," pp. 471–624; "Paper Money," pp. 626–725. The verbose language of American legislation is another factor. One may compare the text of the 1792 act with that of the French law of 1803; see p. 244, n. 43.

CHAPTER 9: WORLD WAR II AND AFTER

1. Nickel in the 5-cent coins needed for war purposes was replaced from 1942 until the end of 1945 by silver and other metals. Similar steps were taken during the war with regard to the 1-cent pieces in order to save zinc. U.S. Bureau of the Mint, *Annual Reports*, 1943, p. 4; 1944, p. 2; 1945, p. 2; 1946, p. 2.

2. U.S. Department of the Treasury, *Administration of the Wartime Financial and Property Controls of the U.S. Government* (1942).

3. U.S. Congress, Senate, *Hearings before the Committee on Appropriations . . . : Occupation Currency Transactions*, 80th Congress, 1st Session (1947); Nussbaum, *Money in the Law*, p. 530 (with references); Lester, *International Aspects of Wartime Monetary Experience;* Friedberg, *Paper Money of the United States*, p. 125.

4. U.S. Department of Commerce, Office of Business Economics, *Survey of Current Business: Monthly Business Statistics*, summarized in *Statistical Abstracts for the United States.*

5. Federal Reserve notes above $100 have been circulated only on a definitely reduced scale. On June 30, 1956, the total of $500 notes amounted to $295 million; $1,000 notes, $419 million; $5,000 notes, $3 million; $10,000 notes, $13 million. U.S. Secretary of the Treasury, *Annual Report*, 1955–56, p. 539.

According to the 1955 Report of the U.S. Comptroller of the Currency (1956), p. 45, 644 shipments, worth $5,697,560,000, of Federal Reserve currency were made from Washington, D.C., during the year ended December 31, 1955, to Federal Reserve agents and Federal Reserve branch banks; in addition, 18 deliveries, totaling $1,000,000,000, were made to the Treasury of the United States. At the same time, 4,469 lots of unfit Federal Reserve currency, consisting of 452,667,253 notes valued at

$5,510,917,355, were received at the Treasury for verification and certification for destruction.

6. *Federal Reserve Bulletin*, 1951, p. 267; Rist, *La Fédéral Réserve and les difficultés monétaires d'après guerre 1945–1950.*

7. A careful and objective investigation is presented by Wronski, *Le rôle économique et social dans les démocraties populaires* (preface by Professor J. N. Jeannenay, Paris, 1954), concerned with the satellites). Cf. also Schwartz, *Russia's Soviet Economy* (2d ed., 1954), ch. XII; Kiesewetter, *Die Wirtschaft der Tschechoslowakei seit 1945* (Deutsches Institut für Wirtschaftsforschung, Berlin, 1954); Adolf Weber, "Geld und Gold in der Sovietwirtschaft," *Finanzarchiv* (N.S.), XII (1951), 631.

8. Main source: International Monetary Fund, *Annual Reports* since 1947; International Monetary Fund, *Summary Proceedings* (annual meetings of the Board of Directors) since 1946. Literature: Young, *The International Economy* (3d ed., 1953), p. 447; Kindelberger, "Bretton Woods Reappraised," *International Organization*, V (1951), 32; Nussbaum, *Money in the Law*, p. 526 (with further references); John H. Williams, *Postwar Monetary Plans*, p. 3; C. Williams, *Bretton Woods*, a useful popular survey; Mossé, *Le système monétaire de Bretton Woods;* Stokvis, *Bretton Woods en het International Monetair Bestel;* Bachmann, *Die Konventionen von Bretton Woods.*

By the Bretton Woods Agreement Act of July 31, 1945, Congress established the National Advisory Council on International Monetary and Financial Agreements, which is concerned also with American participation in the operation of the Fund. Semiannual reports of the Council are published in Congressional documents.

9. Members are: Afghanistan, Australia, Austria, Belgium, Bolivia, Brazil, Burma, Canada, Ceylon, Chile, China, Colombia, Costa Rica, Cuba, Denmark, Dominican Republic, Ecuador, Egypt, El Salvador, Ethiopia, Finland, France, Germany (Federal Republic of), Greece, Guatemala, Haiti, Honduras, Iceland,

India, Indonesia, Iran, Iraq, Israel, Italy, Japan, Jordan, Korea, Lebanon, Luxembourg, Mexico, Netherlands, Nicaragua, Norway, Pakistan, Panama, Paraguay, Peru, Philippines, Sweden, Syria, Thailand, Turkey, Union of South Africa, United Kingdom, United States, Uruguay, Venezuela, Yugoslavia. International Monetary Fund, *Seventh Annual Report* (1956).

10. Regarding the exchange rate systems of the nonmember states, see International Monetary Fund, *Exchange Restrictions: Seventh Annual Report* (1956), pp. 345 ff. There is more about Swiss regulations in Bank of International Settlements, *23rd Annual Report* (1953), p. 133.

11. There has recently been much discussion of this subject. See, e.g., Zupnick, *Britain's Postwar Dollar Problem,* chs. V and VI; Gardner, *Sterling-Dollar Diplomacy;* Bell, *The Sterling Area in the Postwar World;* Polk, *The Sterling Area;* International Monetary Fund, *Exchange Restrictions: Seventh Annual Report,* 1956, p. 295.

12. $180 million were taken from the Stabilization Fund which kept therefore $200 million of its original stock plus $99 million earnings. Secretary of the Treasury, *Annual Report,* 1947, p. 432. Hence the U.S. Treasury has kept a basis for independent financial transactions in the international area.

13. For an instructive discussion of these conditions, see Bloomfield (of the Federal Reserve Bank, New York), *Speculative and Flight Movements of Capital in Postwar International Finance,* especially pp. 22, 67, 68.

14. For the following cf., e.g., Kriz (of the Federal Reserve Bank, New York), "The International Gold and Dollar Movement, 1945–1953," *Commercial and Financial Chronicle,* Nov. 19, 1953, pp. 4, 36; Kriz, "Gold," *Engineering and Mining Journal,* February, 1956 and February, 1957. Valuable information on the free gold market is found in the *Annual Reports* of the Bank of International Settlements, XX (1950), 180; XXI (1951), 155, 158; XXII (1952), 161, etc.

15. See, e.g., the address by N. C. Hanenga, Minister of Finance of the Union of South Africa, in International Monetary Fund, *Summary Proceedings, Annual Meeting*, 1952, p. 81. William J. Busschau (of South Africa), *The Measure of Gold* and *America's Role in Monetary Stabilization* (reprint from *Optima*, March, 1953).

16. In addition, Great Britain received a credit up to $500 million from the Export-Import Bank, a U.S. government institution.

17. The figures are given in Kriz's articles in the *Engineering and Mining Journal*. The output of the Soviets is not included.

18. International Monetary Fund, *Annual Report*, 1956, p. 118.

19. We may leave aside the primitive and abnormal conditions in Saudi Arabia and some other Asiatic countries.

20. Referring to a publication of the Soviet writer Zlubin, I had mentioned this fact in *Money in the Law*, p. 523, n. 51. Cf. also Dewar, *Soviet Trade with Eastern Europe, 1945–1949*, pp. 109, 112. I have been authoritatively informed that Soviet officials try to explain the reference as irrelevant, because the ruble is equal to 25 cents. But from this point of view the reference to the dollar would appear superfluous. Besides it is well known that the ruble is worth much less than 25 cents, see, e.g., Schwartz, *Russia's Soviet Economy*, p. 482.

21. Cf. the very informative study by Klopstock (of the Federal Reserve Bank, New York), *The International Status of the Dollar*.

22. The official denomination was "Preliminary Draft Outline of Proposal for a United and Associated Nations' Stabilization Fund."

23. Officially called "International Clearing Union." The full text of the proposals are found in U.S. Department of State, *Proceedings and Documents on the United Nations Monetary and Financial Conference* (2 vols.), pp. 1536 ff. For comments, see Gardner, *Sterling-Dollar Diplomacy*, ch. V, Lutz, *International*

Monetary Mechanisms: The Keynes and White Proposals, and, very much from a British point of view, Einzig, *Currency after the War: The British and American Plans.*

24. *The Dollar*, p. 104. Communist leanings of which White has been accused have nothing to do with the matter discussed above.

CHAPTER 10: CONCLUSION

1. Reference may be made here to the remarkable study by Firmin Roz, *L'energie américaine* (1914), which was highly honored by the Académie Française.

Selected Bibliography

Adams, Henry. The New York Gold Conspiracy (1870). Reprinted in his Historical Essays. New York, 1891.

American Numismatic Society. Numismatic Notes and Monographs. *See* Bullowa, D. M.; Dillistin, William H.; Gillingham, Harrold E.; McKay, George L.; Nesmith, Robert I.; Noe, Sydney P.; Scott, Kenneth.

American State Papers: Documents, Legislative and Executive, of the Congress of the United States (38 vols., Washington, D.C., 1832–61). Class III: Finance, 5 vols., 1st Congress–20th Congress, 1789–1828.

Andrews, Charles M. The Colonial Background of the American Revolution; Four Essays in American Colonial History. New Haven, 1924.

Ascarelli, Tullio. La moneta. Milan, 1928.

Bachmann, Hans. Die Konventionen von Bretton Woods. St. Gall, Switzerland, 1946.

Bancroft, George. A History of the United States. 10 vols. Boston, 1834–74.

Bank of International Settlements. Annual Reports, 1950–56.

Barrett, Don C. The Greenback and Resumption of Specie Payments, 1862–1879. Cambridge, Mass., 1931.

Barrett, George E. State Banks and Trust Companies since the Passage of the National Bank Act (61st Congress, 2d Session, Senate Doc. 659). Publications of the National Monetary Commission, Vol. VII. Washington, D.C., 1911.

Bassett, John Spencer. The Life of Andrew Jackson. New ed. New York, 1916.

Beard, Charles A. An Economic Interpretation of the Constitution of the United States. Edition with new introduction. New York, 1935.

Bell, Philip W. The Sterling Area in the Postwar World; Internal Mechanism and Cohesion, 1946–1952. Oxford, 1956.

Beyen, J. W. Money in a Maelstrom. New York, 1949.

Bloomfield, Arthur I. Speculative and Flight Movements of Capital in Postwar International Finance. Princeton Studies in International Finance, No. 3. Princeton, 1954.

Bolles, Albert S. The Financial History of the United States, from 1774 to 1789. 4th ed. New York, 1896.

—— The Financial History of the United States, from 1789 to 1860. 4th ed. New York, 1894.

—— The Financial History of the United States, from 1861 to 1885. 2d ed. New York, 1894.

Bollmann, Erick. Plan of an Improved System of the Money Concerns of the Union. Philadelphia, 1811.

Bouchary, Jean. Les faux-monnayeurs sous la Révolution Française. Paris, 1946.

Bradbeer, William West. Confederate and Southern State Currency. Mount Vernon, N.Y., 1915.

Breckinridge, R. M. "The Demand Notes of 1861," in 5 *Sound Currency* (1898), No. 20.

Bronson, Henry. A Historical Account of Connecticut Currency, Continental Money, and the Finances of the Revolution. In Papers of the New Haven Colony Historical Society, Vol. I. New Haven, 1865.

Bullock, Charles J. Essays on the Monetary History of the United States. New York, 1900.

Bullowa, D. M. The Commemorative Coinage of the United States, 1892–1938. American Numismatic Society, Numismatic Notes and Monographs No. 83. New York, 1938.

Busschau, William J. America's Role in Monetary Stabilization. Reprint from *Optima*, March, 1953.

—— The Measure of Gold. Johannesburg, 1949.

Cajori, Florian. A History of Mathematical Notations. 2 vols. Chicago, 1928–29.

Caldwell, Stephen A. A Banking History of Louisiana. Baton Rouge, 1935.

Cannon, James G. Clearing Houses (61st Congress, 2d Session, Senate Doc. 491). Publications of the National Monetary Commission, Vol. VI. Washington, D.C., 1911.

Carothers, Neil. Fractional Money; a History of the Small Coins and Fractional Paper Currency of the United States. New York, 1930.

Cassel, Gustav. The Downfall of the Gold Standard. Oxford, 1936.

Catterall, Ralph C. H. The Second Bank of the United States. Chicago, 1903.

Chaddock, Robert E. The Safety Fund Banking System in New York, 1829–1866. *See* Dewey, Davis R., and Robert E. Chaddock.

Chalmers, Sir Robert. A History of Currency in the British Colonies. London, 1893.

Chevalier, Michel. La monnaie. (Vol. III of his Cours d'économie politique fait au Collège de France.) 2d ed. Paris, 1866.

Clapp, George H., and Howard B. Newcomb. The United States Cents of the Years 1795, 1796, 1797 and 1800. New York, 1947.

Clough, Shepard B., and Charles W. Cole. Economic History of Europe. 3d ed. Boston, 1952.

Collins, Charles M. The History, Law and Practice of Banking. London, 1881.

Conant, Charles A. The Principles of Money and Banking. 2 vols. New York and London, 1905.

Crawford, Arthur W. Monetary Management under the New Deal; the Evolution of a Managed Currency System—Its Problems and Results. Washington, D.C., 1940.

Crosby, Sylvester S. The Early Coins of America; and the Laws Governing Their Issue. Boston, 1875.

Davis, Andrew McFarland. Colonial Currency Reprints, 1682–1751. 4 vols. Boston, 1910–11.

—— Currency and Banking in the Province of Massachusetts-Bay. Publications of the American Economic Association, 3d series, Vol. 1, No. 4; Vol. 2, No. 2. New York, 1901.

—— The Origin of the National Banking System (61st Congress, 2d Session, Senate Doc. 582). Publications of the National Monetary Commission, Vol. V, No. 1. Washington, D.C., 1911.

De Knight, W. F. History of the Currency of the Country and of the Loans of the United States from the Earliest Period to June 30, 1900. Treasury Department Doc. 1943. Washington, D.C. 1900.

Del Mar, Alexander. The History of Money in America from the Earliest Times to the Establishment of the Constitution. New York, 1899.

Dewar, Margaret. Soviet Trade with Eastern Europe, 1945–1949. London, 1951.

Dewey, Davis R. Financial History of the United States. 12th ed. New York, 1934.

—— The Second Bank of the United States. *See* Holdsworth, John Thom, and Davis R. Dewey.

Dewey, Davis R., and Robert E. Chaddock. State Banking before the Civil War, by Davis R. Dewey . . . and The Safety Fund Banking System in New York, 1829–1866, by Robert E. Chaddock (61st Congress, 2d Session, Senate Doc. 581). Publications of the National Monetary Commission, Vol. IV, No. 2. Washington, D.C., 1910.

Dickeson, Montroville Wilson. The American Numismatic Manual of the Currency or Money of the Aborigines, and Colonial, State, and United States Coins. Philadelphia, 1859.

Dillistin, William H. Bank Note Reporters and Counterfeit Detectors, 1822–1866; with a Discourse on Wildcat Banks and Wildcat Bank Notes. American Numismatic Society, Numismatic Notes and Monographs No. 114. New York, 1950.

Domett, Henry W. A History of the Bank of New York, 1784–1884. New York, 1884.

Dorfman, Joseph. The Economic Mind in American Civilization, 1606–1865. 2 vols. New York, 1946.

Du Bois, Armand Budington. The English Business Company after the Bubble Act, 1720–1800. New York and London, 1938.

Einzig, Paul. Currency after the War: The British and American Plans. London, 1944.

—— Primitive Money in Its Ethnological and Economic Aspects. London, 1940.

Faulkner, Harold Underwood. American Economic History. 7th ed. New York, 1954.

Feavearyear, Albert E. The Pound Sterling; a History of English Money. Oxford, 1931.

Federal Reserve System: Board of Governors. Banking and Monetary Statistics. Washington, D.C., 1945.

—— The Federal Reserve System. Washington, D.C., 1954.

Federici, Luigi. La moneta e l'oro. Revised ed. Milan, 1948.

Feis, Herbert. Europe, the World's Banker, 1890–1914; an Account of European Foreign Investment and the Connection of World Finance with Diplomacy before the War. New Haven and London, 1930.

Felt, Joseph B. An Historical Account of Massachusetts Currency. Boston, 1839.

Fernow, Berthold. "Coins and Currency of New York," in G. Wilson, ed., Memorial History of the City of New York, Vol. IV. New York, 1893.

Fiske, John. The Critical Period of American History, 1783–1789. 4th ed. Boston and New York, 1889.

Flick, Alexander C., ed. History of the State of New York. 10 vols. New York, 1933–37.

Fortier, Alcée. A History of Louisiana. 4 vols. New York, 1904.

Franklin, Benjamin. Works. Ed. by Jared Sparks. 10 vols. Boston, 1836–40.

Friedberg, Robert. Paper Money of the United States; a Complete Illustrated Guide with Valuations. New York, 1953.

Friedensburg, Ferdinand. Münzkunde und Geldgeschichte der Einzelstaaten des Mittelalters und der Neueren Zeit. Munich and Berlin, 1926.

Fuller, Claud E. Confederate Currency and Stamps, 1861–1865. Nashville, 1949.

Gallatin, Albert. Suggestions on the Banks and Currency of the Several United States, in Reference Principally to the Suspension of Specie Payments. New York, 1841.

Gardner, Richard N. Sterling-Dollar Diplomacy; Anglo-American Collaboration in the Reconstruction of Multilateral Trade. Oxford, 1956.

Gibbons, James S. The Banks of New York, Their Dealers, the Clearing-House, and the Panic of 1857. New York, 1859.

Gilbart, James William. The History of Banking in America. London, 1837.

Gillingham, Harrold E. Counterfeiting in Colonial Pennsylvania. American Numismatic Society, Numismatic Notes and Monographs No. 86. New York, 1939.

Goldenweiser, Emanuel A. American Monetary Policy. New York, 1951.

Gouge, William M. A Short History of Paper Money and Banking in the United States. Philadelphia, 1833; 2d ed., New York, 1835.

Gragnani, Carlo. La moneta nelle colonie inglesi del Nord America, 1607–1775. Bologna, 1935.

Gras, Norman S. B. The Massachusetts First National Bank of Boston, 1784–1934. Cambridge, Mass., 1937.

Hamilton, Alexander. Works. 3 vols. New York, 1810.

Hardy, Charles O. The Warren-Pearson Price Theory. Brookings Institution pamphlet series, No. 17. Washington, D.C., 1935.

Harris, Seymour E. Exchange Depreciation, Its Theory and Its History, 1931–35; with Some Consideration of Related Domestic Policies. Harvard Economic Studies, Vol. 53. Cambridge, Mass., 1936.

—— Twenty Years of Federal Reserve Policy, Including an Extended Discussion of the Monetary Crisis, 1927–1933. Harvard Economic Studies, Vol. 41, 2 vols. Cambridge, Mass., 1933.

Harrod, Roy Forbes. The Dollar. London, 1953.

Hart, Albert Bushnell, ed. American History Told by Contemporaries. 5 vols. New York and London, 1897–1929.

—— Salmon Portland Chase. American Statesmen Series, Vol. 28. Boston and New York, 1899.

Hasenkamp, Adolf. Die Geldverfassung und das Notenbankwesen der Vereinigten Staaten. Jena, 1907.

Haynes, Frederick E. Third Party Movements since the Civil War, with Special Reference to Iowa. Iowa City, 1916.

Heckscher, Eli F. Sveriges Ekonomiska Historia. 2 vols. Stockholm, 1935. Abridged translation from Swedish by Göran Ohlin: An Economic History of Sweden. Cambridge, Mass., 1954.

Hepburn, A. Barton. A History of Currency in the United States, with a Brief Description of the Currency Systems of All Commercial Nations. Revised ed. New York, 1924.

Hickcox, John H. A History of the Bills of Credit or Paper Money Issued by New York, from 1709 to 1789. Albany, 1866.

Hicks, John D. The American Nation; a History of the United States from 1865 to the Present. 2d ed. Boston, 1949.

Hofstadter, Richard. The Age of Reform; from Bryan to F.D.R. New York, 1955.

Hofstadter, Richard. The American Political Tradition and the Men Who Made It. New York, 1948.

Holdsworth, John Thom. Money and Banking. 5th ed. New York, 1928.

Holdsworth, John Thom, and Davis R. Dewey. The First and Second Banks of the United States (61st Congress, 2d Session, Senate Doc. 571). Publications of the National Monetary Commission, Vol. IV. Washington, D.C., 1911.

Holland, Robert M. The London Bankers' Clearing House (61st Congress, 2d Session, Senate Doc. 294). Publications of the National Monetary Commission, Vol. VIII. Washington, D.C., 1911.

Holt, Bryan W. "Continental Currency," in 5 *Sound Currency* (1898), 51.

Hooper, Samuel. An Examination of the Theory and the Effect of Laws Relating to the Amount of Specie in Banks. Boston, 1860.

Huntington, A. T., and R. Z. Mawhinney. Laws of the United States Concerning Money, Banking and Loans, 1778–1909 (61st Congress, 2d Session, Senate Doc. 580). Publications of the National Monetary Commission. Washington, D.C., 1910.

Hütter, J. P. La question de la monnaie d'argent aux Etats-Unis des origines à 1900. Thesis. Paris, 1938.

International Monetary Conference, Brussels, 1893. Report of the Commissioners . . . and Journal of the Sessions. . . . Washington, D.C., 1893.

——, Paris, 1867. Procès-verbaux. Paris, 1867.

——, Paris, 1878. Proceedings and Exhibits. Washington, D.C., 1879.

——, Paris, 1881. Proceedings. Cincinnati, 1881.

International Monetary Fund. Annual Reports, 1947–1956. Washington, D.C.

—— Exchange Restrictions: Seventh Annual Report. Washington, D.C., 1956.

International Monetary Fund. Summary Proceedings (Annual Meetings of the Board of Directors), 1946–1956. Washington, D.C.

Johnson, G. Griffith, Jr. The Treasury and Monetary Policy, 1933–1938. Cambridge, Mass., 1939.

Keynes, John M. A Treatise on Money. 2 vols. New York, 1930.

Kiesewetter, Bruno. Die Wirtschaft der Tschechoslowakei seit 1945. Deutsches Institut für Wirtschaftsforschung. Berlin, 1954.

Kinley, David. The History, Organization and Influence of the Independent Treasury of the United States. New York, Boston, 1893.

—— The Independent Treasury of the United States and Its Relation to the Banks of the Country (61st Congress, 2d Session, Senate Doc. 587). A revision and continuation of his 1893 work. Publications of the National Monetary Commission. Washington, D.C., 1910.

Kisch, Cecil Hermann, and Winifred A. Elkins. Central Banks; a Study of the Constitutions of Banks of Issue, with an Analysis of Representative Charters. 4th ed. London, 1932.

Klopstock, Fred H. The International Status of the Dollar. Princeton Studies in International Finance, No. 28. Princeton, 1957.

Knapp, Georg Friedrich. Die Staatliche Theorie des Geldes. Berlin, 1905. English translation, by H. M. Lucas and J. Bonar: State Theory of Money. London, 1924.

Knies, Carl. Weltgeld und Weltmünzen. Berlin, 1874.

Knox, John Jay. United States Notes; a History of the Various Issues of Paper Money by the Government of the United States. New York, 1884; 2d ed., 1885; 3d ed., 1899.

Laughlin, J. Laurence. The Federal Reserve Act; Its Origins and Problems. New York, 1933.

—— The History of Bimetallism in the United States. 4th ed. New York, 1897.

Laughlin, J. Laurence. A New Exposition of Money, Credit and Prices. 2 vols. Chicago, 1931.

Laum, Bernhard. Heiliges Geld; eine historiche Untersuchung über den sakralen Ursprung des Geldes. Tübingen, 1924.

Lee, William. The Currency of the Confederate States of America. Washington, D.C., 1875.

Lester, Richard A. International Aspects of Wartime Monetary Experience. Princeton Essays in International Finance, No. 3. Princeton, 1944.

—— Monetary Experiments, Early American and Recent Scandinavian. Princeton, 1939.

Lewis, Lawrence. A History of the Bank of North America. Philadelphia, 1882.

Linderman, Henry R. Money and Legal Tender in the United States. New York, 1877.

Lutz, Friedrich A. International Monetary Mechanisms: The Keynes and White Proposals. Princeton Essays in International Finance, No. 1. Princeton, 1943.

McKay, George L. Early American Currency; Some Notes on the Development of Paper Money in the New England Colonies. American Numismatic Society, Numismatic Notes and Monographs No. 104. New York, 1944.

McMaster, John B. A History of the People of the United States, from the Revolution to the Civil War. 8 vols. New York, 1883–1913.

Martin, François X. The History of Louisiana, from the Earliest Period. 2 vols. New Orleans, 1827–29.

Mill, John Stuart. Principles of Political Economy. Boston, 1848.

Mitchell, L. M. Le chèque dans les pays Anglo-Saxons. Paris, 1927.

Mitchell, Wesley C. Gold, Prices, and Wages under the Greenback Standard. Berkeley, Calif., 1908.

—— A History of the Greenbacks, with Special Reference to the

Economic Consequences of Their Issue, 1862–65. Chicago, 1903.

Mossé, Robert. Le système monétaire de Bretton Woods et les grands problèmes de l'après-guerre. Paris, 1948.

Muhleman, Maurice L. Monetary and Banking Systems. New York, 1908.

—— Monetary Systems of the World. New York, 1895.

Murad, Anatol. The Paradox of a Metal Standard; a Case History of Silver. Washington, D.C., 1939.

Muscalus, John A. The Characters and Events Illustrated on State Bank Notes. Bridgeport(?), Pa., 1938.

National Monetary Commission publications. *See* Barrett, George E.; Cannon, James G.; Davis, Andrew McFarland; Dewey, Davis R., and Robert E. Chaddock; Holdsworth, John Thom, and Davis R. Dewey; Holland, Robert W.; Huntington, A. T., and R. Z. Mawhinney; Kinley, David; Noyes, Alexander D.; Sprague, Oliver M. W.

Nesmith, Robert I. The Coinage of the First Mint of the Americas at Mexico City, 1536–1572. American Numismatic Society, Numismatic Notes and Monographs No. 131. New York, 1955.

Nettels, Curtis P. The Money Supply of the American Colonies before 1720. Madison, Wis., 1934.

Nevins, Allan. History of the Bank of New York and Trust Company, 1784 to 1934. New York, 1934.

Noe, Sydney P. The Pine Tree Shilling of Massachusetts. American Numismatic Society, Numismatic Notes and Monographs No. 125. New York, 1952.

Noyes, Alexander D. History of the National Bank Currency (61st Congress, 2d Session, Senate Doc. 572). Publications of the National Monetary Commission, Vol. V, No. 2. Washington, D.C., 1911.

—— The War Period of American Finance, 1908–1925. New York and London, 1926.

Nussbaum, Arthur. Lehrbuch des Deutschen Hypothekenwesens, nebst einer Einführung in das allgemeine Grundbuchrecht. 2d ed. Tübingen, 1921.

—— Money in the Law, National and International; a Comparative Study in the Borderline of Law and Economics. Revised ed. Brooklyn, 1950.

O'Connor, James F. T. The Banking Crisis and Recovery under the Roosevelt Administration. Chicago, 1938.

Olivecrona, Karl. The Problem of the Monetary Unit. New York, 1957.

Osgood, Herbert L. The American Colonies in the Eighteenth Century. 4 vols. New York, 1924–25.

Paris, James D. Monetary Policies of the United States, 1932–1938. New York, 1938.

Phillips, Henry. Historical Sketches of the Paper Currency of the American Colonies, Prior to the Adoption of the Federal Constitution. 2 vols. Roxbury, Mass., 1865–66.

Preston, Robert E. History of the Monetary Legislation of the United States. Philadelphia, 1895.

Quiggin, Alison. A Survey of Primitive Money; the Beginnings of Currency. London, 1949.

Quiring, Heinrich. Geschichte des Goldes; die Goldenen Zeitalter in ihrer kulturellen und wirtschaftlichen Bedeutung. Stuttgart, 1948.

Ramsden, Henry A. Chinese Paper Money. Yokohama, 1911.

Raymond, Wayte. The Standard Catalogue of United States Coins. 17th ed. New York, 1954.

Ripley, William Z. The Financial History of Virginia, 1609–1776. New York, 1893.

Rist, Charles. La Fédéral Réserve et les difficultés monétaires d'après guerre 1945–1950. Paris, 1952.

Robertson, Ross M. History of the American Economy. New York, 1955.

Roosevelt, Franklin D. Public Papers and Addresses. Compiled by Samuel I. Rosenman. 4 vols. New York, 1938–50.

Root, L. Carroll. "New England Currency," in 2 *Sound Currency* (1895), No. 10.

—— "New York Bank Currency," in 2 *Sound Currency* (1895), No. 5.

—— "States as Bankers," in 5 *Sound Currency* (1895), No. 10.

Roscher, Wilhelm. The Spanish Colonial System. Translated from German by Edward G. Bourne. New York, 1904.

Rosendale, Simon W. "Wampum Currency," in 3 *Sound Currency* (1896).

Roz, Firmin. L'energie américaine. Paris, 1914.

Russell, Henry B. International Monetary Conferences; Their Purposes, Character, and Results. New York and London, 1898.

Schwartz, Harry. Russia's Soviet Economy. 2d ed. New York, 1954.

Scott, Kenneth. Counterfeiting in Colonial America. New York, 1957.

—— Counterfeiting in Colonial New York. American Numismatic Society, Numismatic Notes and Monographs No. 127. New York, 1953.

—— Counterfeiting in Colonial Pennsylvania. American Numismatic Society, Numismatic Notes and Monographs No. 132. New York, 1955.

Sédillot, René. Le franc; histoire d'une monnaie des origines à nos jours. Paris, 1953.

Shaw, William A. The History of Currency, 1252 to 1894. 2d ed. London, 1896.

Sheldon, William H. Early American Cents, 1793–1814. New York, 1949.

Shepherd, William R. History of Proprietary Government in Pennsylvania. New York, 1896.

Shortt, Adam, ed. Documents Relating to Canadian Currency, Exchange and Finance during the French Period. 2 vols. Ottawa, 1925.

Shultz, William J., and M. R. Caine. Financial Development of the United States. New York, 1937.

Simiand, François. Inflation et stabilization alternées: Le développement économique des Etats Unis des origines coloniales au temps présent. Paris, 1934.

Smith, Ernest A. The History of the Confederate Treasury. Harrisburg, Pa., 1901.

Smith, Laurence D. Counterfeiting, Crime against the People. New York, 1944.

Smith, Walter B. Economic Aspects of the Second Bank of the United States. Cambridge, Mass., 1953.

Snowden, James Ross. A Description of Ancient and Modern Coins. Philadelphia, 1860.

Spaulding, Elbridge G. History of Legal Tender Paper Issued during the Great Rebellion. Buffalo, 1869; 2d ed., with "extra sheets," 1879.

Sprague, Oliver M. W. History of Crises under the National Banking System (61st Congress, 2d Session, Senate Doc. 538). Publications of the National Monetary Commission, Vol. V, No. 3. Washington, D.C., 1911.

Stewart, Frank H. History of the First United States Mint, Its People and Its Operations. Camden, N.J., 1924.

Stokvis, H. J. Bretton Woods en het International Monetair Bestel. Leiden, 1948.

Studenski, Paul, and H. E. Krooss. Financial History of the United States. New York, 1952.

Sumner, William Graham. A History of American Currency. New York, 1874.

—— A History of Banking in the United States. Vol. I of A History of Banking in all the Leading Nations, edited by the New York *Journal of Commerce*. 4 vols. New York, 1896.

Sussfeld, Louis E. La réorganisation bancaire aux Etats-Unis et la crise du dollar. Dissertation. Paris, 1935.

U.S. Bureau of the Mint. Annual Reports, 1940, 1943. Washington, D.C.

—— Catalogue of Coins of the United States. Washington, D.C., 1928.

—— Catalogue of Coins, Tokens, and Medals in the Numismatic Collection of the Mint of the United States at Philadelphia, Pa. Treasury Department Doc. No. 2612. 3d ed. Washington, D.C., 1914.

—— Domestic Coin Manufactured by Mints of the United States since Organization. Washington, D.C., 1951.

U.S. Comptroller of the Currency. Annual Reports, 1876, 1905. Washington, D.C.

U.S. Congress, American State Papers. *See* American State Papers.

U.S. Congress, House of Representatives. Committee on Banking and Currency. Money Trust Investigation. Investigation of Financial and Monetary Conditions in the United States under House Resolutions Nos. 429 and 504, before a Subcommittee [the Pujo Committee] of the Committee on Banking and Currency. 3 vols., Washington, D.C., 1913.

U.S. Congress, Senate. Hearings before the Committees on Appropriations, Armed Services and Banking and Currency. 80th Congress, 1st Session. Occupation Currency Transactions. Washington, D.C., 1947.

—— Report of the Silver Commission, 44th Congress, 2d Session. Senate Report 703, Vol. I. Washington, D.C., 1876–77.

U.S. Department of Commerce. Historical Statistics of the United States, 1789–1945. Washington, D.C., 1949.

—— Office of Business Economics. Survey of Current Business: Monthly Business Statistics, summarized in Statistical Abstracts for the United States.

U.S. Department of State. Proceedings and Documents on the United Nations Monetary and Financial Conference. Department of State Publication No. 2866. 2 vols. Washington, D.C., 1948.

—— Annual Reports. U.S. Treasury Department. Administration of the Wartime Financial and Property Controls of the U.S. Government. Washington, D.C., 1942.

Vissering, W. On Chinese Currency: Coin and Paper Money. Leiden, 1877.

Wagner, Adolf. Sozialökonomische Theorie des Geldes und Geldwesens. Leipzig, 1909.

Walker, Francis A. International Bimetallism. New York, 1896.

Warburg, Paul M. The Federal Reserve System, Its Origins and Growth; Reflections and Recollections. 2 vols. New York, 1930.

Warner, John DeWitt. "The Currency Famine," 2 *Sound Currency* (1895), No. 6.

Watson, David K. History of American Coinage. New York and London, 1899.

Webster, Pelatiah. Political Essays on the Nature and Operation of Money, Public Finances and Other Subjects. Philadelphia, 1791.

Westerfield, Ray B. Our Silver Debacle. New York, 1936.

Wheeler-Bennett, John W., and S. A. Heald, eds. Documents on International Affairs, 1933–34. London, 1935.

White, Charles A. "The Archaic Monetary Terms of the United States," *Smithsonian Miscellaneous Collections*, L (1908), 93–104.

White, Horace. Money and Banking, Illustrated by American History. 5th ed. Boston and New York, 1914.

—— "New York's Colonial Currency," in 5 *Sound Currency* (1898).

Whitney, David R. The Suffolk Bank. Cambridge, Mass., 1878.

Wildman, Murray S. Money Inflation in the United States; a Study in Social Pathology. New York and London, 1905.

Williams, John H. Postwar Monetary Plans, and Other Essays. 3d ed. New York, 1947.

Willis, Carrie H., and Lucy S. Saunders. The Story of Virginia. New York, 1943.

Willis, Henry P. The Federal Reserve System, Legislation, Organization and Operation. New York, 1923.

Wronski, H. Le rôle économique et social dans les démocraties populaires. Paris, 1954.

Wyckoff, Vertrees J. Tobacco Regulation in Colonial Maryland. Johns Hopkins Studies in History and Political Science. N.S., No. 22. Baltimore, 1936.

Yang, Lien-shêng. Money and Credit in China, a Short History. Cambridge, Mass., 1952.

Young, John P. The International Economy. 3d ed. New York, 1953.

Zollman, Carl. The Law of Banks and Banking; a Treatise Concerning the Organization, Stockholders, Staff, Customers and Public Control of Banks. 12 vols. Kansas City, Mo., St. Paul, Minn., 1936.

Zupnick, Elliot. Britain's Postwar Dollar Problem. New York, 1957.

References to Congressional Enactments

"Stat." means "Statutes at Large," the official collection.
Additional remarks in brackets have no official character.

* To become later the statutory title.

* Statutory title.

Index